AMERICANS AND OIL

IN

THE MIDDLE EAST

Americans and Oil
in the
Middle East

by

CHARLES W. HAMILTON

GULF PUBLISHING COMPANY
HOUSTON, TEXAS

AMERICANS AND OIL IN THE MIDDLE EAST

Copyright© 1962 by Gulf Publishing Company, Houston, Texas. Printed in the United States of America. This book or parts thereof may not be reproduced in any form without permission of the publishers.

Library of Congress Catalog Card No. 62-18873

FOREWORD

by

HERBERT HOOVER, JR.

In this most interesting book, *Americans and Oil in the Middle East,* Charles W. Hamilton tells a story that will be equally absorbing to historians, the petroleum fraternity and the reading public in general.

The author has an intimate knowledge of Middle East affairs, especially those affecting petroleum, for as an executive in one of the largest American oil companies he personally took part in many of the negotiations which are related in this volume. His deep interest in the historical background of the countries in which he lived and worked, together with a penetrating awareness of the economic, political and social forces which were present around him, add much significance to his comments and conclusions.

In this connection the book also reveals, perhaps unintentionally, some all-too-little appreciated facts about the work of Americans abroad. For the span of more than a century American engineers have found their careers taking them into the furthest corners of the world. They have successfully undertaken a wide variety of enterprises, and in doing so they have had to solve problems of a much greater range than the technical ones that lay immediately at hand. Charlie Hamilton was an engineer in the highest traditions of the profession, and this book should serve as a real inspiration for those who will follow behind him.

Herbert Hoover Jr

LOS ANGELES
JULY 6, 1962

CONTENTS

Kuwait Neutral Zone, Qatar, Saudi Arabia, Abu Dhabi and Aden-Yemen.

INTRODUCTION

A FULL CENTURY ELAPSED after the Western World was permitted to establish missions and schools within the borders of the Old Ottoman Empire before American commercial interests generally and oil companies in particular were allowed a proprietary foothold in Middle East countries. Stemming from the combined humanitarian efforts of missionaries, educators and oilmen one of the great social, cultural and economic renaissance of modern times emerged in the lands east of the Mediterranean. The part played by Americans in this revival is considerable, but remains largely unknown.

It seems apparent from reading current literature and the press that the American public does not fully comprehend the great contributions which their fellow countrymen have made over the years, to the welfare of Middle East peoples. It is this concept which has prompted the author to relate this story of *Americans and Oil in the Middle East.*

The term Middle East as used in this text embraces the present states of Turkey, Syria, Lebanon, Israel, Jordan, Iraq, Iran, Kuwait, Saudi Arabia, and Yemen, also Bahrain and the Shaikhdoms along the fringe of Arabia. The peoples of the Middle East comprise a number of technical groups. Except for a small minority of Christians and Jews, almost all of these peoples are Muslims.

The author is greatly indebted to Dr. Bayard Dodge, President, American University of Beirut, 1923-1948; Norval E. Baker, Chief Geologist, Iraq Petroleum Co., Ltd., 1935-1953; and Floyd W. Ohliger, Vice President, Arabian American Oil Co., 1947-1958, for reviewing portions of this text and for their helpful suggestions and criticism. Also special credit is due to the Near East College Association, Near East Foundation, American University at Cairo and the Arabian Mission, for making available source material for the *Prologue* of this book; and to Kuwait Oil Co., Ltd., British Petroleum Co., Ltd., Arabian American Oil Co., Gulf Oil Corp. and Gulf Publishing Co. for making available reports and data pertaining to the Middle East Oil.

The author also owes much to Mrs. T. F. Culbreth and Mrs. D. B. Fardelmann for their painstaking efforts in editing and typing the manuscript. Finally, but for the encouragement of the author's wife this book would never have been written.

For any errors of misstatement or omission and for all unreferenced views expressed, the responsibility is solely that of the author—he has not been authorized to speak for any individual, company, group or interest. Because the author was so closely identified with oil industry's overseas exploration and development operations for some 45 years, from 1912-1957, (most of which was with Gulf Oil Corp. and its subsidiaries) it should be emphasized that this manuscript is neither vouched for nor sponsored by any oil company or any oil industry association.

CHARLES W. HAMILTON

UPPER MONTCLAIR, N. J.
MAY, 1962

Prologue

Down through the ages, since the very beginning of recorded history, recurrent wars—little and big—have swept back and forth across this world, scourging out the old and establishing the new. Perhaps more than any other area, the Middle East countries have suffered wave after wave of despoilers and empire builders over the past 5,000 years. Some of these conquerors came solely for loot, others surged into the Fertile Crescent and nearby deserts in the name of religion. Each invasion left its imprint upon the sands of time.

A.D. 636-1258

The peoples of the Middle East were not always the conquered. Following the teachings of Mohammed there was a great upsurge of Muslim might, mobilized to seek converts to Islam by conquest of arms. This military movement began in Arabia in the mid-seventh century, and soon overran Syria, Iraq, Persia, Egypt and swept into northern India. Each of these new territories was ruled by a Muslim caliph.

Except for a common bond of religious fervor, these several caliphates were more or less autonomous—more like separate

1

states than as members of an empire. Early in the eighth century the Islamic hords again took to the field and in short order the Saracens overran and dominated all of North Africa, and from there spilled over to Malta and Sicily and thence on to conquer the Iberian Peninsula.

The glory of the Islamic Empire began to dim in the eleventh century.

In the twelfth century the Crusades were at their peak. The Middle East was repeatedly penetrated by invaders from both Europe and Asia. In A.D. 1204 the Europeans captured Constantinople and drove out the Byzantine rulers. However, strangely enough, the recurring waves of Crusaders over the Arab countries fostered trade and brought increased prosperity to the mercantile classes.

The crowning blow to the Islamic Empire in the Middle East occurred in A.D. 1258 when the devastating Tartars under Hulagu invaded Mesopotamia and completely destroyed the ancient irrigation systems along the Euphrates and Tigris rivers and razed the city of Baghdad. So ended the Abbisid caliphate —the last medieval dynasty of the Arab world. However, in those areas unravaged by the "barbarian infidels," notably Spain and Egypt, Arab culture flourished for another 234 years.

With the fall of the caliphate power, the Arab world returned to its feudalistic tribal life, much like its nomadic ancestors of Abraham's time.

A.D. 1517-1841

For nearly 300 years the Middle East lands (except Persia) were dominated by the Ottoman Turks. From 1517 to 1798 Turkish domination was complete except for commercial contacts with western world traders along the coastal fringe.

The conquest of Egypt and the invasion of Palestine by the French in 1798-99 marked the beginning of the struggle between the Western powers for control over the countries bordering the eastern Mediterranean. However, the French conquest was short-lived. Napoleon returned to France from Egypt in 1799 and two years later the French troops were evacuated. Almost immediately, Mohammed 'Ali, (an Albanian by birth) one of the Turkish Sultan's former army officers, declared himself ruler of Egypt. About 1805, the Turkish Sultan persuaded Mohammed 'Ali to assume the responsibilities of viceroy (Pasha) of Egypt. This tended to keep Egypt within the Turkish empire.

Mohammed 'Ali's power rested on his reforms. He initiated the economic prosperity of Egypt by encouraging industry and commerce; he founded the Boulak printing press (1822), hired French officers to train his army, built a naval force, opened new schools with western teachers, sent student missions to Europe and encouraged the translation of western books into Arabic and the Turkish language. Coincidentally, Mohammed 'Ali made an effort to break up the feudal order in Egypt and Syria and to extend and diversify agriculture.

In 1838 Mohammed 'Ali advised the Great Powers (England, France, Austria, Prussia and Russia) of his intention to declare his independence of the Sultan. A year later Sultan Mahmoud died and shortly thereafter the Turkish fleet sailed into Alexandria harbor and voluntarily surrendered. The Ottoman Empire was tottering and was about to concede all of Syria to Mohammed 'Ali when England and France intervened.

France reluctantly agreed to a British attack on the Egyptian forces under Ibrahim (son of Mohammed 'Ali) in Syria and Palestine in 1841. The Egyptian forces were soundly defeated. As a consequence Mohammed 'Ali renounced his claim to all areas of the empire outside of Egypt. Henceforth, the lands along the east coast of the Mediterranean were only nominally administered by the Ottomans and were subjected to increasing influence of the European Powers.

A.D. 1841-1961

So much for the historic background of the Middle East before the advent of the Western world missionaries and educators. The real purpose of this *Prologue* is to point up the influence which these western world emissaries—with emphasis on Americans—have had on Middle East peoples.

In the early part of the nineteenth century, Europeans for the most part, dominated the influx of missionaries, teachers and traders to the lands east of the Mediterranean. However, by 1820 American mission stations began to be established in Syria and Turkey.

> Since the beginning of the 19th century, the near East has felt continuously the impact of the West. Down to the present, Western ideas and ideologies, western literature, science and education, have had an ever-increasing effect upon the people of the Near East.[1]

By the year 1860, Americans had founded no less than 33 schools and scores of mission stations in the Middle East. Coincidently, European schools and mission stations were also established but for one reason or another did not prosper as did the American ventures. The establishment of Christian Mission schools in the Middle East was a new order of crusade.

> The idea of higher education for the Near East was a natural outgrowth of American missionary activity which, since 1820 had exercised an unbroken influence on Lebanon, Syria and Palestine. Pliny Fisk and his devoted successors under the American Board of Commissioners for Foreign Missions may have failed in their immediate aim of converting Moslems in large numbers to Christianity, but they succeeded better than they knew in accomplishing a regeneration

1. Yale, William, *The Near East,* University of Michigan Press, 1958, p. 35.

in the spirit of the people. Through their schools, their printing press, their general interest in the largely forgotten culture of the Arab world, as well as through their deep concern with spiritual uplift, they kindled a vital flame.[2]

For the most part, these early American Mission schools in the Middle East countries other than Turkey, taught all subjects in Arabic. German, French, and English textbooks were translated into Arabic. When it was found that the existing Arabic font was inadequate an American missionary designed a new one, which became universally known as American Arabic.

The Bible was translated into American Arabic by American missionaries.

The American influence on the development of the Arabic language and literature, both in content and style, has been of enormous importance to the revival of Arab culture.[3]

All of these pioneer Americans were dedicated men and women. They lived their religion and they taught the people the Christian code of moral precepts, along with love of fellowman. Most of the early missionaries and educators were ingenious men and women of Yankee stock who demonstrated that man's dignity is not debased by manual labor and gainful employment. Because of Arab dislike of the Turks and the Middle East's general mistrust of European penetration, the teachings and preachings of the early American missionaries and educators were more readily accepted by the peoples of that area.

Noteworthy among the schools of higher learning instigated by Americans in the Middle East and Egypt may be listed the following in the order of their beginning:

2. Penrose, Stephen B. L., *That They May Have Life*, Princeton University Press, 1941, p. 5 and 6.

3. Lewis, Bernard, *The Arabs in History*, Hutchinson House, London, 1950 pp. 172-173.

Bebek Seminary in Constantinople	1840
Robert College in Istanbul	1863
Syrian Protestant College[4]	1864
"The Home School" in Constantinople[5]	1871
Anatolia College in Turkey	1886
International College	1903
American University of Cairo	1919
Damascus College	1946

Bebek Seminary

Constantinople (now Istanbul) was chosen as a residence for missionaries and as a station of the American Mission Board in 1831. In the interval, 1831-1840, little groups of American missionaries, working out of Smyrna and Constantinople, opened Christian churches and schools at many strategic points within the Ottoman dominated areas. It is significant that, in 1834, Mrs. Eli Smith founded the first school for girls in the Middle East.

Among the influx of pioneer American missionaries to the Ottoman Empire was Reverend Cyrus Hamlin and his young bride. On November 4, 1840 Reverend Hamlin opened a seminary for boys at Bebek on the shores of the Bosporus. Twenty-three years later, Bebek Seminary became Robert College.

Hamlin had no sooner started the seminary before he began instructing his boys—mostly boys from poor families—in extra curricular trade school activities. Bebek students learned to make various household utensils of sheet iron and tin, "Boston" rat traps, and some textiles; they also learned book binding and printing. The finished articles from the seminary workshops were sold to clothe and feed the students. However, probably Ham-

4. Name changed to American University of Beirut, November 20, 1920.
5. Name changed to American College for Girls in Constantinople, in 1890.

lin's greatest contribution to a "new life" in the Middle East occurred when he devised a steam flour mill and a steam laundry—the first in that part of the world. At one time during the Crimean War the Bebek bakery was turning out 12,000 loaves of *bira* bread daily for the British hospitals in Turkey, and the Bebek laundry was processing more than 3,000 pieces of soldier clothing each day.

All told, the Hamlin's industries helped build 13 churches with school annexes. But what is vastly more important, his seminary students learned to live by their own efforts.

Following Ibrahim's defeat at the hands of the British (1841), trouble broke out between the Maronites and the Druzes in Syria. The Turks encouraged this religious dissension, while the French favored the Maronites and the English supported the Druzes.

This dissension became a catastrophy in 1860. Terrible massacres took place in Syria. In a matter of months, the death toll amounted to some 23,000 persons and great damage was done to property. However, notwithstanding the hectic turmoil of the times, no Americans were killed. For safety, these missionaries finally concentrated in Beirut where they worked unceasingly to provide relief. Finally, the French landed 7,000 troops in Syria and, with the assistance of Ottoman troops, quelled the uprising. When security was reestablished, the Great Powers sent a commission to Syria to investigate the cause of the trouble, to see that the guilty were punished and to revamp the political setup for the area. In 1861, Turkey agreed to a new organic statute under which Lebanon was recognized internationally as an autonomous state, guaranteed by the major European powers.

SYRIAN PROTESTANT COLLEGE

During the early 1860's the religious turmoil in Syria/Lebanon and the Civil War in the United States seriously disrupted the lives of Americans abroad and at home. Many Middle East missionary stations and schools were temporarily closed and generally Europeans sought haven at Mediterranean ports. Yet it was during this period of turmoil and strife that the American Mission Board conceived the plan to establish a college in Syria.

Apparently the idea of a Christian college for Syria was first brought before the American Board in the United States for action in January, 1862, by Reverend Daniel Bliss and Reverend Dr. William M. Thomson. These men pointed out that missionaries in the Middle East all agreed it was inadvisable to educate young men outside of their environment. Malta College had not been a success, and it was felt that to send young men from Muslim countries to college in Europe or America would be a serious mistake. It was also agreed that the language of instruction should be Arabic and that the maximum number of qualified native instructors and scholastic helpers should be recruited.

The American Board sanctioned the plea of Bliss and Thomson and in April, 1863, incorporated the Syrian Protestant College. During the next 15 months Reverend Bliss carried his message to the American people and managed to obtain pledges in excess of $100,000 (a very considerable sum to be raised in those Civil War days) for the proposed American College in Syria.

In December, 1866, SPC opened its doors in Beirut, Lebanon with Reverend Daniel Bliss as President. The original faculty consisted of seven men, five of whom were proficient in Arabic.

This college initially offered only literary courses, but within a year added courses in medicine and surgery. Now, 95 years later, the American University of Beirut (successor to SPC in 1920) maintains complete schools of Arts & Sciences, Medicine, Pharmacy, Nursing, Public Health, Engineering and Agriculture. From a beginning enrollment of 16 students (1866) the University's enrollment now exceeds 2,500, not including the enrollment at International College—some 1,500—with which the University is closely associated. The current enrollment at AUB and IC includes students from 53 countries—a mingling of some 22 religious groups.

The American University of Beirut and the associated International College stand out in bold relief in the educational and religious world, as successful achievements and unique examples of intercultural relations.

AMERICAN UNIVERSITY AT CAIRO

The American University at Cairo was founded in 1919, largely through the persistent efforts of Charles R. Watson with the authorities in Egypt and industrialists in the United States. The University opened its doors in 1920 with an enrollment of 142 students.

In February, 1922, Britain terminated her protectorate over Egypt and Dr. Joseph Morton Howell was chosen by the United States government to be its first Minister to independent Egypt. Dr. Howell was esteemed by all Americans in the Middle East as a man of character, standing and personality. That he held American missionaries and educators in high regard is evidenced by the following excerpts from his friendly letter of May 25, 1923, to C. R. Watson,

> After travelling over almost the entire world, I know of no place where the missionaries are scoring for the things that are really worthwhile, as they are doing in the Near East, particularly in Egypt.
>
> I think I might say that just now our people should interest themselves in the American University at Cairo, in a way and manner as they have done with Robert College at Constantinople, and the great American University at Beirut.

By 1961, AUC had graduated more than 1,300 individuals,

and some 3,500 other boys and girls had studied one or more years at the University without receiving a degree. Presently, the University has a full time faculty of 39—about one third Americans and two thirds scholars from the Middle East. It is said that AUC mirrors the best of the Middle East, and the best of America.

It is not possible in this *Prologue* to dwell at length on the work of any particular American college in the Middle East or in fact to more than mention some by reference. Besides the schools of college status named herein, over the last 140 years scores of American mission schools have been established throughout the area, many of which are still maintained.

Education proved to be one of the most valuable tools which the American missionaries could have used to present Christianity to the Muslim. With the development of the mission school came the college and then the university, with all their ramified teachings of the arts and sciences. The training of medical doctors, surgeons, dentists, pharmacists and nurses— including the knowledge and practice of sanitation and hygiene —had an immediate and lasting effect on the Arab, the Turk and the Persian. More than anything else, the knowledge of the medical sciences served to convince the peoples of the Middle East the true meaning of the phrase, "brotherhood of man."

ARABIAN MISSION

The work of the Arabian Mission in the countries adjacent to the Persian Gulf stands out in bold relief among the many American mission ventures in the Middle East.

In 1889, at the Reformed Church in America's Theological Seminary in New Brunswick, N. J., three young students— James Cantine, Philip T. Phelps and S. M. Zwemer—met with Professor John G. Lansing to discuss the need of missionary effort in behalf of Muslims and their slaves in Africa and

Arabia. Professor Lansing encouraged the boys in their project and as a result they banded themselves into the "wheel," with Lansing as the "hub," to organize a private Arabian Mission. For personal reasons Phelps dropped out of the wheel soon after it was organized leaving Zwemer and Cantine to carry on the field expedition.

Both boys studied Arabic in New Brunswick and later in the Syrian Protestant College in Beirut, Lebanon. In the summer of 1890 Zwemer and Cantine met with Professor Lansing in Cairo, where he had gone for his health, and from there started out separately by steamer to explore the coast of Arabia. As a result of their survey these young men opened the first Arabian Mission station in Basra on the Shatt-al-Arab (the confluence of the Euphrates and Tigris rivers) in Mesopotamia in August, 1891.

However, within a year, Zwemer and Cantine concluded that something more than preaching was necessary if their Mission was to be effective in Arabia.

> All missionaries in Arabia are agreed, I am sure, that the qualified medical practitioner and surgeon has a passport that opens closed doors and wins hearts no matter how obdurate.[6]
>
> The one greatest need of the Mission is a Medical Missionary staff. Medical work is one phase of missionary effort which meets with no opposition, but for which there comes a fervent plea from the people.[7]

The Arabian Mission's medical work in the field did not get properly going until 1896. During the interim, the Board of Foreign Missions of the Reformed Church in America agreed

6. Zwemer, Samuel, and Cantine, James, *The Golden Milestone,* Fleming H. Revell Co., New York, 1938, pp. 68.

7. DeWitt, Rev. Mason, and Barney, Rev. Frederick J., *The History of the Arabian Mission,* Board of Foreign Missions, New York, 1926, pp. 73.

to receive the Arabian Mission under its care, thus assuring the permanence and stability of the Mission.

From the beginning of the Arabian Mission, Samuel Zwemer was chosen to be the explorer or advance agent. During the formative years of the Mission, Zwemer traveled up and down the Persian Gulf and along the north shores of the Arabian Sea stopping at the several ports of entry. He trekked inland to El Hofhoof (Hofuf) and El Kateef (Qatif) in al-Hasa, made two trips from the Red Sea coast into Yemen, and sailed up the Euphrates and Tigris as far as Baghdad.

In 1903 the first mission hospital—actually the first modern hospital in all the Persian Gulf area—was dedicated at Bahrain. Eight years later a mission station and hospital was established in Kuwait by Dr. Paul Harrison, Reverend Edwin Calverley and Dr. Eleanor Calverley.

By the end of the First World War the Mission was maintaining five stations and three substations along with six Sunday schools, seven day schools, one boys boarding school and five hospitals and dispensaries. These stations, schools and medical service centers were located at Basra and Amarah in Iraq, and Bahrain, Kuwait, Muscat and Matrah in Oman.

Many persons feel that American commercial interests might not have had the opportunity to participate in the development of the great oil fields of the Middle East had it not been for the splendid work of the Arabian Mission. Sir Arnold Wilson, formerly British High Commissioner for Iraq and for many years active in political affairs in the Persian Gulf, said in a 1927 lecture:

> I should not like to speak about the Persian Gulf without bearing testimony to the wonderful work they (Arabian Mission) are doing. I do not suppose they have made converts in appreciable numbers, but they have, by their labors, assisted by the high standard of rectitude displayed

by British officials and British merchants, profoundly modified the Arab outlook in ethical matters. The Arab is a Muhammadan first and an Arab after, like all Islamic races; he regards Europeans likewise as Christians first and foremost. He knows, perhaps better than we do, that our standard of conduct has its basis in the religion of our country; he respects our standard of conduct as higher than his. He does not despise but greatly respects those who devote their lives to spreading, by example and teaching, the Christian religion. There is no greater influence for good in the Persian Gulf than the Christian Missions; no Europeans are so universally respected as are the missionaries, such as Zwemer, Van Ess, Harrison, and Mylrea, and those who decry foreign missions do less than justice to themselves and harm to our good name.[8]

During World War II Arabian Mission doctors were repeatedly allowed to tour at will the hinterland of Arabia to render medical and surgical aid to ill and afflicted Arabs. It was in that period that Dr. Esther Barney Ames was requested by the King to come to Riyadh, twice annually, to attend the palace women. Also, about this time Mrs. Josephine Van Puersem, RN, devised a simplified form of Arabic Braille for the benefit of the thousands of sightless Arabs, victims of Trachoma—the terrible scourge of the Middle East countries.

Since the end of World War II, the work of the Arabian Mission has further expanded in scope, rather than in territory. All the hospitals have been enlarged and facilities improved, both for men and women.

The Arabian Mission was not the first mission to be established in Arabia and in what is now Iraq. Also, it is not the only Christian Mission in that field today. However, the Arabian

8. "A Periplus of the Persian Gulf," excerpt from "The Near East and India," portion of lecture by Sir Arnold Wilson before the Royal Geographical Society in London, January, 1927.

Mission has been particularly successful, through its schools, hospitals and ministry, in exemplifying the character of American Christian people and their selfless interest in the welfare of their fellowmen in the Muslim countries of the Middle East.

NEAR EAST FOUNDATION

During World War I, foreign troops occupied all the countries of the Middle East except Saudi Arabia, Yemen and Turkey. The simple life of all peoples residing in those occupied areas—whether city dwellers, farmers or nomads—was deranged and complicated in the vortex of international conflict. Great masses of population were uprooted and scattered. Normal trade was interrupted, and there resulted a condition of want for both food and clothing, especially among the common folk.

In order to alleviate this want of the necessities of life—brought about by another man's war—the Near East Relief organization was created. It functioned for 15 years before being terminated in 1929. Of the work of this organization, Dr. Bayard Dodge, President (1923-1948) of the American University of Beirut said:

> It had raised a hundred million dollars and carried on one of the most constructive relief programs in history.[9]

Those who were familiar with the work and programs realized that, although Near East Relief had done a splendid job of "giving," more than giving was necessary for any lasting solution to the underprivileged problem. From these convictions, there developed a feeling that the benefits of Near East Relief should be furthered. So, it came to pass that Cleveland E. Dodge* met with some fellow American philanthropists and business men to

9. Dodge, Dr. Bayard, *The American University of Beirut*, Khayat's, Beirut, Lebanon, 1958, p. 64.

* Twin brother of Dr. Bayard Dodge.

consider what might be done by private interests to alleviate the urgent needs of the Near East and Middle East.

This group of men were agreed that, "Our task is to give a way—a way by which the people of the Near East can help themselves. Simply to give away food, money and clothing will never solve their problem."

Without fanfare, and quickly, the Near East Foundation was launched in 1930—dedicated to the principle that the remedy for the backwardness of Eastern Lands must be found in their own people; no relief from abroad could do for them what only they could do for themselves.

The Near East Foundation is a voluntary, philanthropic, non-profit, private agency—chartered under the laws of New York State. It is not a religious organization and has no sectarian or denominational basis although its Board has always been composed of Christian men. The primary support of the Foundation comes from current contributions—largely from American individuals, corporations, college campus chests and endowed Foundations. It has no endowment or invested funds of its own. The Foundation cooperates with the International Cooperative Administration of the United States government, with whom it has had a number of contracts for overseas projects.

The basic principle under which Near East Foundation operates is briefly the following:

> To enter a country only at the invitation of the local government and with its agreement, participate in and support the program.

> To choose as a pilot project, a practical, grass-roots improvement in village life that can be readily understood by the villager.

> To demonstrate this improvement in an actual village set-

ting, with the local government and community as participating partners from the very beginning.

To concentrate on training national technicians and their trainers, once the demonstration has been launched and a national program begins to emerge.

To withdraw as rapidly as feasible as the project becomes the responsibility of national agencies, thus leaving behind a fully indigenous program.

The Foundation holds that its prime objective should be the improvement of conditions in rural areas where—in the Near and Middle East countries—approximately 85 per cent, (roughly, some 30 million people), of the population lives. Hence, the Foundation programs include work in improved agriculture practices, new types of crops, village sanitation, home welfare, rural schools, agricultural cooperatives, public health and livestock husbandry. The Foundation has been most successful in introducing adult education techniques to the Near and Middle East countries as instruments for improving the productive capacity of rural populations.

The Foundation employs the on-the-ground method demonstration. In this method, the Foundation cooperates with the host government to operate a pilot project in a restricted area. The host government supplies all the local currency costs, national personnel, equipment plant and plant maintenance. The Foundation's private funds are used to cover the dollar cost of its technicians. When the demonstrations have been completed, the Foundation personnel withdraws leaving local agencies to carry on the work. This method is aptly called by some, "Operation Spark Plug."

These Near East Foundation's self-help demonstration programs have been singularly successful—the people have been directly benefited and thus have gained a new hope in life.

CONCLUSION

That American missionaries and educators have had a profound and beneficial effect upon the peoples and cultures of the Middle East, there can be no doubt. Since 1820, theirs has been a crusade against poverty, illiteracy and disease. They have been advocates of truth and hope. They have taught self-help and self-determination. Under the inspired leadership of dedicated Americans the Middle East peoples have emerged from a somnambulistic life engendered by the dark ages, which followed the fall of the Muslim Empire, and the throttling effect of Turkish imperialism.

Not that American missionaries or educators were more worthy or more dedicated than their counterparts from Europe, but the record does indicate that Americans sought to inspire and teach and aid with a somewhat different technique. Americans sought to help not to dominate—to lead and not to drive. They ministered to the mind and bodies of the people of the Middle East, regardless of their race, color or creed. They inspired the oppressed to believe in the dignity of man. They demonstrated that good will towards all men is a mightier force than armed conflict.

Because of the American missionary and educator the peoples of the Middle East, whose life from cradle to grave for many generations had followed the pattern of their forebears, began to seek a new and better life. Knowledge, health and hope proved to be the people's "open sesame" to cultural and social advancement. Thus, shortly after the turn of the twentieth century, the Middle East was ready for the great economic impact of finding huge resources of petroleum beneath her stifling deserts and naked hills.

1

Before and After American Entry

As in the case of missionary and educator effort in the Middle East, Americans were not the first in the field of oil finding in that geographic area. It was some 15 years after the British found oil in Iran that Americans were let in to participate in the oil development of Iraq, and it was not until 1933 that an American owned Canadian company found oil in commercial quantities on Bahrain.

In the period 1913-1961 inclusive, the Middle East countries produced more than 18.3 billion barrels of liquid petroleum and of this total some 50 per cent has accrued to American interests through ownership in several concessions. In 1961, American interests were credited with 56.6 per cent of all the oil produced in Iran, Iraq, Bahrain, Saudi Arabia, Kuwait, Qatar, Neutral Zone, Turkey and Israel.

Oil has revitalized the economy of the Middle East, but of equal importance has been the coincidental development of the people's social conscience. European and American oil men brought to the Middle East not only their technical skills, neces-

18

sary to oil finding and development, but also their concept of a better way of life. The oil companies in the Middle East have initiated trade and primary schools for their employees of all nationalities; they have built and maintained hospitals; they have constructed homes for their workmen and have promoted housing schemes. They have erected mosques and churches in or adjacent to the oil camps; they have installed commissaries, ice plants, laundries, central heating and cooling systems, gardens, recreational centers, clubs and movies for the benefit of all employees and their families, and they have encouraged nationals to undertake private contract work.

In addition to the payment of good wages for service rendered, these oil companies have given their workmen a new sense of social security against sickness and old age by fostering savings plans, pensions and incentive benefits. Religion, race or color has been no bar to employment or advancement in the Middle East. In that area, every man can aspire to hold any position in the oil industry which he is qualified to hold or which in time he becomes qualified to hold.

Thus, the western oil men have brought about a new relationship between employer and employee in the Middle East. The Middle Easterner has been quick to learn and develop his natural talents. Through experience, education and adaptability, the nationals have grown in economic and social stature.

From camels to Cadillacs in a single generation is a startling transition—but it has happened in several Middle East countries. It is not too farfetched to conclude that had it not been for the indoctrination and example of the western missionaries, educators and oil men, the sudden wealth from oil, which has poured out from the underground, might have been the undoing of the peoples of the Middle East.

Americans, generally, have a right to be proud of their contribution to the social and economic awakening of the Middle East. The finding and development of huge reserves of oil and gas in the Middle East has had an immediate and profound impact on the entire world.

In the text which follows, an attempt is made to sketch the historic background of the oil producing countries in the Middle East and to tell something of what oil and oil men have done to enhance the future of those countries and their people.

Early Oil Indications

The earliest recorded history has mentioned time and again various surface manifestations of liquid and gaseous petroleum. But, until the last one hundred years, man did not comprehend the significance of these manifestations in terms of fuel and power.

According to the Bible, Noah "pitched" his Ark (maybe from the great asphalt deposits at Hit on the Euphrates River); King Nebuchadnezzar had Shadrach, Meshach and Abednego bound and thrown into the midst of a fiery furnace (there is now good reason to believe that this fiery furnace was none other than burning gas exudes near Kirkuk in Iraq); the "slime" used by the Babylonians to build their walls and great tower was probably bitumen and the reference to "thick water," poured by Nehemiah upon the sacrifices and the wood on the altar which burst into flame when the sun appeared from behind a cloud,[1] can only mean liquid crude petroleum.

The Oracles of Delphi used natural gas for their perpetual fires. In the thirteenth century, Marco Polo reported extensively upon the oil springs near Baku. Said he, "This oil is not good to use as food but is good to burn and is also used to annoint camels that have the mange."[2] The terrible "Greek Fire" em-

1. Redwood, Sir Boverton, *A Treatise on Petroleum,* Charles Griffin & Co. Ltd. London, 1913, p. 1.
2. Redwood, Sir Boverton, *A Treatise on Petroleum,* Charles Griffin & Co. Ltd. London, 1913, p. 3.

ployed so devastatingly in the naval battles during medieval times on the Black Sea and Mediterranean was very probably a mixture of lime and asphalt.

However, it was not until the now famous Drake well discovered oil in the underground (August 28, 1859) near Titusville, Pa., that serious exploration for oil began in Asia and the Middle East.

EARLY OIL EXPLORATION

In 1864, Colonel Gowan, an American, drilled several shallow wells in search of petroleum in the Crimea—some of his borings encountered only gas but others did, in fact, yield some oil. The first important oil flow was found with the drill in the Kuban (Russia) in 1866. Twenty years later the first great oil well came in at 714 feet in the Baku area. That discovery led to the development of the several Baku oil fields which have produced for more than 70 years.

The next major oil discovery came in 1908, when Well M1 blew in at a depth of 1,180 feet at a place in Persia, northeast of the head of the Persian Gulf, called Maidan-i-Naftun—now better known as MIS.

Thus ended an era (1866-1908) of oil exploration and discovery in Asia and the Middle East, all of which had been financed by non-American capital, although a number of Americans were employed as operators. As a matter of fact, American capital did not have an opportunity to participate in the oil ventures of the Middle East until 1928.

BRITAIN'S PERSIAN GULF

The advent of the American oil interests into the Middle East did not happen without a long diplomatic struggle after the First World War. Britain, especially, made it clear to the world that all the territory touching on the Persian Gulf and along the Arabian Sea was considered to be within her zone of influence, commercially, if not politically. What is now known as Iran, Iraq, Pakistan, India, Kuwait, Bahrain, Qatar, and the Trucial coast of Arabia fell within this so-called zone of influence. The only exception was that part of Arabia which is now known as Saudi Arabia. Britain had never laid a heavy commerical or political hand on the interior of Arabia. This may have been due to the belief that the control of Arabian trade was not worth the effort, or perhaps because of Arabia's long history of divided authority which continued until Ibn Saud gathered the political loose ends together after a tribal war of some 30 years.

For 100 years or more, Britain had been in a preferred position commercially in the Middle East because of its East India Co., which straddled the trade routes from the Far East to European markets. This commercial advantage took on a decided political aspect when the administration of India and what is now Pakistan came under the British crown in 1858. India remained a crown colony, in effect, until 1935.

The Shaikhdoms of the Trucial coast have been under British protection by reason of treaties signed with Britain in 1853 and 1892—these treaties provided that the Shaikhs should not sell or cede any part of their land to any other power. Aden still remains a British colony. The Sultanates of Oman and Muskat have been under British protection since the nineteenth century. Kuwait became a protected State of Britain by reason of the treaty of 1899. The Bahrain Islands have been virtually a protectorate of Britain—having been in treaty relations with the British government since 1820. The office of the British Political Resident in the Persian Gulf is in Bahrain.

Although Iran has never been completely dominated by Britain, the Anglo-Russian convention of 1907 which divided Iran into two spheres of influence did not prosper, and the British attempt to impose a protectorate over all of Iran was defeated in 1919. Nevertheless, the prestige and policies of Britain have long been important factors in the political and commercial development of Iran.

After the fall of the Ottoman Empire as the result of World War I, Syria was mandated to France. It was not until 1930 that France recognized Syria as an independent republic, but still subject to the mandate. The Vichy control over Syria continued until 1941.

British troops occupied Egypt in 1882 and Britain's resident agents became the actual administrators, though the country remained under nominal Turkish sovereignty until December 18, 1914 when such fiction was ended and Egypt became a British protectorate. On February 28, 1922, Britain declared Egypt an independent state, although reserving the right to maintain military bases within the country, "for the protection of the Suez Canal and the defense of Egypt."

"The British invasion and occupation between 1914 and 1918 during World War I of what was then called Mesopotamia had political and economic as well as military objectives. The British during the four years of war brought about more progress in the Tigris and Euphrates Valley than had centuries of Turkish rule. Locally, the British were laying the foundation of an imperial colonial government patterned after India."[3]

In 1919 that part of old Mesopotamia, now known as Iraq, came under mandate to the British. Even after the British had established Faisel (from Syria) as King over Iraq in 1921, Britain still maintained very considerable influence over the political and commercial life of Iraq until the Kasim military coup in 1958.

From the foregoing, it is evident that Britain's zone-of-influence did, in fact, exist for many years, over all the Middle East countries pinchered between India on the east and Egypt on the

---

3. Yale, William, *The Near East,* University of Michigan Press, Ann Arbor, 1958, p. 314.

west, with the exception of the area now known as Saudi Arabia.

Because international trade has been and still is Britain's economic life blood, it is understandable that the Crown sought to dominate the source of this life blood and the channels through which it flowed. Thus, it was only natural that Britain should have exerted both her political and commercial influence over the countries of the Middle East so long as she controlled the policies and economics of Egypt and India.

Such was the situation which confronted American capital seeking a foothold in the Middle East during the first two decades of this twentieth century. The American oil compaines only got into the Middle East because of diplomatic pressure (as in Iraq) or because the British failed to properly evaluate the potentialities of the region (such as the oil discoveries in Bahrain, the Arabian mainland and Kuwait) or because Britain could not pull her chestnuts out of the fire without the help of other nationals (as in the case of Iran).

However, it should not be concluded that British influence in the Middle East or for that matter, in Iran, India, and Egypt was bad, either for the individual country or the area as a whole. On the contrary, the British brought order out of chaos and did, in fact, protect the weaker nations from their aggressors. Had it not been for British protection, most, if not all, the Shaikhdoms and Sultanates around the coastal fringe of the Arabian Peninsulas would have long since been gobbled up by stronger nations.

Britain encouraged the missionary, the educator and the doctor in the Middle East countries. They introduced democratic processes in civil administration. For the most part, British agents in the Middle East have been sincere, able and honest. But two world wars have demonstrated that the people of this world want to be free—free even from beneficent alien power influences, whether commercial or political or both. Hence, as British influence in the Middle East has waned, private American free enterprise has been welcomed.

ENTER: AMERICAN CAPITAL

During the past 30 years, American capital has participated in all new oil discoveries in the Middle East, with the exception of Persia prior to 1954. The oil discovered in Iraq and Qatar was the result of exploration by a mixed company of British, French, Dutch and American capital. The oil discoveries in Bahrain, Saudi Arabia, and the Kuwait Neutral Zone were made exclusively by American-owned companies. Oil was discovered in Kuwait by a jointly owned British-American company. Since the fall of 1954, the former oil properties of Anglo Iranian Oil Co., Ltd. (now known as British Petroleum) in Iran (Persia) have been operated by a consortium in conjunction with the National Iranian Oil Co. The consortium is composed of 40 per cent British, 14 per cent Dutch, 6 per cent French and 40 per cent American capital. As of this writing, American capital and personnel are engaged in all oil exploration and development in the Middle East, with the exception of some of the new Persian Gulf offshore exploration operations.

In order to fully appreciate the circumstances and conditions which have led to the entry of American oil capital in the Middle East, it has been advisable to deal briefly with the history of each of the oil producing countries in the area.

2

Iran (Persia)

PERSIA, OR IRAN AS IT IS NOW CALLED, has been
a cradle of man for as far back as archeologists have been able
to determine. It is believed that prehistoric man was living on
the Iranian plateau as long ago as 10,000 B.C., maybe even
before then. Pieces of pottery and other evidences of early man
which can be reliably dated from 5,000 B.C., have been found
in Iran.

Among the ancient relics in the excellent museum in Teheran
is a small sculptured lion of asphalt (maybe gilsonite) inlaid
with a delicate design of silver wire. This piece is said to date
from several thousand years before Christ. It could be the
earliest evidence that oil was known to man even before recorded history.

The immigration of the Medes and Persians occurred during
the first millennium B.C. They are believed to have come from
the north. With the decline of Assyrian power, the Median
Kingdom became a reality with its capital at modern Hamadan.
Cyrus the Great was the son of Astyages, King of Media and

under him the Achaemenian Empire flourished. In 537 B.C., Cyrus led the attack along the western frontiers of his domain and caused the fall of Babylon. In the course of time, Darius succeeded Cyrus as King; his armies expanded the Achaemenian Empire to include all of present day Egypt, Greece, Turkey, Iraq, Lebanon, Palestine, Trans-Jordan, Iran and a large chunk of Asia south and east of the Caspian Sea. The ruins of the once great city of Persepolis—first established by Darius—are noted for its grand scale, monumental art and bold sculptures.

The wave of the Achaemenian Empire began with the death of Darius. The armies of his successor, Xerxes, suffered a serious defeat at the hands of the Greeks (480 B.C.) under Alexander, and for more than 150 years thereafter no King of Kings commanded his army as Cyrus and Darius had done. "Rivalries, intrigues and struggles were even centered around the throne."[4] By 330 B.C., Alexander the Great had become the virtual overlord of Persia. The Greek language began to spread in Iran and in due time replaced Aramaic. Also, there were many marriages between the women of Iran and the Macedonians. In official circles Iran became Hellenized but the Greek influence had little effect on the peasant folk living in the country.

About 100 B.C., nomads from central Asia swept into Iran. About a century later, the Parthians emerged from the north as the dominate rulers, but their empire in turn was overthrown in A.D. 226.

During the second and third centuries A.D., the Roman Empire impinged on the Parthian Kingdom and proceeded to slice off all of the western portion, including all the areas fronting on the Mediterranean, Turkey and northern Mesopotamia. The Sassanian dynasty became the overlords of Persia. Under their regime, the idolatry of the Parthians was put down and in

4. Ghirshman, E., *Iran,* English Version, Penguin Books, Ltd., Harmondsworth, Middlesex, England, 1954.

its place came the revival of Zoroastrianism—a religion which had been nearly forgotten for five centuries.

The Sassanidae were the rulers of the Persian Empire from A.D. 226 until the Saracen hordes, followers of the new Islamic faith, swept over Persia in A.D. 641. The Saracens appointed Arab governors to take over the control of Persia and its colonies. For more than two centuries, Persia remained under the dominion of the Khalifs during which the Persian people became Mohammedans, and their literary culture flourished.

The dynasty of Yakoob ben Leis, which had gained control of the Persian government from the Arab, was short lived. Then came the rise of Mahmoud of Ghizni—during most of which Persia was divided between the two families of Samanee and Dilamee—the first reigning over eastern Persia and Afghanistan, and the other over western Persia. This empire ended A.D. 1160. Next came the Korasmian Empire which flourished until the devastating invasion of Mongols and Tartars, under the leadership of Zingus Khan, about A.D. 1220. "It is said that the ravages of the four years of Zingus Khan's Korasmian war were so great that five centuries were not sufficient to repair its ravages."[5]

The Mongol-Tartar dynasties in Persia held power until the country was ravaged by the Uzbecks and Turkomans about the year 1500.

In 1503, Ismail Suffee established the independence of Persia and became the founder of the Suffeean (or Safair) dynasty. Within four years all of Persia had submitted to his authority, thus giving rise to the modern Persian Empire. Shah Abbas the Great, who came to power in 1582, successfully defended his kingdom against the Ottomans and defeated the Turks in many battles. As a consequence, all of the Turkish territories on the Caspian, in Azerbijan Georgia, Kurdistan, Baghdad, Mosul

5. Clare, I. S. (compiler), *Library of Universal History*, New York, 1897, 8 Vols., Vol 5, p. 1883.

and Diarbekr were annexed to the Persian Empire. During the reign of Shah Abbas, Persia waxed great among the international powers and flourished within her own far-flung borders. Isfahan, the capital, under Shah Abbas became one of the most beautiful cities in the world; many of the famous buildings of his day are still to be seen there. However, Persia's prosperity ended with the death of Abbas the Great in 1628.

After the death of Abbas the Great, Persia was ruled by a series of tyrants until 1722 when under the rule of Hussein, the country was invaded by a strong force of Afghan tribesmen. Millions of Persians were slain before Tamasp II, Hussein's son, drove all Afghans from Persian soil in 1730. Six years later, Khouli Kahn deposed Tamasp II and restored much of the old Persian Empire—driving out all the Turks. Khouli Khan or Nadir Shah, as he was now called, was assassinated in 1747, after brilliant successes in battle but a miserable administration. Persia then lapsed into anarchy and civil war. This deplorable state of internal affairs was brought to an end by Kerim Khan of Shiraz, said to be one of the best rulers Persia ever had.

In 1795 Aga Mohammed Khan made himself Shah of Persia (founder of the Kadjar dynasty which occupied the Persian throne until 1925), removed the capital from Isfahan to Teheran* and restored order to the kingdom.

Except for several minor wars with Russia early in the 1800's during which Georgia was lost to Russia, the modern history of Persia is relatively uninteresting. It was during the long reign of Naser-ed-Din Shah (1808-1896) of the Kadjar dynasty, that the modernization of Persia began in earnest. Roads and railroads were built, the telegraph was instituted and concessions for banking and the exploitation of minerals were granted.

Reza Pahlavi seized the government on February 26, 1921 and was elected hereditary Shah in 1925. From that date until the exigencies of World War II caused his abdication in favor

* Now sometimes spelled 'Tehran'—either spelling is correct.

of his son, Reza Shah, he did much to modernize his country and abolished all foreign extra territorial rights. In 1941, the present Shah, H. I. M. Muhammad Reza Shah Pohlavi, took over the rulership of Persia and under his leadership modernization, social and political reforms continue in Persia (Iran).

During the past two centuries, Iran has lost most of her dependencies. Her once great empire has shrunk to the present day Iran of 636,293 square miles, populated by 20,633,000 people (1960 United Nations estimate)—Iranians, Kurdish and Azerbaijani.

No doubt to some, the foregoing historical sketch will seem dry of current interest—it certainly is by no means complete—however, the author has felt it necessary to review Iran's past in order to bring into proper focus, the present. Iran stands today as one of the world's oldest nations—it is a treasure house of ancient culture and architecture. It has been ravaged by barbarians, and evangelized by two great religions—the Zoroastrianism and Islam. Yet in spite of the ebb and flow of foreign conquerors and disrupting internal intrigue, the homeland of Iran remains a large geographic unit, with great potentialities economically, socially and politically.

The erosion of many centuries—while changing the physical appearance of Iran's landscape, did not cause any loss in the greatest of all her hidden natural resources—namely, petroleum.

OIL IN PERSIA

Baron Julius de Reuter, of German-Jewish origin, was intrigued by possibilities of investment in Persia as far back as 1870. Through his agent, M. Cotte, de Reuter, negotiated a concession in Persia which granted him a monopoly for the construction of railways and tramways, canals and irrigation works, the exploitation of forests and uncultivated lands, and the operation of a bank and all public works. In addition, it included, "The exclusive working of all Persian mines," except those of gold, silver and precious stones.

The public objected, and so did Russia, hence, finally, the negotiations were cancelled. In 1889, with the help of the British Minister in Teheran,[6] Baron de Reuter obtained a new concession which embraced the right to operate a bank and the exclusive working of Persian mines. The bank was soon organized and was successfully operated for 60 years, but the several ventures in oil prospecting failed and the oil concession expired at the end of its first ten years.

Baron de Reuter, best known outside Persia as the founder of a famous news agency, died in 1899. His agent, M. Cotte, carried on with de Reuter's Persian ventures. Cotte interested Antoine Kitabdji Khan[7] in the prospects of finding oil in Persia. At the time, Kitabdji, although an Armenian by birth, was Director General of the Persian Customs administration. He sought French capital without success. Finally, Kitabdji was able to secure a monopoly of oil rights in Persia from a small private Persian company that had been carrying on exploration for oil after the expiration of the de Reuter concession. Cotte and Kitabdji again tried to interest European investors in Persian oil. Among others, Kitabdji approached Calouste Gulbenkian, who is reported to have said in his memoirs:[8]

> An Armenian, Mr. Kitabdji, the Director of Persian Customs, had a concession for which he wanted £15,000. I knew Kitabdji very intimately myself and I submitted this business to my friend Lane[9]—also, I believe to Deterding,[10] but we all

6. Elwell-Sutton, L. P., *Persian Oil,* Lawrence & Wishart, Ltd., London, 1955, p. 12.

7. Sometimes spelled Ketabji instead of Kitabdji.

8. Hewins, Ralph, *Mr. Five Per Cent,* Rinehard & Company, Ltd., New York, 1958, p. 67.

9. Frederick Lane, British representative of the important oil interests of Messrs. Rothschild of Paris.

10. Henri Deterding of the Royal Dutch Shell group.

thought it was a wildcat scheme and it looked so speculative that we thought it was a business for a gambler and not at all for our trio.

It was on my refusal that Mr. D'Arcy,[11] a great speculator in mining businesses in Austraila and elsewhere, interested himself and succeeded in forming a syndicate—I believe with the help of Scottish concerns.

Once he was interested in the Persian oil prospects, D'Arcy got busy and sent a team of geologists to investigate the possibilities on the ground. Their report was so favorable that D'Arcy closed the deal with Cotte and Katabdji. However, D'Arcy felt the concession needed to be put on a firmer basis with the Persian government, and so dispatched his own representative to Persia with Cotte and Kitabdji for discussion with the prime minister. After considerable talk, and maybe some money, an exclusive concession to carry on all stages of oil exploration, production, refining and marketing in Persia was confirmed by the government to D'Arcy on May 28, 1901, except as respects the five northern provinces which border on Russia.

The First Exploitation Co. was formed by D'Arcy and associates in May, 1903. Drilling was started even before this company was incorporated. It was five years and several unsuccessful wells later before the M.I.S. oil field was discovered.

Before the M.I.S. discovery, D'Arcy funds began to run short. When this became known in banking circles, German interests approached D'Arcy but before he could avail himself of such capital—if, in fact, he was ever so inclined, the British government intervened. About this time, Sir John Fisher, First Lord of the Admiralty, began to press for the conversion of the Royal Navy from coal fueling to oil burning. He urged British interests to augment the Burma oil supply from other sources in the

11. William Knox D'Arcy.

East and, as a result, the Burma Oil Co., and Lord Strathcona, jointly, organized Concessions Syndicate, Ltd., to operate in Persia outside the 1,000 square mile area where the First Exploitation Co. had been operating.

First Exploitation Co. and Concession Syndicate, Ltd., carried on their respective explorations and drilling separtely until mid-1907, when D'Arcy indicated his desire to assign his private interest in the Persian oil venture. By mutual agreement and for a substantial consideration, D'Arcy transferred to Burma Oil Co. all his shares in the First Exploitation Co. on July 31, 1907.

Meanwhile, Britain and Russia were trying to resolve their respective "zones of interest and influence in Asia." Britain particularly wanted to maintain the Persian Gulf as a "British Lake,"—as it had been considered since the early nineteenth century—against all other foreign entities.[12] For this reason and other reasons, the British government urged that prospecting for oil in Persia be diligently pursued. So, field work continued in spite of unsuccessful drilling results.

As fate would have it, only ten months after D'Arcy sold out his private Persian interests, the M.I.S.-1 well blew in. A new oil field had been discovered, the first in the Middle East.

On April 4, 1909, the Anglo-Persian Oil Co. was formed and acquired all the rights granted in the D'Arcy concession and all of the issued shares of the several companies which had been organized to operate in Persia under the D'Arcy concession. Still the British government had no visible interest in either the old companies or in the Anglo-Persian Oil Co.

Some two years later Winston Churchill became First Lord of the Admiralty, and revived his predecessor's proposal to fuel the Royal Navy with oil. He appointed a Royal Commission to inquire into sources of oil supply readily available to the Crown. In the spring of 1913, the Royal Commission reported

12. Elwell-Sutton, L. P., *Persian Oil,* Lawrence & Wishart, Ltd., London, 1955, p. 18.

favorably on the use of oil for Navy fueling. Anglo-Persian promptly offered to meet all the Royal Navy's fuel oil requirements from Persian sources, provided the British government would assist its expansion and development financially. Several months later, Churchill went before the House of Commons and said,

"Our ultimate policy is that the Admiralty should become the independent owner and producer of its own supplies of liquid fuel . . . or at any rate, the controller at the source of at least a proportion of the supply of natural oil we require."[13]

In view of the Commission's report and Churchill's statement, it was not unexpected that within the year—actually on May 20, 1914—the British government signed a contract to acquire a controlling share interest in Anglo-Persian, but with the specific understanding that the government would not ever interfere in purely commercial and operating matters of the company. The day after the outbreak of World War I—August 5, 1914—the House of Commons voted the funds to complete the deal. Coincidentally, the Admiralty executed a 30-year contract with Anglo-Persian for an undisclosed quantity of fuel oil to be supplied at undisclosed prices.

With the advent of war, exploration, drilling, pipe line and refinery construction in Persia proceeded. I believe it was Lord Curzon who said, after the war was over that, "The Allies floated to victory upon a sea of oil." Certainly, most of that fuel oil for the Allied navies came from the Americas and Persia.

The original D'Arcy concession (1901) excluded the five northern provinces of Persia but that fact did not deter the Anglo-Persian Oil Co. from trying to prevent others from obtaining such rights. Russia continued to diplomatically and privately press her claims to this area until 1921 when the new Russian Republic signed a treaty with Persia renouncing all

13. Elwell-Sutton, L. P., *Persian Oil,* Lawrence & Wishart, Ltd., London, 1955, pp. 22 and 23.

concessions (except one) acquired by the Tsarist regime in Persia. However, this treaty further provided that no concessions in the five northern provinces of Persia (the so-called "Russian" area) were to be granted in the future to any third power. Hence, Anglo-Persian claims to that area were blocked.

Next, the Persian government sought to interest American oil capital in the five northern provinces. A resolution was presented to the Majles (Persian Congress) to give Standard Oil Co. (New Jersey), a 50-year concession over the former "Russian area." With that, diplomacy exploded—both Russian and British. The deal with Jersey-Standard was blocked.

American private interests and the United States government were obviously peeved at being shut out of participation in the Middle East. Washington came out in favor of the "open door" policy in Persia. Such was the situation in 1921.

A year later, the Persian government sought again to negotiate an oil concession over the five northern provinces with the Standard Oil Co. (New Jersey) on the one hand and Sinclair Consolidated Oil Co. on the other. The proposals made by these companies were similar except that Standard offered the government a percentage of the value of crude oil whereas Sinclair offered a percentage of net profits. Politically, it was felt that Sinclair might have an edge because of its friendly relations with Russia. (At that time, Sinclair had the agency for the sale of Russian oil products abroad and had acquired an oil concession on the island of Sakhalin in the Pacific, north of Japan).

It is a fact that the Persian government signed the oil concession with Sinclair over the so-called "Russian area" in September, 1923. The Majles ratified this agreement the following March. About three months thereafter, an unfortunate incident occurred resulting in the death of the American Vice Consul in Teheran. He had tried to photograph a religious gathering—an offensive action to the Muslim—and the crowd became fanatical. This incident aroused all of Persia.

The Persian government was quick to make amends to the Vice Consul's family and to the American government but the public generally continued to be emotionally upset. Under those conditions, it was believed to be too dangerous for Sinclair field men to work. To make matters worse, Sinclair apparently was unable to raise the promised $10 million loan and the Russians turned on Sinclair by cancelling the Sakhalin concession and the sales agency and announced that no foreign oil could be transported through Russian territory. Sinclair gave up early in 1925 and abandoned its concession in Persia.

A Difficult Time for Anglo-Persian

At the time the American companies abandoned their attempts to obtain oil concessions in Persia Anglo-Persian employed in its petroleum operation about 29,000 persons of whom 6,000 were foreigners. Even then (1925) the Persian government was urging the company to train more Persians for higher positions.

The Persian government alleged that its "take" from oil was being affected by the company's accounting practices and the large sales of fuel oil to the Admiralty at below market prices. At the refinery in Abadan and in the fields, labor relations worsened and strikes occurred. The differences between the Persian government and the company deteriorated. When Persia passed its first income tax law in April 1930, (four per cent) Anglo-Persian refused to pay, claiming that the company, under the terms of the concession, was exempt from all Persian taxation. A crisis was in the making.

On November 27, 1932, the Company's representative in Tehran, B. R. Jackson,[14] received a letter from the Minister of

14. Basil R. Jackson, later Deputy Chairman, then Chairman of Anglo-Irania Oil Co., Ltd.,—deceased in 1957.

Finance informing him that the D'Arcy concession no longer satisfied the rights and interests of the Persian nation; that a new basis must be reached between the two sides; that the government no longer felt itself bound by an agreement concluded under conditions prevalent during the Qajar regime.[15]

This letter went on to say that so far, the company had shown no disposition to meet the demands of the government and had even reduced Persia's share, hence, the government saw no alternative but to annul the concession while expressing its readiness to grant a new concession to Anglo-Iranian based on equity and justice.

The substance of this letter became public knowledge in Persia. A two-day holiday throughout the country was declared. Persia's position in this oil matter was supported by the Russian press and to some extent, by the American press. However, the company's position was adamant. British warships were dispatched to the Persian Gulf. After some months had passed, the British government notified Persia that unless it withdrew its threat to annul the D'Arcy concession, the matter would be referred to the Hague.[16]

When the Persian government rejected the competence of the International Court to deal with, what they called, "a purely domestic dispute," the British government threw the problem into the lap of the League of Nations on the grounds that annulment of the D'Arcy concession removed the safeguards for the safety of British subjects provided by the concession. It is generally conceded that the Persians made a good case for their side before the League.

The hearings at Geneva dragged on from mid-December 1932 until the spring of 1933, when Sir John Cadman—Chairman of Anglo-Persian—went to Teheran and handed the Persian

15. Elwell-Sutton, L. P., *Persian Oil,* Lawrence & Wishart, Ltd., London, 1955, p. 75.

16. Permanent Court of International Justice.

government the draft of a new concession. The new concession terms were finally accepted by the Majlis (the Iranian legislature) and was signed by the Shah on May 28, 1933.

The obvious gain to Persia under the terms of the new concession was the reduction in the size of the concession area—from 500,000 square miles to 100,000 square miles. Less obvious was the financial gain to Persia derived from the new royalty basis. According to L. P. Elwell-Sutton:

"The company was now to pay four shillings on every ton of oil sold in Persia or exported, and a sum equal to 20 per cent of the dividends over £671,250 distributed to the holders of the ordinary shares. The total sum paid in this way was not to be less than £750,000 in any year."[17] However, some faults of the past were carried over into the new concession—there being no provision to avoid disproportionate payments to the British government vis-a-vis the Persian government and no way of checking the effect on profits arising from the sale of Persian oil at below market prices. Under the new concession, the Anglo-Persian Co. was entirely exempt from Persian taxation—although liable to the British government for all British taxes on profits and income.

Notwithstanding Sinclair's abortive attempt to obtain and hold an oil concession over the northern area of Persia, in 1936 another American oil company, Amiranian Oil Co. (subsidiary of Seaboard Oil Co. of Delaware) sought and obtained an oil concession covering an area of some 200,000 square miles in North Persia. Geological work was initiated and drilling equipment shipped to the Persian Gulf but then in 1938, before the drilling equipment was removed from seaside, Amiranian announced it was surrendering its concession. Presumably this decision was partly prompted by financial difficulties and political

17. Elwell-Sutton, L. P., *Persian Oil*, Lawrence & Wishart, Ltd., London, 1955, p. 80.

hazards and partly by the problems and cost involved in shipping any north Persia oil out through the Persian Gulf.

In spite of the new concession terms, the Persian government continued to fret—particularly with regard to Persia's share of the "take" from its indigenous natural resource. However, before this dissention got out of hand there loomed on the horizon World War II. So, from 1939 until after the cessation of hostilities in 1945, concession terms were hardly debated between Anglo-Iranian Oil Co. Ltd.,[18] and the Iranian[19] government.

During the war the oil fields and oil terminals in Iran were feverously active in supplying the navies of the Allies with fuel and the Allied land and air forces with gasoline. The Abadan refinery became the largest, in point of volume throughput, in all the world.

In 1941, Russia again pressed her claim to the oil rights of northern Iran but the Iranian government was not moved.

Two years later the representatives of the Royal Dutch Shell group visited Teheran to open negotiations for oil rights outside of Anglo-Iranian's area in southern Iran. Some months thereafter representatives of Standard Vacuum Oil Co.[20] and the Sinclair Consolidated Oil Co. arrived in Iran, evidently interested in the oil prospects of northern Iran outside of Anglo-Iranian's area.[21]

The advent of these American oil company missions caused the Iranian government to engage two American oil experts[22] to advise them. Among other things, these experts may have drawn Iran's attention to the new Petroleum and Income Tax

18. Name changed from Anglo-Persian to Anglo-Iranian in 1935.
19. Name changed from Persia to Iran in 1935.
20. Joint subsidiary of Standard Oil Company of New Jersey and Socony Vacuum Oil Co.
21. Shwadran, Benjamin, *The Middle East, Oil and the Great Powers*, Frederick A. Praeger, New York, 1955, p. 65.
22. Herbert Hoover, Jr., and A. A. Curtice.

laws of Venezuela which provided for a fifty-fifty[23] division of profits between the respective oil company and the government of the country.

Then in 1944 the British and American governments got together in Washington for an oil conference which caused the Iranian government to get quite disturbed when they learned of it. This conference consisted of many of the best brains in government and industry from both sides of the Atlantic sitting down together around the table, first in April and then in July 1944. This oil conference had for its object the establishment of a foreign oil policy. It was to be a cooperative agreement. While it is true that this agreement considered overseas oil concessions and oil reserves, it was not directed at any particular country— as feared by the Iranians—nor was it directed at any particular area. Part of the agreement provided, in essence, that with respect to the acquisition of explorations and development rights in areas not now under concession, the principle of equal opportunity shall be respected by both governments; and further, that the government of each country and the nationals thereof shall respect all valid concession contracts and lawfully acquired rights, and shall make no effort unilaterally to interfere directly or indirectly with such contracts or rights.[24] Although the "Agreement on Petroleum" between the US government and UK government was drawn and agreed by the conferees, it was never fully ratified or implemented.

The worry of the Iranians about the possible effect of the "Agreement on Petroleum" drawn in Washington was further

23. The so-called 50-50 basis was born out of discussions between American companies and the Venezuelan government in 1942, but was not fully effective until the passage of an amended income tax law in 1948. In principle, the 50-50 basis provides that the country of origin's share from royalties, taxes and other payments arising out of oil should equal one-half of the company's new profits.

24. Fanning, Leonard M., *Foreign Oil and the Free World*, McGraw-Hill Book Co., Ltd., New York, 1954, p. 285.

aggravated by Russia's insistence that it be given the oil rights to the five northern provinces following exhaustive explorations carried on by them in that area.

It was a real dilemma for the Iranian government. As they saw the situation, Iran was in between power pinchers with two American companies on one hand and the Russians on the other. Each side wanted oil concessions over areas not covered by the existing Anglo-Iranian concession; futhermore, Iran's American oil experts had reported that a 50-50 division of profits between the companies and the government obtained in Venezuela.[25] Finally, the British and American governments had reached an "Agreement on Petroleum," which in time must surely have a bearing on international trade and foreign oil concessions and foreign oil resources. Iran envisaged political implications in whatever it might do. So, the Iranian government did nothing, except to ratify the cabinet ruling to not grant any further concessions until after the war. On October 16, 1944, all applicants for oil concessions in Iran were notified of this decision.

On December 2, 1944, Dr. Mossadegh introduced a bill into the Majlis to prohibit any future granting or even discussions of oil concessions with foreigners. After lengthy debate, this bill was passed by a large majority.

By the end of 1945, all American wartime troops, most of whom had been transporting supplies from the Persian Gulf to the Russians on the Caspian Sea, were withdrawn. Persia settled down to her local affairs. But not for long. Qavam as-Saltane, then prime minister, showed himself pro-Russian. Among other things which demonstrated his leaning to the neighbor on the north, was his utter disregard for the Mossadegh-Majlis law

25. It was alleged by the Iranians that under the terms of the contract with Anglo-Iraniun Oil Co., Iran's take from the oil produced and sold locally or shipped abroad was only about one-third of what it would be under the 50-50 basis at market prices.

of December, 1944 in signing an agreement (on April 4, 1946)
with Russia promising her an oil concession extending right
across north Persia.[26] Incidentally, this concession called for 51
per cent Russian and 49 per cent Persian for the first 25 years
and thereafter 50-50. True, this was not the 50-50 basis currently prevalent in Venezuela but it was a radical departure
from the terms of the Anglo-Iranian agreement. What the
Russians offered was an equal partnership in costs and profits
(though some feel the contract was so drawn that Russia could
control the profits), not much different in principle to the consortium arrangement with the National Iranian Oil Co., which
came into being in the late fall of 1955.

Some historians hold that Qavam as-Saltane never meant to
have the Russian oil concession ratified by the Majlis. At any
rate, the Russian oil concession was not ratified and all Russian
troops were evacuated from northern Iran. The Tudé party was
broken and defeated. Russian influence was now at its lowest
ebb.

On August 12, 1947, the Russian ambassador to Iran, undaunted by previous rebuffs and delays in the Majlis, presented
to Qavam the text of an oil agreement for his signature. This
agreement met with violent opposition in the Majlis—debates
dragged on and on.

A month later, the American ambassador to Iran made a
forthright speech in which he defended the right of the Iranian
people to decide for themselves as to how and to whom they
should dispose of their natural resources. This statement shook
the British who, apparently, were encouraging the Iranians to
concede the northern oil rights to Russia, perhaps in order to
take the pressure off the Anglo-Iranian Co's. oil concession in
the south.

On September 21, 1947, a leading deputy in the Majlis at-

26. Longrigg, Stephen Hemsley, *Oil in the Middle East,* Oxford University Press, Oxford, 1954, p. 145.

tacked both the proposed Russian oil concession and the existing British oil concession. Another deputy demanded that wholly owned Iranian companies be formed to exploit Iranian oil. Thus, after years of maneuvering in and out of the Majlis, the real objective of the national politicians was out in the open. No doubt, a wave of nationalization was beginning to shape which would sooner or later threaten foreign investments. However, nothing happened immediately except that the Majlis turned down the Russian oil agreement by an overwhelming majority.

With the close of World War II, there was increasing evidence that the Iranian government intended to exercise more authority over the Anglo-Iranian Oil Co. and over the country's oil reserves. Word leaked out of Teheran that the Ministry of Finance was discussing the formation of a national company for the exportation of oil. Anglo-Iranian was so concerned over this new development that it sent out to Teheran from London, Sir William Fraser,[27] then Chairman, to discuss this turn of affairs with the Shah and his ministers.

During this time, and subsequently, labor relations in the fields and at Abadan were deteriorating. The workmen were being organized into unions, with apparent Communist leanings. These new unions were quick to make demands, and in 1946 there was a series of strikes in the oil fields. In July of that year, a general strike of all oil workers was called. Fearing that the situation would get completely out of hand, British warships anchored off Abadan in Iraqi waters and word came in over the "grapevine" that Indian troops might be called in. However, in due time the tension lessened; the troops were not mustered and the warships sailed away. But, looking back, we can now realize that the upsurge of nationalism continued to simmer like a dormant volcano giving vent to steam and rumblings but not yet ready to erupt.

27. Now Lord Strathalmond.

In the early fall of 1948, N. A. Gass[28] went to Iran from London to discuss labor problems with union officials and the company staff. Generally, the workers wanted improved conditions, amenities in the oil fields, and fewer Indian workmen on the payroll. However, nothing tangible came out of these talks.

Under the law of October 22, 1947, the Iranian government was required to open discussions with Anglo-Iranian, "with a view of securing Persia's natural rights." These discussions began early in 1948. The government complained that Iran's share of the profits from oil was all too small in comparison to the take of other sovereign states overseas. The bill of particulars enumerated some 25 points[29] in all, which are here listed by title only.

1. Fluctuation in the price of gold.
2. British government taxation.
3. Limitation of company dividends.
4. Sales agreements with the British Admiralty and American companies.
5. Oil products consumed in company operations.
6. Inspection of accounts and technical information.
7. Export of crude oil.
8. Installations outside of Persia.
9. Price of oil products.
10. Oil distribution facilities.
11. Reduction of foreign employees and welfare of Persian staff and labor.
12. Prevention of gas wastage.
13. Foreign contractors.
14. Insurance.

28. Later Sir Neville Gass was Chairman of Anglo-Iranian. He is now retired.

29. These points are as listed on p. 165-169 in *Persian Oil*, by L. P. Elwell-Sutton, Lawrence and Wishart, Ltd., London, 1955. According to Elwell-Sutton, these points were drafted by the Iranian government with the assistance of two French advisers, namely, Professor Eidel and Jean Rousseau and appeared in a fifty page memorandum which was preseented to and debated in the Majlis.

15. Length of concession.
16. Royalty basis.
17. Exemptions.
18. Company shares.
19. Foreign exchange.
20. Sale of oil for export.
21. Naft-i-Shah.
22. Associated companies.
23. Change in status.
24. Company reserves.
25. Air, telegraph, telephone and other communications.

These points and the exposé appearing in the memorandum were presented to Gass and his company delegation in Teheran late in September, 1948. After several weeks of discussion, it was agreed the company delegation should take the memorandum back to London for study and to return to Iran for further talks within three months. This was done.

In April of 1949, Gass returned to Teheran. The Iranian government promptly asked that Anglo-Iranian Oil Co.'s Chairman, Sir William Fraser, also come. The first meeting with Sir William and the prime minister, Sa'ed took place May 5, when the company presented a draft of the Supplemental Agreement. This document proposed a substantial revision of royalty terms and a larger per cent of the distributed profits. However, the government felt that this new deal fell considerably short of a 50-50 division of profits. The company stood fast on the terms of its offer although the Iranian government retreated somewhat from its original proposal. By July when it was apparent that the company would not budge from its stated terms, representatives of the Iranian government signed the agreement supplementing the 1933 concession on July 17, 1949.

The new agreement was forthwith laid before the Majlis. Neither the Majlis nor the public reacted favorably. All concerned noted that the proposed new agreement dealt only with five of the 25 points at issue (namely, points 2, 3, 9, 16 and 24) and while the company did propose an upping of the royalty, their proposal did not approximate the government's views as set forth in point 16, i.e., Royalty Basis.

Debate in the Majlis on the Anglo-Iranian Oil Co. Supplemental Agreement began on July 23, 1949 and continued until July 26 when the assembly was adjourned until its final meeting two days later. No action was taken by the fifteenth Majlis on the oil matter before it adjourned and so no legislative action could be expected until after the sixteenth Majlis convened some time in the late winter or early spring.

It was in early June of 1950 when the Supplemental Agreement (Anglo-Iranian's proposal) next came before the Majlis. Two weeks later, the Majlis tossed the question into the lap of an 18-member oil commission for study—of which Dr. Mossadegh was one of four from the National Front (the Iranian political party of Dr. Mossadegh). From late June until mid-November, the Majlis oil commission discussed the Supplemental Agreement at length. The oil commission solicited views from the prime minister and the minister of finance. On November 25, the oil commission reported to the Majlis that, "The Sa'ed-Gass Supplemental Agreement is not adequate to secure the rights of Persia and it (the commission) therefore expresses its opposition to it."[30]

This report was obviously disappointing to the company, to the Shah and to his Minister of Finance, Gholan Hosein Forouhar. The latter, when defending the Supplemental Agreement before the Majlis in late December, 1950, attacked any suggestion of nationalization and announced that the government would withdraw the agreement and reopen negotiations with the company for increased royalties. Coincidentally, the public began demonstrations for immediate cancellation of the

30. Elwell-Sutton, L. P., *Persian Oil*, Lawrence & Wishart, Ltd., London, 1955, P. 184.

company's concession and nationalization of Iran's oil industry. On December 30, 1950, Saudi Arabia and the Arabian American Oil Co. executed their 50-50 agreement—similar in many respects to the 50-50 basis which had been in vogue for several years in industry in Venezuela. This Saudi Arabia-Aramco agreement was a decided breakaway from the concession terms heretofore in force in the Middle East.

The new oil commission, appointed by the Majlis following Forouhar's announcement to withdraw the company's proposal, had its first meeting on January 19, 1951.

By this time it was apparent that religious authorities in Iran were in favor of nationalization. The public fervor was fanned by the press. Dr. Mossedegh became the spokesman for nationalization of oil in Iran.

In February, 1951, the British government came alive over the seriousness of the oil situation in Iran and instructed Sir Francis Shepard, the British ambassador in Teheran to warn the Iranian government that, "While the company is prepared to discuss an agreement of an equal sharing of profits in Iran, they obviously cannot be expected to do so except on the clear understanding that the terms of the existing concession would be unaltered. They could not enter into any such agreement under threat of nationalization."[31]

In Iran, this new suggestion by Britain was considered as an attempt to put pressure on another sovereign government and was so played up by the advocates of nationalization. The proposal of a 50-50 sharing of profits from oil had come too late— several years too late to stem the tide of nationalization.

During February, March and April of 1951, oil was the principal subject of discussion in the Majlis, the Oil Commission and by the Iranian public. It also was the subject of conferences

31. Elwell-Sutton, L. P., *Persian Oil*, Lawrence & Wishart, Ltd., London, 1955, p. 205-206.

and discussions in official London and official Washington circles.

George C. McGhee, Assistant Secretary of State for Near Eastern Affairs visited Teheran in March for talks with the American ambassador to Iran, Dr. Henry F. Grady. Then in April, high officials of the British Foreign Office plus the Ministry of Fuel and Power, and Mr. Gass for Anglo-Iranian, met in Washington with U.S. State Department officials and representatives of American oil companies. The British delegates came prepared to give Iran a larger share in Anglo-Iranian Oil Co.'s profits and to admit some Iranians to their board. However, they were chagrined when they learned the American attitude envisaged that any solution to the Iranian oil problem must be within the framework of Iran's announced desire to nationalize its oil industry. The British refused to accept the principle of nationalization and so went home.

On April 26, the Iranian Oil Commission, headed by Dr. Mossadegh, approved the draft of a nine-point law[32] and submitted it to the Majlis where it was unanimously approved. Four days later, the nine-point law was approved by the Senate. On May 1, the nine-point law went to the Shah for his signature. He duly signed. Meanwhile, the Shah appointed Dr. Mohammed Mossadegh as prime minister of Iran.

> "Every correct form of approach was in due course tried. The company (Anglo-Iranian) protested to the Persian government that one-sided repudiation was specifically forbidden in the 1933 concession and further that, since by terms of that concession disputes should be submitted to arbitration, they desired the appointment of an arbitrator.

32. Elwell-Sutton, L. P., *Persian Oil,* Lawrence & Wishart, Ltd., London, 1955, p. 216-217. Because this nine-point law played such an important part in the discussions between the Consortium group and the National Iranian Oil Co. and the Iranian Government, it is reproduced in substance in the appendix of this book.

This request was summarily dismissed. A delegation of directors headed by Deputy Chairman, Basil Jackson, flew to Tehran in June (1951) with proposals consistent with the nationalization principle to set up a company with mixed British and Persian directors to operate on behalf of the National Iranian Oil Company, after vesting in the latter all Anglo-Iranian's local assets—a far-reaching, practical and from the Persian point of view, face-saving proposition. The sole reply was a demand for the complete execution of a nine-point law which the Persian's had hastily passed on May 1, without the advice of experts on the oil industry. The Jackson Mission returned after ten days[33]

Meanwhile, labor conditions in the oil fields, refinery and loading terminals had deteriorated. Oil exports had ceased by July 1. With no shipments of crude or refined products, the producing areas were forced to stop operations and the refinery slowed down almost to a standstill. Withdrawal from the fields left the Iranian government with 29,000 idle employees to pay and a salary bill of some $2,100,000 a month.

By September, of all the foreign staff, only a hard core remained. On October 4, 1951, by order of Mossadegh, the few remaining British staff embarked from Abadan on the British cruiser, H.M.S. Mauritius, for Basra and from there to England. The day following, Alick Mason, the company's senior representative and K. B. Ross, the General Refineries' Manager drove away. Thus Britain's largest overseas commercial enterprise ground to a standstill.

Subsequent developments during the next three year period will be noted in the following text under, "The Vacuum."

33. Longhurst, Henry, *Adventures in Oil*, Sidgwick & Johnson, London, 1959, p. 140-141.

THE VACUUM 1951-1954

Notwithstanding that the Iranian oil crisis of 1951 made great splashes of headlines in the United States, outside of the informed in Washington and a segment of the oil industry, only a relatively few of the general American public knew what the shouting was all about. As very little Iranian oil had come to the Western Hemisphere, the failure of that oil to flow into the world markets did not directly affect the consumers in America. Since only British properties were involved, Iran's proposed action to nationalize its oil caused only slight repercussion in Wall Street. John Q. Citizen was, for the most part, unperturbed by the histrionics of Mossadegh, although almost everyone knew the meaning of "stolen oil."

However, international oil companies and American diplomats were seriously concerned with this turn of events in Iran. Nationalization of oil[34] in Iran could set a new pattern for all other Middle East producing countries. Willy-nilly governmental flouting of commercial contracts by unilateral action, could demolish the foundation for all international business. An eco-

34. Author's Note: According to the dictionary, the word nationalization literally means, "the act of putting the ownership or control under the nation—abolishing private ownership."

In the case of Iran, the minerals in the underground always had been considered to be the property of the nation. However, Iran had leased to Anglo-Iranian, for a term of years and within a defined area, the right to search for and win hitherto undiscovered liquid and gaseous hydrocarbons at the sole expense of the company. In return for this right to "search and win," the company contracted to pay to the nation certain fees and royalties on such natural resources brought forth from the underground. Over the years at a huge cost, the company was successful in developing large oil and gas reserves and coincidentally, had created in Iran a vast estate of physical property necessary to the production, transportation and refining of petroleum. The act of nationalization in Iran would void the company's ownership to and control over these underground and surface assets.

In 1938 a similar action against the oil companies in Mexico was called "expropriation."

nomic crisis or political debacle in Iran could create a vacuum which might result in that country becoming so communistic as to lose its national independence.

Hence, although the threat of oil nationalization in Iran was primarily a matter between Great Britain and Iran, the United States government was deeply concerned. However, Uncle Sam could do little or nothing until the nationalization of oil in Iran had become virtually a certainty. When the British broke off negotations early in 1951 and when soon thereafter Anglo-Iranian began to shut down the oil fields and evacuate British employees from its oil operations in Iran, the United States moved to act as intermediary.

In May, 1951, President Truman wrote to Premier Mossadegh counseling patience and recommending Iran carry on its discussions with representatives of both the Company and the British government. On June 27, the US attitude stiffened. Dean Acheson, Secretary of State, denounced Iran for its tactics of "threat and fear" in trying to coerce the British into accepting Iran's oil nationalization program, and again urged Iran to make a further effort to come to terms with the British. The following day Mossadegh replied to President Truman repeating that his government was duty-bound to implement the nationalization act, adding that his government was willing to discuss terms of compensation and the continued use of foreign experts to supervise the "former oil company's" operations.

"On July 1, 1951, the Anglo-Iranian Oil Co. had ordered a 40 per cent cutback in the Abadan refinery and on the 3rd had decided to transfer all field operations to the Iranians and to withdraw all British personnel from the oil fields to Abadan for possible evacuation to Britain."[35]

Meanwhile, the International Court had considered the application of Anglo-Iranian in the matter, and on July 5, pro-

35. Shwadran, Benjamin, *The Middle East, Oil and the Great Powers,* Frederick A. Praeger, New York, 1955, p. 119.

posed temporary measures—such as the appointment of a Board of Supervisors—to maintain the status quo without prejudice to either party, pending final decision by the Court. The company readily accepted the recommendations of the Court but, as might be expected, the Iranian government did not.

Again on July 9, President Truman, in a letter to Premier Mossadegh, urged that Iran reconsider the International Court's recommendations as a basis for settling the dispute and offered to send W. Averell Harriman to Teheran as his personal representative to talk things over. Mossadegh replied that he would welcome Harriman but said that Iran had received no proposal or suggestion from the "former oil company" indicating acceptance of the principle of nationalization.

In the talks between Harriman and Mossadegh, Iran conceded it would not insist that the British accept the Enabling Law along with the Nationalization Law, but reiterated that acceptance of the Nationalization Law was a must. Harriman volunteered to submit this proposal to the British government. As the result of Harriman's visit in London, and further work by American Ambassador Grady in Teheran, a compromise was worked out and Richard R. Stokes, Lord Privy Seal, headed a new British delegation to Iran which arrived August 4.

Premier Mossadegh was jubilant. He told the Majlis that through Harriman's efforts the long-standing dispute of 42 years duration with reference to the southern oil concession had been totally and successfully settled. As it happened, this rejoicing was premature. Stokes submitted a proposal which the Iranian cabinet rejected. On August 21, Stokes withdraw his eight-point proposal and as a consequence, negotiations terminated. Stokes returned to England and Harriman left Teheran for the United States.

Almost immediately, the Iranian Senate gave Mossadegh a unanimous vote of confidence on his oil policy. Following this, on September 5, 1951, he threatened to expel all remaining

British technicians unless the British government resumed negotiations within 15 days. The British Foreign Office refused this ultimatum and hence, negotiations were completely broken off.

A few days later, Mossadegh submitted another proposal to Harriman which he requested be submitted to the British. On September 15, Harriman informed Premier Mossadegh that his latest proposal was no different than that previously proposed by the Iranian delegation and rejected by the British delegation, and therefore he regretted that he was unwilling to submit it to the British government.

On September 25, the latest remaining British oil technicians in Abadan were ordered by the Iranian government to leave the country by October 4. A few days later, Iranian soldiers took over the company works and locked out all British.

Soon after this action, the British declared their intention to call on the Security Council to compel Iran to abide by the interim decision of the International Court of Justice. The Council took up the British request on October 1, and at once a procedural wrangle developed.

Premier Mossadegh journied to New York to personally present the Iranian case before the Security Council. In essence, he claimed the issue was solely a domestic affair of Iran and thus neither the Court nor the Security Council had any competence.

Skipping all the details and pros and cons of the debate it must be admitted that the British attempt to force the issue through the United Nations was a failure.

The American government sincerely desired this Middle East commercial muddle settled equitably, and as soon as possible, because of its disturbing political, as well as economic effect. Hence, arrangements were made for Premier Mossadegh to meet with President Truman. This meeting took place in Washington on October 23, 1951; the next day the Premier met with the Secretary of State, Dean Acheson, and later he met with George

C. McGhee, Assistant Secretary of State. All the meetings were barren of results—no new basis of settlement could be reached. Then Mossadegh applied for a $120 million loan and left the country.

Apropos of the requested loan, it was suggested to Mossadegh by neutral diplomats, "That the International Bank of Reconstruction and Development might possibly assist in a settlement of the Anglo-Iranian oil controversy and act as an intermediary between the two member states."[36] Dr. Mossadegh expressed his willingness to have the Bank attempt to work out a solution and Robert L. Garner, Vice President of the Bank, so advised the British government. After Mossadegh had left Washington, the British Office agreed to the intercession by the Bank and Torkild Rieber, President of Barber Oil Co. and former Chairman of the Board of The Texas Co., (Texaco) was retained to act as adviser.

In January, 1952, Messrs. Rieber and Hector Prudhomme (of the staff of the Bank) visited Iran as guests of the Iranian government. They inspected the oil fields and the refinery and found them in such good physical condition as to permit operation at will. However, the Bank representatives and the Iranian officials could not agree on the price of oil, so these negotiations also stumbled to a halt.

During the mid-summer of 1952, the International Court of Justice got around to holding hearings on the competence of the Court to deal with the United Kingdom-Iranian Government case. After several weeks of hearings, the Court ruled that it had no jurisdiction. On the very day of the judgment, the Shah called on Mossadegh to form a new government and on August 3, the Majlis gave him dictatorial powers to rule the country for six months. This action was confirmed by the Iranian Senate a week later.

About the first of September, the British and American Ambassadors in Teheran delivered to Premier Mossadegh a compromise plan worked out by Prime Minister Churchill and President Truman for restoring oil operations. Within the week Mossadegh condemned the Anglo-American proposals as the worst Iran ever received. Soon thereafter, Mossadegh advised the Majlis that he might break off diplomatic relations with Britain.

On September 24, 1952, Mossadegh formally rejected the Anglo-American proposal and made counter proposals which he said were valid only for ten days from delivery. About October 14, the British Government rejected these Iranian counter proposals, whereupon the Premier announced to the world that because of this rejection he was forced to sever diplomatic relations. The official act took place on October 27.

Even after the breaking-off of diplomatic relations between Iran and Great Britain, the United States did not completely give up the possibility of working out some solution to start the oil flowing again. During the meeting of the Foreign Ministers in Paris in the middle of December 1952, Secretary of State Dean Acheson and Foreign Secretary Anthony Eden discussed the Iranian issue, and subsequently the United States Ambassador in Tehran, Loy Henderson, began a series of conversations with Premier Mossadegh which extended into 1953. At the end of December (1952), the Assistant Secretary of State for Near Eastern, South Asian and African Affairs, Henry A. Byroade, opened discussions in London with British representatives. By the middle of January 1953, it looked as if a solution was near, for Premier Mossadegh declared, though cautiously and with reservations, 'That the oil question might be resolved within two or three days,' and on February 12 he appointed a Committee to prepare a full list of Iran's claims against the A.I.O.C.[37]

On February 20, 1953 the British transmitted through the American Ambassador the proposed solution which had been worked out in conjunction with the United States. Two weeks later, following a meeting between President Eisenhower and Anthony Eden, a joint communique was issued approving this final offer and stating that the United States considered the proposal reasonable and fair. However, before the end of March, Mossadegh had rejected the new British proposal. Again Iran made counter proposals—which proved unacceptable to the British.

Finally, perhaps in desperation, Premier Mossedegh wrote a letter (May 28, 1953) to President Eisenhower complaining that because of the legal efforts of the British in blocking sale of oil from his country, Iran had suffered great loss in revenues, and appealed to the President either to persuade the British to accept Iranian terms or to advance Iran financial aid to develop her other resources in order to prevent economic collapse.

President Eisenhower finally told the Premier of Iran that it would not be consistent to use American taxpayers' money to aid his country, "So long as Iran could have access to funds derived from the sale of its oil." Furthermore, the President said that compensation merely for the loss of Anglo-Iranian's physical assets could not be called, "A reasonable settlement and that an agreement to such a settlement might tend to weaken mutual trust between free nations engaged in friendly economic intercourse."[38]

The Premier's failure to secure aid from the United States caused considerable unrest in Iran. Soon there resulted a number

37. Shwadran, Benjamin, *The Middle East, Oil and the Great Powers,* Frederick A. Praeger, New York, 1955, p. 140-141.

38. Shwadran, Benjamin, *The Middle East, Oil and the Great Powers,* Frederick A. Praeger, New York, 1955, p. 143.

of more or less serious demonstrations for and against Mossadegh. For a time the Shah's position became so precarious that he and his queen fled to Baghdad en route to Rome. Almost immediately, the Shah's men clashed with, and overcame the supporters of Mossadegh and he was forced out of office. Several hundred persons were killed or wounded in the civil strife before General Zahedi took over the government and recalled the Shah from Rome.

After the fall of Mossadegh, if anything, the United States seemed to be even more desirous than Great Britain of finding an equitable solution to the Iranian oil problem. It was evident that unless Iran's revenues could be substantially and quickly improved, this financially sick State might become prey to Communism in its more virulent and violent form. So, again the United States sought to bring the disputing parties together.

National Iranian Oil Co. had possession of the oil properties and was producing some of the wells in the fields and refining some of that oil at Abadan, but being without foreign markets for crude or refined products and being unable to cut its burdensome payroll in keeping with the reduced operations, all the while it was going deeper and deeper into the red. Quite obviously Iran had killed the golden oil goose and had thereby, lost the precious eggs.

Hence, again the United States ventured to offer its good services in an effort to bring order out of what was rapidly becoming an international calamity. The American government promised Iran some direct financial aid and concurrently sought out Herbert Hoover, Jr.—an oil consultant with wide experience in international oil legislation—to go to Teheran and there, with the help of the American Ambassador, Loy Henderson, to seek a formula which would permit oil operations to be resumed. Somewhat reluctantly, Hoover accepted (Labor Day, 1953), this assignment at the urgent request of Secretary of State John Foster Dulles.

After prolonged discussions with all concerned in Teheran, Hoover reached four basic conclusions:

First, the oil properties would have to stay nationalized, and the British could not return to the oil fields in a clearly dominant position. These were 'musts' dictated by the Iranian political situation. Any other course would sign the new government's death certificate.

Second, compensation would prove to be a major snag. Any attempt to put a figure on what Iran owed Anglo-Iranian might well prove to be fatal to the negotiations.

Third, any solution to be acceptable to Iran must be so framed as to allow Iran 'to save face.'

And fourth, that a temporary solution would be as difficult to work out as a permanent solution.

After many conferences in Iran and subsequently in London, there emerged to Hoover and his consultants the idea of Iran transferring full operating rights to the properties of the 'former oil company' to some new, politically acceptable international oil group for a long term approximating that of the old concession—this new group to compensate Anglo-Iranian directly for rights and 'interests' it acquired.

Thus the idea of an international consortium was born. Many times after that it almost died of asphyxiation. But Hoover—whose easy-going, engaging manner belied a determined streak—kept at it, pushing, pulling and cajoling.[39]

Neither the Anglo-Iranian Co. nor the British government was quick to seize on Hoover's idea of a possible solution. There was considerable spoken and silent opposition to this American intervention. However, by December, 1953, Sir William Fraser, Chairman of Anglo-Iranian, was persuaded that it would be in the best interests of his company and his country to give the Hoover plan a trial. Accordingly, he extended an invitation to

39. Jablonski, Wanda, *"Master Stroke in Iran,"* *Colliers* Magazine, January 21, 1955 issue.

the heads of the major international oil companies to sit down with Anglo-Iranian at Britannic House in London to discuss the possibility of forming a consortium to operate his former Iranian properties.

Politicians and oil men alike, agreed that it was high time something be done to salvage Iran from its financial and economic plight resulting from the three year debacle under the leadership of a tyrannical, almost fanatical, Premier-Dictator Mossadegh.

During those three years, Iran's oil production had slumped from more than 600,000 barrels per day (i.e., 219,000,000 barrels yearly) which was obtained by Anglo-Iranian in 1950, to a low of 26,200 barrels per day (i.e., 9,490,000) in 1953 under the management of National Iranian Oil Co. In the same period, Kuwait's oil production increased from 345,000 barrels daily to 861,700 barrels daily; Iraq's oil production was boosted from 136,200 barrels daily to 576,000 barrels daily and Saudi Arabia's oil production went from 546,700 barrels daily to 844,600 barrels daily.

Iraq, Kuwait and Saudi Arabia had made up in those three years more than twice the volume of Iranian oil produced in 1950. Because of this unprecedented rise in Middle East oil production from Kuwait, Iraq and Saudi Arabia, the world did not come knocking on National Iranian's door for oil, as had been expected.

The consortium idea, broached at those now famous meetings of international oil men at Britannic House in London during December, 1953, became the consortium in fact a few months later.

Largely because of American persistence at governmental level, the Anglo-Iranian wreck was salvaged to live again as British Petroleum (with greater assets and more vigor than ever before), while Iran 'saved face' and kept her nationalized oil properties.

THE CONSORTIUM

Once the consortium idea was born and accepted in principle by the international oil group, it became necessary to sort out the pieces with the respective governments and companies before the Iranians could be approached.

Initially, the Anglo-Iranian proposed that it should have (1) control of the proposed consortium, (2) a large cash payment from the consortium, (3) substantial compensation from Iran, and (4) a huge quantity of free oil or else a very large deferred payment out of oil from the consortium as compensation for the underground oil reserves discovered.

Representatives of the interested companies threshed these matters out, tooth and nail, in London from mid-February until the end of March 1954. The American group rightly felt that if it was to assist the British in this salvage project the terms would need to be such that they could stay within the laws of their country and still remain competitive with their European opposites.

Meanwhile, a team of international oil experts had gone to Iran to inspect the fields and the refinery. Their report indicated that contrary to general belief, the conditions of the wells in the field and all the plant in the fields and at the refinery were in surprisingly good condition and apparently had been well maintained. This technical committee also reported that many of the National Iranian staff were very well qualified and could run the operations with some supervision and technical aid. This observation came as a surprise, both to Anglo-Iranian and the other members of the group.

The American government took the position that Anglo-Iranian Oil Co.'s share of the consortium should be limited to 40 per cent and that the American companies should together hold a similar share with the remaining 20 percent to be held by the Dutch and the French. This division of the consortium came to be agreed, with the understanding, however, that the original five American companies, (Standard Oil Co. (New Jersey), Socony-Mobil Oil Co., the Texas Co., Standard Oil Co. of California and Gulf Oil Corp.) might each be required to reduce its 8 per cent to 7 per cent in order that an independent group of American oil companies might come to hold, collectively, 5 per cent. The 20 per cent to the Dutch and French was agreed to be split 14 per cent to the Royal Dutch Shell group and 6 per cent to the Compagnie Francaise des Petroles.

The *Observer* in London for March 7, printed this timely and terse summary of the then situation.

NEW STEP IN PERSIAN
OIL SETTLEMENT
By A Diplomatic
Correspondent

Preparations for a Persian oil settlement enter a decisive phase this week-end. The final formation of the international consortium which is to take over the marketing of Iranian oil is expected to take place in London in the next few days. A delegation of the consortium will then leave for Teheran to start negotiations with the Persian Government before March 21.

The principals of the eight oil companies interested in forming the consortium are flying to London over the week-end. Mr. Herbert Hoover, oil advisor to the United States State Department, arrives today. Mr. Denis Wright, Counsellor at the British Embassy left Teheran for London by air yesterday. Both Mr. Hoover and Mr. Wright are expected to accompany the delegation when it goes to Teheran.

Technical Problem

The plan is for the Anglo-Iranian Oil Company, which will be a member of the proposed consortium, to cede its rights in its Persian enterprise to the consortium and eventually to get its compensation from the consortium. The marketing quotas will be so distributed that Anglo-Iranian will not have a majority share in the consortium, but neither will there be an American majority. Besides the five interested American companies—Standard Oil of New Jersey, Standard Oil of California, Socony-Vacuum, the Gulf Oil Company and the Texas Company—the Compagnie Francaise des Petroles and Royal Dutch Shell are certain to participate.

Apart from the issue of compensation, the main problem for the forthcoming Teheran talks will be that of technicians. The Consortium will be able to reopen the world market to Persian oil only if it is assured of regular output. It will therefore presumably wish to secure some influence in the employment of technical and supervising staff. It will be necessary to find a way of reconciling that need with the Persian Government's wish that ultimate control over the production and refinement of Persian oil should be in the hands of its own board set up under nationalization.

On March 20, 1954, the basic terms as between Anglo-Iranian Oil Co. and the other members of the consortium were agreed and a "Memorandum of Understanding," was drawn. That memo was soon initialed and almost immediately the first consortium negotiating team consisting of Messrs. Hardin, Loudon and Snow, under the leadership of Orville Hardin,[40] set off for Teheran to open discussion with the Iranian government and National Iranian Oil Co. Although the first team made some progress during the few weeks they were in Teheran, still the prospects of a deal with National Iranian did not look too bright when they returned to London in early May.

Again in June, the principals of the consortium companies met in London with representatives of both the British and American governments. Finally, after much debate agreement between the international groups was reached and Howard

40. A director of Standard Oil Co. (New Jersey).

Page of Jersey-Standard was chosen to succeed Orville Hardin as spokesman in Teheran for the consortium.

The second consortium negotiating team arrived in Teheran on Sunday, June 20 and the next day all members of the team and observers met the British and American ambassadors and the Dutch Minister at the U.S. Embassy. Also present at this memorable meeting were Herbert Hoover, Jr., and William Roundtree representing the U. S. Department of State, Denis Wright and Angus Beckett for the U. K., and several other aides.

The first full scale meeting of the negotiations got under way between the consortium and the Iran/National-Iranian group on June 22.

All the negotiating sessions were held at the National Iranian Oil Co.'s guest house, called Elahieh, in the suburbs of Teheran. At each session eleven or more persons sat around the big table. Usually, the Iranian group was represented by Dr. Bayat (then head of National Iranian and formerly twice prime minister); Dr. Ali Amini (lawyer and finance minister); Nuri Esfandiari, (former diplomat); Mr. Rouhani, (interpreter); and Mr. Nafisi, (secretary).

For the consortium, there were the three negotiators, Howard Page (Jersey-Standard); John Loudon[41] (Shell); and H. E. Snow (Anglo-Iranian); and one, "observer"[42] for the other American and French companies, a consortium interpreter and a consortium secretary. The interpreters were seldom used except to translate memos or documents from the Persian language into English or vice versa. Practically all discussions were carried on in English although at times the speakers resorted to French. Generally, the meeting went off quietly and without undue bitterness.

41. Later replaced by D. E. J. Brouwer.
42. These "observers" were rotated among the consortium companies not represented on the three-man negotiating team—the order of rotation was determined by lot.

Considering the complexities of the situation resulting from nationalization and the three frustrating years which followed under National-Iranian's administration, any deal which could be worked out satisfactory to both Iran and the international consortium, was nothing short of marvelous. It required a world of patience and flexibility of thinking on both sides.

Summer in Teheran is hot and dusty, although the city stands at an elevation of some 5,500 feet above the sea. Fortunately, with the Iranian government's assistance, the consortium party was put up at the Darband Hotel and Villas about 12 miles outside of Teheran on the slope of the mountains some 500 feet above the city. It is not customary for hotel villas in Iran to be furnished except by the tenant. Under those circumstances, it took the consortium party quite some time to secure adequate furnishings to make life comfortable. There were, all told, about 30 men and women in the consortium group, including the lawyers, secretaries and aides.

For a workshop, the consortium obtained a short lease on Bagh-i-Djaffer Akravan, a private summer home near the Darband Hotel. The house was not in good repair but the ground floor served the consortium's purpose, especially since it was planned to do most of the group's work out in the open under the trees in the lovely gardens alongside a large inviting swimming pool. The garden and buildings were surrounded by a high wall with huge wooden gates that could be guarded day and night. What really sold the consortium on the place as a working center was the delightful cool stream of mountain water which dashed through the gardens.

From the gardens one could look up north and see the snow on the mountains. This retreat was a sort of Eden. There the group could escape from the tensions of negotiating and relax in shade to ponder and plan. A lot of work was accomplished by the consortium group in Akravan and they had some fun also.

During the negotiations a favorable omen occurred—the total

eclipse of the sun on June 30 between 4:30 and 5:00 pm. On July 4, the U.S. Embassy in Teheran held its traditional Independence Day party. The American Ambassador, Loy Henderson, and his gracious lady were charming hosts to a gathering of some 2,000 persons of all nationalities and walks of life—statesmen, diplomats, princes, government officials, officers from various armed services, agency representatives, merchants, missionaries, educators, doctors, lawyers, scientists, engineers, civilians and the consortium group. It was a gala occasion in a very friendly atmosphere.

While this delightful lawn party was held to commemorate America's Declaration of Independence in 1776, as subsequent developments demonstrated, July 4, 1954 marked the beginning of a new era in Iran—when, for the first time, Americans would be admitted on equal commercial footing with the British.

Between June 22, the date of the first consortium/National-Iranian meeting and July 7, 1954, 11 negotiating sessions had been held and so much progress had been made toward a possible agreement that the consortium members requested their respective principals to send along tax and legal counsel to assist in drafting the final papers.

The twenty-first negotiating session took place on July 22. Although there still remained a number of points to be resolved, these were not major issues and appeared to be solvable without too much difficulty. By that time, the consortium lawyers had drafted an aide-mémoire which, when finalized, would be initialed and referred by members of the consortium back to their respective companies and governments for approval.

At this stage of the negotiations it was the consensus of the consortium that only the principal negotiators and some of their legal advisers need remain in Teheran to secure the Iranian government's and National Iranian Oil Co.'s agreement to the aide-mémoire. As a result, most of the consortium observers and assistants left Iran for America and Europe the last week in July.

In August, 1954, the representatives of the several international oil companies, who were to be members of the consortium, again met in London. Committees were appointed to implement the organization of the operating companies which would take over from National Iranian in Iran, under the provisions of the aide-mémoire. Then followed many long meetings of these committees and the member companies in London. Meanwhile, the main agreement was being drafted in Iran for approval of the Council and the Majlis, after which it had to be submitted both to the U.K. and U.S. governments for final approval. It was contemplated that the earliest effective date of agreement would be September 18 or 20.

It was the unanimous opinion that there should be two operating companies in Iran—one for the fields and one for the refinery—and that both should be of Dutch nationality. D. E. J. Brouwer (Shell) was chosen as the General Manager of both operating companies and it was recommended that his board and staff consist of properly qualified American, British, Dutch, French and Iranian oil men.

It was also agreed that there should be two companies in London—one a sort of holding company and the other a servicing[43] company. Both of these London companies were to be headed by Britishers, aided by Americans, Dutchmen and Frenchmen.

On September 19, word came through from Howard Page in Teheran that the Agreement had been signed by Dr. Ali Amini for Iran at 2:00 a.m. and was being immediately dispatched by chartered plane to London for signature by the consortium.

Twenty-four hours later, the documents got to London from the Hague and were signed by Anglo-Iranian et.al., before daybreak the 20th. As soon as signed by the European members of the consortium, the document was forwarded by airmail to

43. To procure material, equipment and foreign personnel necessary to carry on the Iranian operations.

the United States for signature by the principals of the five American companies. It was a most important and dramatic day. Within a month, the consortium had the Iranian fields producing, and the Abadan refinery operating. On November 1, 1954, the first tanker loaded a cargo for export. Howard Page, representing the consortium, and Dr. Amini for the Iran government, went to Abadan for the momentous ceremonies.

As this first cargo of oil for export was being loaded out of Abadan, the author was at sea, homeward bound. It seems pertinent to quote herein the front page article appearing in the North Atlantic Edition of *The Ocean Times,* HMS "Queen Mary," on that Monday, November 1, 1954.

PERSIAN OIL FLOWS AGAIN
FROM ABADAN
First British Tanker to Leave for Nearly
Three and a Half Years

ABADAN—Intensive efforts to restore Persia's oil industry has started in refinery, oil fields and ports and 40,000 Persians have received their first orders from international companies officials operating the industry for the National Persian Company and the Persian Government.

Ten tankers from Britain, America, France and Holland will load over 130,000 tons during the next three days, which exceeds the total sold during the period following the nationalization by former Premier Mossadeq.

Oil flow began when the Anglo-Iranian tanker British Advocate left with 12,000 tons, becoming the first British tanker to leave Abadan for nearly three and a half years.

Persian royalties, on present prices, estimated at £150,000,-000 over the first three years of the resumed operation, with £31,000,000 being the first year's target.

Operating companies guarantee to produce 68,000,000 tons of crude oil during the same period, including 30,000,000 tons of refined, compared with former Anglo-Iranian production of 32,000,000 tons of crude each year, including 25,000,000 tons of refined, reports the Daily Telegraph.

Persia received 5,000,000 dollars from America as part of 110,000,000 dollars economic aid, expected during the current fiscal year.

Subsequent to execution of the consortium-Iran-National Iranian agreement, at the request of the United States government each of the five original American companies in the consortium surrender one per cent of their respective 8 per cent. The 5 per cent so surrendered was reallocated to nine independent American companies, as a group.

Since the consortium companies began to function in Iran during the latter part of 1954, there has been some realignment of operations at Abadan, the fields and at Bandar Mashur as between National Iranian Oil Co. and the consortium. Much of the non-basic operations have been turned over to National Iranian and gradually more and more of such non-basic services will be divorced from direct consortium responsibility.

During the consortium's first seven full years of operation in Iran, additional producing wells were completed in the Naft Safid, Agha Jari and Gachsaran fields, previously discovered by Anglo-Iranian. Some of the old wells in these fields, as also in the Masjid-i-Sulaiman (M.I.S.), Lali and Haft Kel fields have been reworked. Under consortium management one promising new field, Ahwaz, was discovered and went into production early in 1960.

The major engineering and construction efforts of the consortium companies have been devoted to the over-all development of Gachsaran, including the laying of a 99-mile, 26-28-30-inch pipe line from that field to Kharg Island—25 miles offshore from the mainland. Seventy-four miles of this big inch pipe line traverses rugged, broken terrain and desert and the balance is laid under the sea. This pipe line system has an initially designed capacity of 330,000 barrels a day, all by gravity flow from Gachsaran (elevation 2,215 feet) to the Kharg Island tank farm (elevation 200 feet).

Housing, workshops, clinic, hospital, storage facilities, air strips, offices and a tanker loading pier were also scheduled for construction on Kharg Island in connection with the over-all development scheme.[44] The oil loading terminal, pipe line system and related facilities were completed in the last half of 1960.

The consortium's operations in Iran have been very successful both for Iran and National Iranian, as also for the member companies.[45] Iran's economy has benefited tremendously by her income from oil.

During 1961, the seventh full year of operation under consortium administration, the former Anglo Iranian properties produced some 428 million barrels of crude, whereas in 1953, the last full year under National Iranian administration, all Iranian fields produced only 9.8 million barrels of crude—a difference of about 418 million barrels.

1961 consortium production by fields, expressed in million barrels:

Agha Jari	258.2
Ahwaz	2.6
Gachsaran	92.1
Haft Kel	45.7
Lali	4.0
Masjid-i-Sulamian	12.7
Naft Safid	12.2
Total	427.5

In 1962 the consortium continues its search for new fields. Exploratory wells are being drilled at Khalafabad, 15 miles

44. From Iranian oil operating companies 1958, annual report. (Actually the Gachsaran/Kharg Island pipe line system and deep-sea terminal was put in service during August, 1960).

45. Originally there were five American companies each having 8 per cent interest, now there are 14 American companies—five having 7 per cent interest each and the other nine having 5 per cent altogether.

northwest of Agha Jari, on Kharg Island and on Queshm Island at the entrance to the Persian Gulf. Also wildcat tests are scheduled at Mushtaq, about 50 miles northwest of Ahwaz near the Iraqi frontier, and at Bushgan, about 55 miles southeast of Bushire.

It is also interesting to note the comparison of production and overseas personnel for years 1950 and 1958:

	1950 Anglo-Iranian	1958 Consortium	Difference
Crude Produced— Barrels	242,476,000	299,499,000	57,023,000
Foreign Personnel Employed(A)			
U. K.	2,725	285	—2,440
Others	1,778	306(B)	—1,472
Total	4,503	591	—3,912

(A) At end of year (for A.I.O.C. this figure may include some overseas personnel working for contractors).
(B) Includes 198 U.S., 95 Dutch, 9 French and 4 other alien employees.

NATIONAL IRANIAN OIL COMPANY

Today, the official government oil industry agency in Iran is the National Iranian Oil Co. In addition to its non-basic operational activities in the consortium area, National Iranian Oil Co., operates actively and directly in northern and central Iran in all phases of the oil business—exploration, production, refining, oil products and gas distribution and intracountry marketing.

During 1961, National Iranian production from the Naft-i-Shah field totaled some 2.9 million barrels as compared with 2.4 million barrels produced in 1960.

For some years National Iranian has been drilling in the Qum area of north central Iran—roughly 175 miles north of the consortium Lali field and about 90 miles south of Teheran. Two producing fields have been discovered—oil in the Alborz field and gas condensate in the Saradjeh. Both discoveries are important to Iran internal economy.

The Alborz oil field has proven to be tricky. In March, 1962, Alborz well No. 10 was drilling. Of the nine previous wells, No. 3 is reported to have found oil but no yield was announced; No. 5 encountered high pressure oil and gas and went wild; No. 5A drilled nearby was suspended; No. 8 has an estimated potential of some 20,000 barrels a day, and No. 9 has found oil but is still testing. Wells Nos. 1, 2, 4, 6 and 7 were all failures. In 1961 oil production from Alborz was reported to have been 198,500 barrels.

In 1958 a gas condensate field was discovered at Saradjeh, about 25 miles southeast of Alborz. During the last three years a number of additional wells have been successfully drilled in this area. As the result of these completions the Saradjeh reserves are conservatively estimated at 300 trillion cubic meters of gas and 8.2 million cubic meters of light oil. A 20-inch, 87-mile gas line is to be built to Teheran, the capital of Iran.

During 1961 National Iranian drilled three wildcats at Gorgan, Mazanderan and Yortishah in northern Iran—all were failures.

National Iranian owns half interests in the partnership firms Societe Irano Italienne des Petroles (SIRIP) and Iran Pan American Oil Co., (IPAC). Both SIRIP and IPAC continued active exploration and drilling during 1960 and 1961, mostly in their offshore areas. Their activity will be mentioned in more detail in Chapter 8.

TOTAL IRAN

Iran has produced through 1961, a total of more than 4.5 billion barrels of crude oil. For the oil production record of Iran by years since 1913 and the estimated proven reserves in the ground at the end of 1960, see Appendix IV.

Persian Oil In Retrospect

From 1870 until 1951, the British monopolized oil in Persia. For 81 years neither Russian nor American capital was able to hold oil concessions over Persian lands. However, in all fairness, it must be said that the inability of other nationals to hold oil concessions in Persia was not directly due to opposition from or pressure by the British. More than anything else, the Russian and American oil men were defeated by politics and geography. However, other foreign oil interests certainly were not encouraged to secure, explore or exploit concessions nearby Anglo-Iranian's holdings. It was only human nature for the British to want to protect and hold their oil empire, which they alone discovered and so ably developed.

The fact that the British so long enjoyed a virtual monopoly over Persian oil may not have been good for the British. Such control over a major natural resource in any country tends to make the controller complacent. That, "The King can do no wrong," is a fallacy in commerce as well as in politics.

However, and notwithstanding, it is the author's belief that no oil company anywhere was a better operator than Anglo-Iranian. Also that no company was more jealous of the welfare of its employees in Persia—regardless of nationality—than that company.

The great Abadan refinery and oil loading terminal were built on a swamp. The oil fields lay in stark, broken, desert hills where there is little or no vegetation except in the brief rainy season. In these forbidding hills and the swamp lands of the Shatt-el-Arab (confluence of the Tigris and Euphrates rivers) the British built homes for their workmen, set up hospitals, commissaries, schools, churches and clubs, drilled wells, laid pipe lines, erected tankage, established material and equipment depots, maintained huge machine shops and set up one of the world's largest oil refineries.

The company created at its own expense, a whole township at Abadan. A city of more than 125,000 people, complete with homes, streets, sewer and water service, electricity, shops, movies —in fact everything usually provided by the municipality or state. The company not only footed the bill for the first cost, but also paid for the maintenance. Furthermore, the company subsidized a food and clothing "basket" for native employees, which cost the company (when the author was in Abadan in 1947) some $2,800,000 per year. No other oil company in the Middle East had done so much for so many employees.

Some have charged that Anglo-Iranian did not integrate Persians into skilled and staff work fast enough. While it may be true that British and Indian employees were favored, that was largely because they already had the knowhow and could accept authority readily. Still, the company persevered in training Persians both in skilled work and for staff jobs. For example, in 1947 there were 3,466 trainees in addition to some 1,100 regular employees in the Abadan machine shops.

If the Anglo-Iranian erred in its employee relations, it probably was in the direction of doing too much rather than too little for its workmen. The workmen became too dependent upon the company until the individual lost all values as to what was due him from his employer and as to what should have been provided by his government. From cradle to grave, the families, as well as the Anglo-Iranian workmen were dependent upon the company. The entire community was beholden to the company—company workmen and their families were, in a sense, captives of the industry. Anglo-Iranian was the grand patron throughout an area of 100,000 square miles, an area only slightly smaller than all New Zealand.

The region that had once been economically poor became rich. The people of that area never had had it so good.

At the end of 1950, Anglo-Iranian had on its payroll direct and indirect employees in Iran, including trainees, a total of

61,740 bodies, of which 57,237 were Persians, 2,725 were British and 1,778 were other foreigners, mostly Indian. In other words, the total foreign employees was only 7.3 per cent of the total of all Anglo-Iranian personnel.

Without doubt, for several years before nationalization, Anglo-Iranian Oil Co. operations in the fields and at Abadan were over-manned. However, the Iranian labor laws were then such that personnel could not be released for lack of work or inefficiency; only through disorderly conduct, disablement, death or retirement could the payroll be reduced. This situation led to discontent among the more or less idle workmen and their families and was a considerable financial burden on the company.

No one who knows can claim that Anglo-Iranian Oil Co. was not humanitarian in the treatment of its employees of all nationalities. However, the fact remains that the workmen were unhappy. Maybe because they wanted to earn more and be given less or it may have been because the captive workman felt himself indispensable to the operation.

Generally, from the standpoint of employee work output, the order of sequence was rated by the management, first British, then Indian and finally Persian.

Many times the question has been asked, "Need nationalization of oil in Persia have occurred?" Some do not think so.

The pattern of equal sharing of profits from oil, as between the company and the country of origin, had been established in Venezuela as early as 1942. Thus, in spite of everything Anglo-Iranian had done, employee wages and emoluments in other foreign oil areas had outstripped Persia. The proportion of non-nationals to nationals was as low or lower in most foreign oil developments than in Persia.

Apparently, Anglo-Iranian closed its eyes to these important factors or at least considered that they did not apply to their empire. When the company management was finally aroused to the point of trying to remedy the comparative disparity in treatment, both as respects the country and the employee, the die had been cast. That is, both the Persian government and the workers had gone too far in their respective demands to compromise without loss of face—something which the people of the East abhor above all else.

Sir William Fraser is reported to have said on a number of occasions that Anglo-Iranian's proposed Supplemental Agreements (1949) constituted a better deal for Persia than obtained elsewhere in the oil countries of the Middle East or even in South America. No doubt he was sincere in his belief but unfortunately Persia and the Persians did not think so.

Some oilmen feel that this original Anglo-Iranian complacency, more than anything else, led to the nationalization of oil in Persia.

In order to convey to the reader the British viewpoint and, no doubt, the general feeling of the Anglo-Iranian Oil Co., in respect to the take-over of the oil properties in Iran, it seems pertinent to quote liberally from Henry Longhurst's recent book (1959), *Adventures in Oil—The Story of British Petroleum,* pages 144 and 145.

Before considering, if not answering, the inevitable question, "Need it all have happened?", it might be of interest briefly to survey both what the Persians found in their hands as a legacy of the Company's activities and what they lost as a result of its departure.

The Company left behind oilfields producing 32 million tons a year and the biggest refinery in the world with a throughput of 24 million tons. In addition to Masjid-i-Sulaiman and Haft Kel, they had discovered, surveyed and were expanding the enormous Agha Jari field and the others at Lali, Naft Safid and Gach Saran, and geological, geophysical and topographical survey parties were at work in many other parts. A new crude-oil loading terminal capable of exporting 6 million tons of crude oil a year had been constructed at

Bandar Mashur. A huge catalytic cracking plant and a lubricating oil unit were being brought into production at Abadan and 189 miles of extra pipe lines being laid down. In 1951 the Company was employing some 70,000 Persians. The annual wage bill amounted to about £20 million. In royalties over £16 million was paid to the Persian Government for 1950, making a total of over £100 million since the beginning of the 1933 concession. Had the Supplemental Agreement been ratified Persia would have received over £70 million for the years 1948-1950 instead of £38 million. The profit made by Persia out of the Company's purchases of Persian currency in 1950 (£21 million), which had to be made at an arbitrary rate of exchange fixed by the Persian Government, was £7 million.

By the beginning of 1951, the Company had built, equipped and handed over to the Persian Ministry of Education thirty schools, and its Technical College was probably the finest east of Suez. They had also built, equipped and staffed 3 hospitals and 35 dispensaries and had virtually created all the public health services of South-West Persia. The cost of their housing programme between 1945 and December 1950 was over £28 million. They had built and were maintaining more than 1,250 miles of roads and 40 major bridges.

IRAN—POSTSCRIPT

This story about Persian oil has been longer than was intended but the author was at a loss to portray the oilmen's influence in Persia without summarizing the history of oil exploration and development which occurred in Persia prior to 1954. For more than 80 long years after oil was discovered in Baku on the Caspian, American oil companies, except briefly, held no concessions in Iran until they were "invited" to join the international consortium.

3

Iraq—Qatar

IRAQ WAS ESTABLISHED BY THE BRITISH after
World War I as a modern kingdom.[46] In area, the country is
only slightly larger than the combined area of California and
Maryland. However, Iraq embraces much of the old Bible lands
which straddle the valleys of the Euphrates and Tigris rivers.

Within its borders are to be found such ancient places as the
Ur de Chaldees (birthplace of Abraham), Hit (from which
bitumen was taken to build the walls of Babylon), Baba Gurgur
(traditional fiery furnace of Shadrach, Meshach, and Abednego), Nineveh (the reputed Tomb of Jonah and one time capital of Assyria), Kish (capital after the great flood), Erbie or
Arbela (which has existed as a town since before 2200 B.C.)
and the traditional site of the Garden of Eden (on the shore of
Lake Habbaniya adjacent to the Euphrates River). It is a land
rich in history and at one time the granary of the Middle East.

For more than 5,000 years the region we now know as Iraq
was prized for its irrigated fertile valleys and its overland trade
routes. Several dynasties, at one time or another, had their capi-

46. The coup d'etat of July, 1958, overthrew the kingdom and set up a
republic form of government in Iraq.

77

tals along its mighty rivers. Assyrians, Chaldeans, Babylonians, Tartars, Persians, Arabs, Crusaders and Turks, all waged wars within its borders.

The Greeks had a word for it, namely, "Mesopotamia," meaning "middle rivers." In the Arabic language Iraq means the banks of a river, "for the whole length thereof."[47] But Iraq is only a small part of what was known as Mesopotamia under the Ottoman Turks.

Unlike the Nile, when floods come in the Euphrates and Tigris valleys, the rivers more often than not, are given to meandering. In the past, great damage has been done by these floods—irrigation canals have been obliterated, fields destroyed and often there has been heavy loss of life and property. Noah knew of the toll the "Great Flood" could take and, forewarned, he built the Ark to perpetuate life in that part of the world.

So much detrital material has been carried along by the flood waters of the Euphrates and Tigris that their deltas have filled the whole northern end of the Persian Gulf embayment. Ancient Gulf seaports are now more than 150 miles inland from tidewater.

The great valleys of the Euphrates and Tigris rivers were once favored overland trade routes. Boats plied up the Persian Gulf waters from India and China and thence up the rivers to the head of navigation from whence caravans of camels, heavily laden, trekked out across the deserts and mountains westward to the Mediterranean or northward to the Caspian. Medieval Baghdad became the trading center for all the Middle East. Baghdad remains today, the capital of modern Iraq and the largest city in that country.

The Ottoman Turks partially conquered the peoples in the valleys of the Euphrates and Tigris in 1534, but were unable to completely oust the Persians until 1638. From that date until 1918, Mesopotamia was dominated by the Ottomans.

47. Yale, William, *The Near East,* University of Michigan Press, Ann Arbor, 1958, p. 306.

The British armies invaded and occupied much of what we know as Mesopotamia during World War I. One historian says, "The British during the four years of war brought more progress to the Tigris and Euphrates Valleys than had centuries of Turkish rule."[48]

At the Paris Peace Conference in 1919, under President Wilson's leadership, the League of Nations adopted a Covenant, Article XXII of which provided for mandates to be established over, "Certain communities formerly belonging to the Turkish Empire," until such a time as those areas can stand alone as independent nations.

"Before World War I, the Persian Gulf area was almost a private British preserve and in the Ottoman province of Mesopotamia the British were predominant, politically and commercially."[49] Britain desired to retain some considerable vestige of control over the area drained by the Euphrates and Tigris—but the League of Nations' Covenant threatened their control.

On April 25, 1920, at San Remo, Mesopotamia was mandated to Britain. A few months later insurrection broke out in Iraq. This was quickly crushed by the British-Indian forces but not before nearly 10,000 lives had been lost in the fighting.

At Baghdad on October 17, 1920, Sir Percy Cox (British High Commissioner), declared Britain's intention to establish a national government for Iraq. In due course the British prompted by T. E. Lawrence, chose Emir Faisal, recently of Syria, as a likely candidate for the throne of Iraq. Faisal had been an ally of the British in the war against the Turks. Percy Cox was notified of His Majestys Government's choice and was instructed to make such arrangements as he deemed advisable

48. Yale, William, *The Near East,* University of Michigan Press, Ann Arbor, 1958, p. 314.
49. Yale, William, *The Near East,* University of Michgan Press, Ann Arbor, 1958, p. 317.

for declaring Faisal as king. A plebiscite of sorts was held and on August 23, 1921, Faisal was proclaimed King of Iraq.

So much for the historic background of Iraq. This country— birthplace of prophets, despoiled by the hordes, once a vast granary, ancient trading center for the Middle East and more recently the pawn of power politics—was again to loom large in the world news because of its petroleum deposits.

Oil In Iraq

In 1869, an Armenian lad—born at Scutari on the Asiatic shore of the Bosporus—was christened Calouste Sarkis Gulbenkian. His formative years were spent in England. While still in his twenties this same young man reported to Hagop Pasha, Turkish Minister of the Liste Civile (guardian of Sultan Abdul Hamid's private finances), on the oil prospects of Mesopotamia. In his memoirs, Gulbenkian says, "I elaborated a comprehensive report which was nothing else than a compilation of various travelers' books, principally of reports made by Colonel Chesney on his East Indian missions, and particularly from what I heard from different engineers of the Antolia Railway who had been in Mesopotamia."[50]

Although it is not certain that Gulbenkian had, in fact, ever visited the surface manifestations of oil and gas in the valleys of the Euphrates and Tigris, he had been in the Baku area and his father was a petroleum merchant, hence, Calouste could appraise the economic importance of petroleum in quantities. So impressed was the Sultan with Gulbenkian's report that he decreed the transfer of the petroleum revenues from the treasury to his own Privy Purse by firmans of 1890 and 1899, besides obtaining possession of a number of the known oil bearing

50. Hewins, Ralph, *Mr. Five Per Cent,* Rinehart & Co., Inc., New York, 1958, p. 29.

lands.[51] Thus Gulbenkian laid the foundation of his great fortune and incidentially, also of his subsequent nickname in the oil industry—"Mr. Five Per Cent."

At the turn of this century, the Ottoman Empire embraced all of what is now Turkey, Syria, Iraq, Lebanon, Palestine, Jordan and the Arabian peninsula. It was a vast empire of mountains and desert lands—an empire, which has since been proven to hold the largest petroleum reserves in all the world.

Europe had come alive to the potentialities of Mesopotamia through the reports of German experts as early as 1871, and later by the reports of de Morgan (1892), Stahl (1893), Colonel Maunsell (1897) and Baron von Oppenheim (1899). The Germans were especially interested in their railroad project—Berlin to Baghdad—and above all they desired a seaport on the Persian Gulf.

In 1904, the Young Turk Revolution took place and as one of the results, the Mesopotamia oil lands were transferred from the Sultan's private Civil Lists to the Ministry of Finance.

"By 1912 there were four different groups seeking concessions in Mesopotamia: (1) German-Deutsche Bank, (2) British-D'Arcy, (3) Dutch-Anglo Saxon Oil Co., and (4) American-Chester group."[52] That same year a British company named the Turkish Petroleum Co. was formed, but it was not until two years later that the British obtained control of the shares of this company, leaving the Dutch and Germans with the little end. The American group was frozen out entirely.

On June 28, 1914, the Grand Vizier of the Ottoman government informally granted The Turkish Petroleum Co. a concession for the exploitation of the oil fields in the vilayets of Mosul and Baghdad.

51. Longrigg, Stephen Hemsley, *Oil in the Middle East,* Oxford University Press, London, 1954, p. 13.
52. Shwadran, Benjamin, *The Middle East, Oil and the Great Powers,* Frederick A. Praeger, New York, 1955, p. 194.

The claim of the American group to oil rights in Iraq grew out of Rear Admiral Colby M. Chester's efforts in 1908 when he went to Constantinople for the purpose of obtaining railway and mining concessions. "He had the backing of the New York Chamber of Commerce, the New York State Board of Trade, and was supported by President Theodore Roosevelt and Secretary of State Elihu Root."[53] A year later, Admiral Chester entered into agreements with Turkey involving the construction of a port and three railway lines with mineral rights for 20 kilometers on both sides of these projected rail lines. To implement these concessions, Chester organized the Ottoman-American Development Co.

On March 9, 1910, these concessions were signed by the Turkish Minister of Public Works and a year hence were sent to Parliament for ratification. The Turko-Italian War, the Balkan War and World War I so enmeshed the Turkish government that the Chester concession was never officially ratified. However, later developments demonstrated that the American claims to oil rights in Iraq were not to be entirely ignored.

The French, too, laid vigorous claim to oil rights in Mesopotamia because of the important part her soldiers had played in the Middle East and also by reason of her mandate over Syria and the Lebanon. There was no way to get oil out of northern Iraq to the Mediterranean except by pipe line through territory more or less controlled by the French.

On April 25, 1920, the British and French signed an agreement parceling out the shares of Turkish Petroleum Co., 75 per cent British (including the Dutch share) and 25 per cent French.

When this agreement became known in the United States,

53. Quoted from *The Middle East, Oil and the Great Powers,* by Benjamin Shwadran, Frederick A. Praeger, New York, 1955, in turn referenced to *American Oil Claims in Turkey,* by Henry Woodhouse, Current History XI, March 1922, p. 197.

tension mounted. Both the government and the public knew that US petroleum reserves had been severely taxed by the war. It was generally felt that unless America could win substantial foreign oil reserves, domestic sources might fail within a score of years. Also, as was subsequently pointed out to the allied governments, America had contributed much in the way of manpower, fuel and material in the World War effort and so should rightfully share in the "spoils."

Strong notes of protest were passed to the UK government by our State Department. America advocated the Open Door Policy.

Following the San Remo conference in 1920, Iraq was mandated to the British.

In 1921, Secretary of Commerce, Herbert Hoover, invited representatives of the big American oil companies to meet with him and to consider the Mesopotamia oil prospects. Literally, "representatives of the industry were called to Washington and told to go out and get it,"[54] meaning foreign oil reserves. These American oil companies advised Secretary Hoover that they were ready and willing to dispatch a party of engineers and geologists to Mesopotamia forthwith to make a reconnaissance, always provided such action had the blessing of Washington. A letter[55] reiterating this intention was dispatched by those same oil companies to Secretary of State Hughes the same day (November 3, 1921).

Slowly the diplomatic wheels began to turn, during which

54. The author's statement before "Special Committee Investigating Petroleum Resources" United States Senate, 79th Congress, First Session, June 27-28, 1945—United States Government Printing Office, Washington, 1946.

55. This letter was signed by W. C. Teagle, Standard Oil Co. (New Jersey); G. W. Van Dyke of the Atlantic Refining Co.; H. F. Sinclair of Sinclair Consolidated Oil Co.; C. F. Meyer, Vice President of Standard Oil Co., (New Jersey); George S. Davidson, President, Gulf Refining Co.; Amos L. Beatty, President, The Texas Co.; and E. L. Doheny, President, Mexican Petroleum Co.—seven companies in all.

the American companies could only mark time. In August, 1922, Turkish Petroleum Co. offered the American companies 12 per cent interest—this was refused. After some weeks the offer was raised to 20 per cent and finally in December, the Turkish Petroleum Co. stated it was willing to grant the Americans 24 per cent (from the shares of Anglo-Persian). However, the conditions were that Anglo-Persian should receive, free of charge, 10 per cent of the crude produced by the concession and also that the US State Department should agree not to question Turkish Petroleum Co.'s title and advise the American representatives at Lausanne to strongly support this arrangement to the exclusion of all other interests, American or otherwise. Secretary Hughes balked at these last two conditions.

Early in 1922, Admiral Chester had caused the Ottoman-American Development Co. to be reorganized. Representatives of this new company went to Turkey to negotiate at the same time the conference was being held in Lausanne. Curiously enough, in January, 1923, the US State Department is said to have advised the American acting High Commission in Constantinople it would give support to all Americans seeking concessions.

"In November 1922, Kemal abolished the Sultanate and thus set about shaping a modern state. At the Treaty of Lausanne he obtained all he sought. Turkey kept East Thrace. The British evacuated Constantinople. The Turkish Straits were demilitarized and guaranteed by the Great Powers. Turkey ceded Syria, Mesopotamia, Palestine and Arabia and renounced nominal suzerainty over Egypt, Cyprus and the Sudan. But Turkey proper survived."[56] This pronouncement was made nearly a year after the British had installed Faisal as King of Iraq.

In the spring of 1923, the Chester Agreement was signed in Ankara. However, the Ottoman-American Development Co.

56. Hewins, Ralph, *Mr. Five Per Cent,* Rinehard & Co., Inc., New York, 1958, p. 122.

did not have the necessary financial backing to prosecute work under its concession and, accordingly, the Chester concession was annulled in December of that year.

These diplomatic and political moves had until now stymied the American oil interests from reaching agreement with the Turkish Petroleum.

GULBENKIAN

Meanwhile, Gulbenkian continued to assert, in high places, his claims to an interest in the Mosul concession. Many Americans have long wondered how and why Gulbenkian obtained a 5 per cent interest in the Turkish Petroleum Co., which later became the Iraq Petroleum Co. It was not until *Mr. Five Per Cent,* by Ralph Hewins[57] was published in 1958 that the how and why became apparent to the public. Under the circumstances, liberal references are made herein to the passages in that book.

The reader should bear in mind that Calouste Gulbenkian had favorably reported on the oil prospects of Mesopotamia to the Ottoman government in the 1890's. Later, he became financial and economic adviser to the Turkish embassies in Paris and London and then, a few years later, was nominated by the Turkish government as its Chief Financial Adviser. For these reasons, Gulbenkian had a remarkable prestige both in Europe and in Turkey.

In 1910, Gulbenkian went to Turkey as technical adviser to the British mission headed by Sir Ernest Cassel. On the mission's return to London from Constantinople, the National Bank of Turkey was formed, solely with British capital. Gulbenkian was

57. In the preface to his book, Hewins notes that much of the material for *Mr. Five Per Cent* was obtained from Nubar Gulbenkian's (son of Calouste) notes or was gleaned from Calouste Gulbenkian's Memoirs, written in 1945. (Except as otherwise noted, the quotations in this text under the heading, "Gulbenkian," are from the book *Mr. Five Per Cent).*

nominated to the new bank's Executive Committee and was made a Director. Gulbenkian emphasized to his colleagues in the Bank that Banking business in Turkey was not at all remunerative—owing to keen competition from the German, French and Italian banks—and urged their bank to take a decided interest in the development and oil prospects of the declining Ottoman Empire.

The first major step of the National Bank of Turkey was in the direction of making an agreement with the Deutsche Bank whereby the Anatolia-Baghdad Railways and their mining rights (20 kilometers on both sides) would be merged with British interests. Soon as the British and German bankers had agreed, the respective rights were temporarily transferred to the African and Eastern Concession (an African mining venture belonging to Sir Ernest Cassel). In 1912, the name, African and Eastern Concessions, was changed to, Turkish Petroleum Co. Of the original 80,000 shares issued, 32,000 shares were allotted to Gulbenkian and an oil group of his choosing.

The Royal-Dutch Shell group was relying on Gulbenkian as one of its three creators, to support their interests, as against the Anglo-Persian Oil Co., in this scramble for Mesopotamia oil rights. According to Gulbenkian's memoirs:

> 'I therefore offered them, that is to say, 25 per cent of the company, to Lane and the Royal Dutch Shell Group, keeping for myself 18,000 shares, i.e., 15 per cent'.

The Company (Turkish Petroleum) was, therefore, constituted as follows:

		Shares
Deutsche Bank and Anatolia Railway	(25 per cent) Free	20,000
Royal Dutch Shell Group	(25 per cent) Cash	20,000
C. S. Gulbenkian	(15 per cent) Cash	12,000

Sir Ernest Cassel and National
Bank of Turkey   (35 per cent) Cash   28,000

                                                80,000

The founders of the Bank did not want to indulge in oil speculation, but their intention was to be connected with this enterprise in order to have future banking advantages.

As an oil man, I knew the 15 per cent was a big participation because I could very well gauge the enormous capital outlays necessary. However, I thought that I could keep the 15 per cent temporarily and watch events, as I felt sure that I could at any time dispose of the whole amount.

As early as 1900 the D'Arcy group had sent representatives to Constantinople in an effort to obtain all concessions in Mesopotamia—but their mission obtained nothing. About the same time, the Royal Dutch Shell Group sent a representative on a similar mission to Turkey—they, likewise, obtained nothing.

Again, to quote from Gulbenkian's Memoirs:

About 1912-13, the Anglo-Persian Oil Company, having been acquainted with the fact that an organization was set on foot for the development of Mesopotamia, in which they had no interests, at once got exceedingly upset and decided by hook or crook to get the upper hand in our Company . . . The problem of the Anglo-Persian Oil Company was to exclude the interests of the National Bank of Turkey, the Royal Dutch Shell and mine, thus appropriating 60,000 shares out of 80,000, the total capital of the Turkish Petroleum Company.

In 1913, considerable pressure was brought to bear on Sir Ernest Cassel, a personal friend of King Edward VII, to place the Turkish National Bank's shares (28,000) at the disposal of the British government. Sir Ernest Cassel agreed and urged Gulbenkian and the Royal Dutch Shell Group to do likewise.

When Deterding (Chairman of the Royal Dutch Shell Group)

was apprised of the situation, he became furious and said he would never agree to it and urged Gulbenkian not to do so either, lest it mean a definite rupture between them.

Deterding took steps to inform his government, "That a Dutch corporation with legitimate participation in a British company was being unfairly subjected to pressure to renounce its rights."

While these maneuvers for control were going on in London, the German group (Deutsche Bank) in the Turkish Petroleum Co. was pressing Gulbenkian et al., to come to terms with Anglo-Persian or find some other means of putting an end to this troublesome situation which was causing great difficulties for the Turkish government.

According to the Gulbenkian memoirs:

> In 1913, the official negotiations between the British government, the Turkish Petroleum Company and the Royal Dutch Shell group passed out of my hands to those of Mr. Deterding, who relied on the support, if necessary, of the Dutch Government.

During the ensuing negotiations, Gulbenkian was in daily contact with Deterding, urging him to settle with Anglo-Persian on some equitable basis. As proof of his desire for peace and satisfaction, Gulbenkian placed at Deterding's disposal, two-thirds of his participation in the Turkish Petroleum Co., namely, 10 per cent of shares of the company. "This is how my 15 per cent became 5 per cent," according to the Gulbenkian Memoirs. In deference to Gulbenkian, it should be noted that he neither asked nor received any remuneration for the 8,000 shares of Turkish Petroleum Co. which he relinquished.

In confirmation of Gulbenkian's Memoirs there is quoted below a passage from the book written by Glyn Roberts, published by Covici Friede in New York 1938, entitled, *The Most*

Powerful Man in the World—The Life of Sir Henri Deterding,
p. 150:

> By the time Gulbenkian had finished, the Turkish Petro-
> leum Company was a completely different proposition. The
> 50 per cent given to the National Bank of Turkey, or most of
> it, was now the property of the D'Arcy (Anglo-Persian) group.
> In other words, three quarters of the oil of Mosul was to go,
> after all, to British or semi-British groups. Certainly Gulben-
> kian had done a slick thing. For it, he was given a 5 per cent
> holding in the Company . . . this was fixed up on March 19,
> 1914 . . . Gulbenkian had served London and Deterding well.

On March 24, 1914, there was a conference held in the
Foreign Office attended by representatives of the Turkish government, the British government, the German government, the
Deutsche Bank and the Royal Dutch Shell Oil Group. Here it
was formally agreed that the shares of Turkish Petroleum Co.
would be held 50 per cent by Anglo-Persian Oil Co. which put
up £160,000; 25 percent by the Deutsche Bank and 25 per
cent by the Royal Dutch Shell Group. Gulbenkian's 5 per cent
was to be provided equally by Anglo-Persian and Royal Dutch
Shell for life. The National Bank of Turkey's share holding
disappeared.

Two months later (May 20, 1914) the British government
acquired control of Anglo-Persian Oil Co.—still the Foreign
Office agreement, vis-a-vis Turkish Petroleum Co., had not been
ratified by the Ottoman regime. In fact, no shares had been
transferred and no concession formally signed. Under such circumstances operations could not begin.

To make matters even more confused, the international situation was rapidly worsening. Before anything tangible was decided, war was declared on August 4, 1914. However, in the
interim, the Ottoman Grand Vizier wrote a letter to the British
and German ambassadors in which he said the Minister of

Finance agreed to lease petroleum deposits, "discovered or to be discovered" in the vilayet[58] of Baghdad and Mosul, to the Turkish Petroleum Co. While this was not a legal document, it did form the basis for the Turkish Petroleum Co.'s approach to the newly formed government of Iraq ten years later.

Nothing was accomplished by the Turkish Petroleum Co. during the war years. It was a stagnant organization.

Following the war, Gulbenkian again exerted his influence with the British and the French to pass the German interest in Turkish Petroleum on to a French company. By this time, the Deutsche Bank share in the company had been taken over by the British treasury and the Custodian of Enemy Property.

With the knowledge and consent of the Foreign Office and also the Royal Dutch Shell Group, the French came to hold the German shares in the Turkish Petroleum Co.—this transfer is believed by some to have taken place after the San Remo Treaty (April 24, 1920). The Turkish Petroleum Co. was at once reconstituted:

Anglo-Persian	47.5 per cent
Royal Dutch Shell	22.5 per cent
French Group	25 per cent
Gulbenkian	5 per cent

AMERICANS IN IRAQ OIL

World War I had lost to the free world, the oil fields of Rumania, Poland and Austria, and the oil from Baku could only be had on Soviet terms. Except dollar oil from the Western Hemisphere, only Persian oil was readily available to supply the European markets, and there still was not enough Persian oil to satisfy those markets.

"World War I had been won with United States oil, assisted

---

58. "Vilayet"—an administrative division of Turkey.

by Mexican oil. Tanks, trucks and airplanes—all new to war—had left the Great Powers exceedingly oil conscious. Now a world-shortage scare was in full cry . . . Alarmed because of a possible oil shortage, Washington told American companies in effect, 'go out and get foreign oil'."[59]

To Europeans and Americans alike, the Middle East appeared to offer the best prospects of finding new oil reserves and in all that area, the oil prospects of Mesopotamia loomed most inviting.

Thus, when the San Remo Agreement dealt with the petroleum reserves in Rumania, Asia Minor, France and the British colonies—ignoring entirely the Western Allies—Americans began to clamor for the Open Door in the Middle East. In so many words, they demanded an equal share with the British, Dutch and French in the Mesopotamia oil venture.

"It was, nevertheless, apparent on both sides of the Atlantic that some form of admission of American interests into Mesopotamian oil was desirable and must be arranged."[60] This situation was discussed in America with the American companies by Sir John Cadman (Anglo-Persian) in 1921 and again in 1922. During 1922 a provisional agreement was reached with the American oil group whereby they would share, to the extent of one quarter, in Turkish Petroleum Co., more or less.

In 1923, the way was cleared for a final settlement of the oil rights in Mesopotamia. Iraq was by now a British mandate, the Iraq kingdom had been set up with Faisal as Ruler, an Anglo-Iraq treaty had been signed and Kemal had formally ceded Mesopotamia, among other territory.

That same year, oil in commercial quantities was encountered with the drill on the Iraq-Iran border at a place called Naftkhana, by the Anglo-Persian group on their small but exclusive

59. Fanning, Leonard M., *Foreign Oil and The Free World*, McGraw-Hill Book Co., Inc., New York, 1954, p. 46 and 47.

60. Longrigg, Stephen Hemsley, *Oil in the Middle East*, Oxford University Press, London, 1954, p. 45.

concession. This discovery caused the American companies to be more than ever anxious to finalize their still tentative position in the Turkish Petroleum Co.

The exact status of the American oil companies in the Turkish Petroleum Co. had not yet been agreed when, on March 14, 1925, the Iraq government granted to that company a 75 year concession.

Although Kemal had ceded Mesopotamia, nevertheless the New Turkish government tried to hold onto Mosul. Although Turkey's efforts to hold Mosul were delaying, they were in fact abortive. "The inclusion of Mosul in Iraq was a condition for the approval of the Anglo-Iraqi treaty by the Constituent Assembly, and this greatly helped the British in their efforts to retain Mosul for their empire defense and for its oil fields, as well as to fulfill its obligations to the League as mandatory for Iraq."[61]

Diplomatic notes regarding American participation in the Turkish Petroleum Co. continued to be passed back and forth across the Atlantic, between the governments of the United States and Britain, during 1925 and 1926. Sporadically during this period, the American oil company group continued to negotiate with its opposites in the Turkish Petroleum Co. Both sides were endeavoring to find a formula which would satisfy the Gulbenkian factor and at the same time equate the self-denial provisions of the Foreign Office (March, 1914) with the principles of the Open Door policy as put forward by Secretary of State Hughes (November, 1922).

Finally, in April, 1927, the American oil companies interested in Mosul oil were advised by their government that they could proceed to implement their compromise agreement with the Turkish Petroleum Co. A year later, the State Department

61. Shwadran, Benjamin, *The Middle East Oil and The Great Powers*, Frederick A. Praeger, New York, 1955, p. 241.

wrote to Guy Wellman (then spokesman for the American companies) in part as follows:

> . . . the Department considers that the arrangement contemplated in view of the special circumstances affecting the situation are consistent with the principles underlying the open door policy of the government of the United States.[62]

On July 31, 1928, all the American, British, French and Dutch participants in the Turkish Petroleum Co., including Gulbenkian, signed the Group Agreement. This Agreement limited the individual activity of the participants within a specified area, marked by a red line on a map of the Middle East. Hence, this Agreement became known as the "Red Line Agreement."[63]

The Turkish Petroleum Co. was now constituted:

23¾ per cent Anglo-Persian Oil Co.[64]
23¾ per cent Royal Dutch Shell Co.
23¾ per cent Compagnie Francaise des Petroles
23¾ per cent Near East Development Corp.[65]
5 per cent C. S. Gulbenkian

62. "Papers Relating to the Foreign Relations of the United States," 1927, II, p. 823, 824. Washington, 1942.

63. Hewins, Ralph, *Mr. Five Per Cent,* Rinehard & Co., Inc., New York, 1958, Map p. 51.

Fanning, Leonard M., *Foreign Oil and the Free World,* McGraw-Hill Book Co., New York, 1954, p. 49, 52-54, 285, 286.

64. For relinquishing one-half of its original shareholding in Turkish Petroleum Co., Anglo-Persian was compensated by an overriding royalty of 10 per cent on all of Turkish Petroleum Co.'s oil. In 1931, by agreement, this override was reduced to 7½ per cent.

65. Near East Development Corp., when organized in February, 1928, was composed of five American oil companies: Standard Oil Co. (New Jersey), Socony Oil Co. of New York; Gulf Oil Corp.; Atlantic Refining Co.; and Mexican Petroleum Co.—Sinclair and The Texas Co. having withdrawn from the original group of seven companies. A few years later, Atlantic, Mexican Petroleum and Gulf sold their interest in the Near East Development Corp. to the two Standard companies.

Thus, after some eight long years of diplomatic exchanges, numerous frustrating conferences between the international commercial entities, and the disconcerting pressures of power politics, the Americans were at last firmly entrenched in the scramble for oil in the Middle East.

In June, 1929, the name of Turkish Petroleum Co. was changed to Iraq Petroleum Co., Ltd.

EXPLORATION

Prior to the Americans' formal acceptance in the Turkish Petroleum Co.—in fact, very shortly after the concession had been granted (1925)—geological exploration of the Mosul area began. In April, 1927, drilling was begun at Palkhana, some six miles from Tuz. A second well was spudded three weeks later. Both holes were abandoned because of mechanical failures. A third test well was located at Tarjil, near Kirkuk but proved to be "off structure" and only encountered edge water. A fourth well at Khashm al-Ahmar was given up after encountering gas and heaving shale, as was the fifth test at Injana and for the same reasons. The sixth well at Qaiyara, west of the Tigris, found encouraging quantities of oil—but of heavy gravity and sulphurous.

These several failures were a bitter disappointment to the company. But then, out of the blue so to speak, Baba No. 1 at Baba Gurgur (just north of Kirkuk) blew in on October 14, 1927, and was wild for a week at the reported rate of 110,000 barrels a day. Thus was discovered one of the great oil fields of the world.

From then on, the company concentrated most of its drilling rigs in the Kirkuk area, while continuing to prospect with the drill on outlying structures to the north, south and west.

In 1929—a year after the Americans came in—the Turkish Petroleum Co. changed its name to Iraq Petroleum Co., Ltd.

Because the original so-called Mosul concession only gave the right to the company to choose 24 blocks (each eight miles square) within a 32-month period, it seems advisable to relate something of the territorial expansion in the company's oil holding which eventually took place.

On May 19, 1931, a new Convention (Supplementary Agreement, amending the 1925 Agreement) was ratified between Iraq Petroleum Co. and the government whereby the block system was abandoned and in lieu thereof the company received a single territory of 32,000 square miles in the Mosul and Baghdad vilayets, east of the Tigris—with the provisos that, (1) the company's rights were restricted to that single area; (2) the company be obliged to build a pipe line to the Mediterranean before the end of 1935, and (3) the company to pay the Iraq government £400,000 (gold) a year—of which one-half would apply against future royalties. Thus, by this convention, *all the territory of Iraq west of the Tigris River was opened to other oil companies.*

Promptly, an independent group of British formed the British Oil Development Co., (to which they later admitted Italian, French, Dutch and German capital), and sought to obtain oil concessions in Iraq. On May 28, 1932, British Oil Development was granted an oil concession on all of Iraq west of the Tigris and north of the 33rd degree line (some 42,000 square miles). The terms of the British Oil Development concession were stiffer than those of Iraq Petroleum, as to drilling obligations and royalty. Furthermore, British Oil Development had to also build a pipe line to the Mediterranean and pay an annual amount to the Iraq government of £100,000 rising to £200,000, pending production.

During the next three years British Oil Development carried out considerable exploration and some drilling in Iraq but without significant results. By 1935, the Italians had become majority shareholders of British Oil Development, but by this time the financial strain was serious—and growing greater as field operations progressed. The company found it increasingly difficult to raise the necessary funds to pay for exploration and drilling and also to make the very large annual payments to the Iraq government.

Similar difficulties confronted the Mosul Oil Fields, Ltd. which had been organized to acquire British Oil Development. In 1936, the Italian element which held the majority shareholdings in Mosul Oilfields, approached Iraq Petroleum for a way out.

"By the beginning of 1937, the I.P.C. interests were in effective charge and in 1942 Mosul Holdings, renamed, 'Mosul Petroleum Company,' received the assignment from B.O.D. of its 1932 concession. Both B.O.D. itself and M.O.F. were liquidated and disappeared in the same year."[66]

Iraq Petroleum Co. now controlled oil concessions over some 80,000 square miles of Iraq, as well as a 75 year oil concession over Qatar (granted May 17, 1935).

"On November 30, 1938, the Basrah Petroleum Company, a subsidiary of Iraq Petroleum Company, obtained a 75-year concession covering all lands not included under previous concessions (about 93,000 square miles)."[67] Thus, before 1939, Iraq Petroleum held all concessions over all Iraq and over all Qatar —an aggregate area of some 77,000 square miles, larger than the Anglo-Persian Oil Co.'s holding in Iran—and in this vast empire of oil prospects Americans held 23¾ per cent.

Iraq Petroleum Co. Development

It is not the author's intent to detail the exploration and development of the Iraq Petroleum Co., either before or after the American group was officially accepted as partners. Such detail is readily available in the several books mentioned by

66. Longrigg, Stephen Hemsley, *Oil in the Middle East,* Oxford University Press, London, 1954, p. 80.
67. Shwadran, Benjamin, *The Middle East, Oil and the Great Powers,* Frederick A. Praeger, New York, 1955, p. 250.

reference, as also in the files of oil industry publications. As previously stated, it is the author's primary purpose to limit this story to an outline of the antecedents of America's entry into the Middle East.

Nevertheless, a very brief sketch of Iraq Petroleum Co. development seems to be justified to round off the story of Americans in Iraq.

With but few exceptions, Iraq Petroleum Co. affairs in London and the operations in the field, have been ably directed by Britishers for the past 32 years. For the most part, the operating staff has been British, although there has been included a sprinkling of Dutch, French and American technical men.

The notable exception is the company's choice of men to head geological and, subsequently, geophysical work. For example, geological exploration was begun in 1925—even before the Americans had become partners officially. The exploration team from 1925 through 1928 was headed by Dr. DeBoeck (Austrian) who had a mixed field staff of several nationalities, including Messrs. E. W. Shaw, A. C. Trowbridge and Shirley Mason (Americans).

From 1929 until 1953, Iraq Petroleum's chief geologists were Americans. Under their supervision, all geological and geophysical work in Iraq, the Levant and elsewhere within the Red Line territory was carried on. During those years, E. W. Shaw (1929-34) and Norval E. Baker (1935-53) successively headed Iraq Petroleum's Exploration staff. They and their organization were responsible for making well locations to be drilled in "wildcat" areas, as also in the proven and semi-proven oil fields. To them and their staff, may be ascribed much of the credit for the discovery of the several new fields in Iraq and Qatar following the original discovery well at Baba Gurgur (near Kirkuk) in 1927.

From 1927 until 1934, annual oil production was less than one million barrels of crude—all consumed locally. However, in 1934, the first trans-desert pipe lines were completed. These were 12-inch lines. They were laid parallel from Kirkuk until, after crossing the Euphrates at a place called "Haditha," they forked. One line ran in a southerly direction 620 miles across Iraq, Jordan and Palestine to a point near Haifa.[68] The other line ran 534 miles almost due west across Iraq, Syria and Lebanon to a tanker loading terminal at Tripoli. The capacity of each of these pipe lines was somewhat more than 14 million barrels a year.

With these trans-desert lines completed, production increased to more than 30 million barrels annually until the outbreak of World War II. Annual production dropped to a low of 12 million barrels in 1941.

During the period 1945-49, new 16-inch trans-desert lines were laid along the same routes as the two 12-inch pipe lines. The additional 16-inch pipe lines were designed to increase the total trunk line capacity to about 90 million barrels a year. A few years later, Iraq Petroleum's trans-desert pipe line system was further augmented by laying a combination 26-inch, 30-inch, and 32-inch diameter pipe line from Kirkuk to Banias in Syria, an open roadstead on the Mediterranean some 55 miles north of Tripoli. When this major construction work was completed, Iraq's annual oil production zoomed to more than 200 million barrels.

During 1958 and 1959 additional big-inch pipe line loops were installed by Iraq Petroleum between Kirkuk and the Syrian border as also along the main line in Syria. As a result of this loopline construction, Iraq Petroleum's pipe line capacity to the Mediterranean was increased to an annual rate of approximately 263 million barrels.

After the war, the oil fields in the Ain Zahal area of northern

68. The Palestine end of this pipe line and the subsequent 16-inch pipe line (laid in 1947) was cut and removed by the company when the Israeli-Arab troubles flared up in 1948 and have never been used since.

Mosul—on the former properties of British Oil Development, later the Mosul Petroleum Co.—were connected by pipe line to the Kirkuk fields, which lay well over 100 miles to the south. To date, these northern Mosul oil fields have not proven to be large volume producers.

On the other hand, the concession in southern Iraq, obtained by Iraq Petroleum interests through the acquisition of the Basrah Petroleum Co., proved to have very significant oil prospects. In 1948, oil was first discovered by drilling in this area at Zubair (15 miles southwest of Basra)[69] and at Nahr Umar (30 miles up river from Basra). The Zubair discovery proved to be the more important of the two—however, both discovery wells yielded oil of better quality and higher gravity than Kirkuk production.

It was not until December, 1951, that the first oil was exported from the southern Iraq fields. This oil moved to tankers at Fao on the Persian Gulf, instead of being pumped northward to Iraq Petroleum's trans-desert pipe lines—the nearest point of which was nearly 500 miles away. Further drilling in southern Iraq has considerably extended the Zubair area by the discovery of Rumaila in December, 1954.

Iraq Petroleum Co. and associated companies have so far developed five producing fields in northern Iraq, namely Kirkuk, Bai Hassan and Jambur in the Kirkuk area and Ain Zalah and Butmah in the Mosul area. At the end of 1960 there were reported a total of 57 flowing wells, 1 pumping well and 31 shut-in producers in these two producing areas. During 1960, the three Kirkuk fields produced 256,767,989 barrels of crude and the two Mosul fields produced 9,569,735 barrels of crude. All northern Iraq production—not locally consumed—is moved by pipe line to Iraq Petroleum's Mediterranean terminals at Tripoli and Banias.

Basrah Petroleum Co., an associated company of Iraq Pe-

69. Either Basrah or Basra is accepted spelling.

troleum, produced 86,434,127 barrels in 1960 from the Rumaila and Zubair fields in South Iraq. At the year end there were 13 flowing wells in Rumaila and 14 shut-in; and 26 flowing wells at Zubair and 11 shut-in. Basrah Petroleum Co. has elaborate plans for increasing production in Southern Iraq through a step-up in development drilling, the building of more big-inch pipe lines from Rumaila and Zubair to tidewater at Fao on the Persian Gulf, and improved delivery facilities at that terminal. Such work, so far completed, has already increased delivery capacity to some 150 million barrels annually.

The total production from all Iraq fields approximated 367,-830,000 barrels in 1961; an increase of 13,238,000 over 1960 production.

(QATAR)

In the spring of 1935, Anglo-Iranian Oil Co. obtained a 75-year oil concession over the territory of Qatar[70] from the local Shaikh and duly assigned same to Qatar Petroleum Co., Ltd., an affiliate of Iraq Petroleum Co., Ltd. Exploration began almost immediately. In the fall of 1938, the first wildcat (test) well began drilling. A little more than one year later that well came in at a depth of nearly a mile below the surface and was rated at some 5,000 barrels a day of 36 degree A.P.I. gravity oil. Thus, another virgin oil field had been discovered by Iraq Petroleum Co. interests.

Subsequently, the second well located 10 miles to the south was drilled and completed as a producer, rated at about 12,000 barrels a day. By then, it was thought enemy war activity might envelope the Persian Gulf. For that reason, all work on Qatar

70. A peninsula-like area of some 8,000 square miles which literally sticks out from the mainland into the Persian Gulf like a "sore thumb," just south and east of the Bahrain Islands.

was suspended and much material and equipment were removed to Bombay and Basra.

Exploration work on Qatar was begun again in 1946, and in 1947, drilling in the vicinity of the discovery well (now called Dukhan Field) was resumed with several strings of tools. Pipe lines were laid from Dukhan to Umm Sa'id on the east coast of Qatar, some 50 odd miles from the oil field. There, the Doha sealoading terminal was built and in December 1949, the first tanker was loaded for export shipment.

Iraq Petroleum Co. was now a two country operation.

During 1961, Qatar Petroleum Co., Ltd. delivered more than 65 million barrels of Dukhan crude oil to its Doha terminal from a total of some 50 producing wells. Also, during 1961, Qatar Petroleum relinquished more than 1,400 square miles, or approximately one-third of its original concession area on the Qatar Peninsula.

In addition to Iraq Petroleum's extensive exploration and development work in Iraq and Qatar, during the period 1933-1945 the company obtained exploration licenses and in some cases oil concessions in Palestine, Trans-Jordan, part of Syria, Cyprus, Lebanon, Yemen, Western Saudi Arabia, Aden Protectorate, Oman and the Trucial coast.

Geological and geophysical work and some drilling was done in all these areas but so far as publicly known, the results were unfavorable. All of these oil rights have been surrendered by the Iraq Petroleum Co. group, except as pertains to oil concessions in the Sultanate of Oman and the Trucial coast which are still held by Petroleum Development (Oman) Ltd., and Petroleum Development (Trucial Coast) Ltd. Commercial oil production has not yet been established in either Oman or the Trucial Coast but some encouraging drilling results have been obtained in the Shaikhdom of Abu Dhabi, as noted in Chapter 8 of this text.

Annual production figures for both Iraq and Qatar by years

since production began in those areas, as well as estimated
proven oil reserves appear in Appendix V.

IRAQ PETROLEUM'S PROBLEMS

Ever since Iraq Petroleum Co.'s inception it has been plagued
by differences of policy opinion among the numbers of its four-
nation board, including the voice of Gulbenkian, and by serious
national and international disturbances. Differences among the
member companies could be and were coped with in each
instance and in due course. But the political events were un-
avoidable and extremely disruptive to the oil operations.

For instance, in the 33 years of Iraq Petroleum Co.'s oil history, there have occurred six major events of international consequence having particular significance in Iraq: (1) World War
II (1939-1945); (2) Israel proclaimed an independent state
(May, 1948); (3) nationalization of the Suez Canal (July,
1956; (4) cessation of pipe line operations between Kirkuk and
the Mediterranean terminals at Banias and Tripoli due to sabo-
tage of pumping stations T2, T3 and T4 in Syria (November,
1956); (5) the overthrow of the Iraq kingdom by a military
coup headed by Abdul Karim Kassem (July, 1958), and (6)
Iraq's claim to the territory of Kuwait (June-July 1961).

It is a great credit to the courage, integrity and intelligence
of Iraq Petroleum Co.'s management and staff in the main
offices and in the operating areas, that these world shaking
events have not destroyed the company. As a matter of fact,
although there has been considerable property damage to the
oil installations and some loss of life due to these international
and national incidents, the oil concessions and the oil fields remain in the undisturbed possession of Iraq Petroleum Co. The
author ventures to say that no other international oil company
in the Middle East has been plagued so much by political events
and has withstood those shocks so well.

IRAQ PETROLEUM CO.'S
RELATIONS WITH LABOR AND GOVERNMENT

Iraq Petroleum Co. may not have done more for its employees in Iraq and Qatar than Anglo-Iranian did for its employees in Iran, but some impartial oilmen believe that it did, what it did, somewhat differently and with more effect. It could be that the difference between the ideologies, customs and culture of the peoples of two countries accounted for the different results. Whatever the reason, there has been less difficulty with the oil workers in Iraq than in Iran. Conditions have never been allowed to get out of hand.

Possibly the American influence may have been a factor. The reader should bear in mind that American oil companies were expropriated in Mexico as the result of labor troubles. The lessons they learned from their ineptitude in Mexico, they profited by in their operations in Colombia and Venezuela. In the latter country particularly, the workman in the oil fields never had it so good and have generally reacted accordingly.

Within the industry, Iraq Petroleum's employee relations have been outstanding down through the years, especially so in Iraq.[71]

The workmen welfare policies of the company were likewise put into practice in the Qatar operations but were not as successful as in Iraq, largely because that country was almost entirely devoid of natural amenities, being a flat waterless, sandy wasteland with no agriculture and no business enterprise. The native Qataris, generally, were ignorant, shiftless and primitive people. Nevertheless, the company welfare policies in Qatar have produced a marked improvement in worker health and living standards.

71. Stephen Hemsley Longrigg has made an excellent analysis of I.P.C.'s employee relations, with emphasis on the Kirkuk area, in his book, *Oil in the Middle East*, Oxford University Press, London, 1954, p. 177-179.

Before 1950, much of Iraq's revenue from oil was syphoned off to finance consumption imports and operating expenses of state. However, in May of that year, Iraq created a Development Board, "To which was to be assigned the revenue derived from the oil companies."[72] This board requested the International Bank for Reconstruction and Development to send to Iraq, a mission to survey the economic potentialities of the country. The mission arrived in February, 1951, and a year later submitted its report, proposing a five-year plan for reinvesting some $470 million of oil revenues in irrigation schemes, roads and other public works for the benefit of the public. Considerable progress was made to attain the objective of the "Five-Year Plan" with the revenues from oil, but other economic and political factors made the going rough.

Coincidentally, word got around the Middle East that there was to be a new deal in Saudi Arabia—that the American oil companies there were going to share their profits equally with the State. In Iraq, unlike Anglo-Iranian in Iran, the oil companies quickly opened negotiations with the government to revise the oil concession terms. Although the Iraq situation was somewhat more complex than that in Saudi Arabia—largely because of the diversity of international interest—nevertheless in 1952 specific provisions were spelled out and agreed upon for calculating profits. However, it was not until early in 1955— after the consortium agreement with Iran—that a new price fixing formula was arrived at. Incidentally, this new basis for determining profits increased the Iraq government oil revenue by about one-fifth.

Even under the new regime in Iraq, the bulk of the oil revenues continued to be plowed back into public works. And so it should be, for oil is a wasting natural resource and revenues

72. Shwadran, Benjamin, *The Middle East, Oil and the Great Powers,* Frederick A. Praeger, New York, 1955, p. 271.

therefrom should largely accrue to the benefit of the people generally.

Notwithstanding Iraq Petroleum's annual rate of production in Iraq has increased from 265 million barrels to some 368 million barrels in the four years since Kassem came to power, the government still insists that it should receive a larger share of the oil revenues. A summary of the current situation appears in *World Oil* for August 15, 1961, as follows:

> The following were the main points of contention between the government and IPC during the nine months of negotiations which began about August 15, 1960.
>
> Increase in government income from industry earnings. The government has cited agreements effected in the Middle East since 1957 providing more than 50 percent of profits to the government. IPC questions whether such agreements will actually provide the affected governments more revenue or whether they will merely get a larger proportion of smaller profits and will hence enjoy no net gain over 50-50 contracts.
>
> More employment of Iraq nationals by the IPC companies, and appointment of Iraqi directors to the board.
>
> Relinquishment of undeveloped areas. IPC has agreed to drop 100,000 acres of the operating companies' choosing. The government has asked to choose some or all of the acreage to be returned.
>
> Better conservation of casing-head gas to reduce flaring.
>
> Priority for Iraqi tankers in charters to move Iraq crude. There are several other issues.
>
> Owing to inability of the two parties to agree, the Iraq government ordered the operating companies to suspend exploration in 1961. This is a violation of the original concessions and apparently affects geophysical work as well as wild-cat drilling. IPC, BPC, and MPC conducted a total of 15 party months of geological work, 71 crew months of seismic reflection and 1 party month of refraction work in 1960.

The Iraq Petroleum group's effort to placate Kassem's government and to satisfy its demands came to an abortive and abrupt end on December 12, 1961. The following extract of an article entitled "Iraq Seizes Unexploited Areas" appearing in the January, 1962, issue of *Petroleum Press Service* (London) tells that story in terse and unequivocal words.

The dispute which has been simmering for three years between the Iraq Government an the Iraq Petroleum group of companies working in Iraq has now boiled over. Overriding the companies' legal rights under the concession agreements, General Kassem has taken high-handed legislative action, and by Law No. 80 of 1961, passed on 12th December, has, re-defined and greatly restricted their areas of operation. They are allotted a total of 47 parcels: the Iraq Petroleum Company is granted 12 Kirkuk, six at Bai Hassan and four at Jambur, totaling 747.75 sq. kms.; The Mosul Petroleum Company four at 'Ain Zalah and four at Butmah, totaling 62 sq. kms.; the Basrah Petroleum Company seven at Rumaila and 10 at Zubair, totaling 1,128 sq. kms. The companies would, on this basis, be left with only about 1,938 sq. kms., out of their original concession areas totaling some 435,780 sq. kms. From the information available it is not clear if this allocation covers the area of the present producing fields. Provision is made for the conditional grant of additional areas which would double this total, but even taking this possibility into account they have been stripped of more than 99 per cent of the area of their concessions which only legally expire at or after the end of the century.

This treatment is both excessively harsh and unmerited by standards of fair dealing. For the companies had accepted, in principle, that their enormous "blanket" concessions covering virtually the whole country were, in the absence of the now common provisions for surrendering territory, due for adjustment by agreement. Responding to a counter-proposal made by General Kassem in the course of last year's discussions the companies agreed, as part of a general settlement of various matters under discussion, to relinquish 90 per cent of their areas, in two stages, namely 75 per cent immediately, and a further 15 per cent within seven years.

The companies have protested and have reserved their rights, for the loss of which no compensation has been offered. Production is continuing. But further legislation is threatened regulating exploration, and is dismally awaited. While some of the Iraq press has been congratulating the Leader on his clemency in leaving the companies with their present producing areas intact, the Oil Minister has reiterated that there is no wish to harm the companies! What does not seem to be appreciated is that the peremptory seizure of acquired rights by a government contending for the leadership of the Arab world, damages not only the oil companies, but even more the Arabs' good name.

The government of Iraq owns and operates the former Khanaqin Oil Co. concession. The Naft Khaneh field, which is presently the only producing field in this concession, is credited with a production of some 1,830,000 barrels in 1960. It is understood that development in the Naft Khaneh field will be stepped up.

4

Bahrain (Bahrein)

EVEN BEFORE THE AMERICAN OIL COMPANIES had been allotted a definite share in the Turkish Petroleum Co. (now known as Iraq Petroleum Co.), and some 28 years before the American companies became a party to the consortium in Iran, a colorful, brusk, New Zealander appeared in New York City offering—in behalf of Eastern and General Syndicate, Ltd. —a two year option for an oil concession over the Bahrain Islands. The story of the vicissitudes of that oil concession and how its acquisition by an American oil company eventually led to the discovery of the important oil fields of Bahrain, Saudi Arabia, Kuwait and the Neutral Zone, is one of the great sagas of our times.

But, before telling about the Bahrain oil concession and the train of events which flowed from that venture, the reader should be briefly informed of the historic and political importance of the Bahrain Islands.

The total area of the five principal islands in the group is about 231 square miles. Of the five, the Island of Bahrain is the largest (some 30 miles long by 8 to 10 miles wide). The second largest island is Muharraq and is now linked to Bahrain by a causeway one and one-half miles long. Like the famous pearls for which these islands have been noted for many centuries, the Islands of Bahrain are set like jewels in the blue waters of the Persian Gulf nearly 20 miles offshore from the mainland of Arabia and slightly less distant from the Qatar Peninsula. Although low lying for the most part, near the center of Bahrain there is a pronounced rocky promontory known as "Jebal ad Dukhan" (the mountain of smoke), so designated because of the mist which often veils these hilltops. These hills rise some 450 feet above the sea and about 250 feet above the surrounding plain.[73]

Ever since man began to navigate the high seas, Bahrain has been known. The islands afforded safe anchorage for the early navigator and soon it became an entrepot along the trade route from China and India to Europe. Possession of these islands was considered strategic and many battles were fought to seize and hold these tiny bits of land. Of great importance to the inhabitants and exploiter alike were the offshore fresh water springs, welling up from the bed of the Gulf. For many centuries it has been the most important center of the natural pearl industry.

> Pearl diving is probably the oldest industry in Bahrain and has been the reason why an otherwise small and comparatively unproductive group of islands has been the scene of so many bitter wars and has been overrun by so many invading armies. From the earliest times, Bahrain has been famous for its pearls; in an Assyrian inscription of some 2,000 B.C., a parcel of "fish eyes" from Dilmun is believed to be the first reference to the pearls of Bahrain. Tylos, the classical name for Bahrain, was stated by Pliny to be, "Famous for the vast number of its pearls." In more recent years, the merchant, Suliman, an Arab traveler of the ninth century, mentioned the pearl fisheries of Bahrain, while in the tenth

---

73. The Bahrain oil field was developed in the plains of Dukhan.

century we have the first description of the actual methods of diving left by a certain Abu Zaid Hassan. From an examination of his description, it can be seen how little the methods of diving have changed during the past 1,000 years. Many later travelers and geographers have been interested by the pearl fisheries; the famous geographer Idrisi, after mentioning the political state of affairs, describes the method of diving; Bakri in 1273, Abu'l Fida in the early fourteenth century and Ibn Batuta all mention the pearl fisheries. In 1485, Duarte Barbosa, a Portugese explorer, says of Bahrein, (Bahrain), 'Around it grows much seed pearl, also large pearls of good quality. The merchants of the island itself fish for these pearls and have there from great profits.'

At the turn of the sixteenth century, the Portugese had firmly established themselves in India and were expanding into the Persian Gulf. In 1514, Don Albuquerque, Governor of India, visited Bahrain . . . it is probable that the subsequent seizure of Bahrain by the Portugese in 1522 was due to the wealth of the pearl traders.[74]

A Dutch traveler reported in 1598 that the Portugese had established a "factor" in Bahrain. The Portugese built a fort in Bahrain and maintained a small garrison there. However, the Portugese rule over Bahrain was very insecure all during the sixteenth century.

In the early 1600's, the Portugese domination of Bahrain was severely threatened by the Persians and in 1622 a force of Anglo-Persians captured Hormuz and so were able to overlord Bahrain. For most of the seventeenth century the Persians ruled Bahrain with the aid of a military force of some 300 men. Near the end of the seventeenth century, the wild tribes from the Oman invaded Bahrain and wrecked the place. Most of the inhabitants of the islands fled to Qatif and settled. "In 1720,

74. Belgrave, James H. D., *Welcome to Bahrain—A Guide for Tourists and Travelers,* Mark and Moody, Ltd., K.B.E., Stourbridge, Eng., 1953, p. 46 and 47.

the Persians purchased Bahrain from the Omanis for, "a large sum of money."[75]

The Persian rule over Bahrain was unhappy and fraught with repeated attacks from Arab tribes further north along the mainland of Arabia, and also from the Omans. Zubara on the west coast of the Qatar peninsula became a large town, fortified by a great fort, Qalat Marir, the ruins of which can still be seen. The Persians attacked the Arab forces at Zubara but were defeated and driven from the shore to their ships. From about 1776 until 1796, both Bahrain and Zubara were ruled by Shaikh Ahmed al Khalifah.[76] Ahmed's son, Sulman, carried on the Khalifah rule in Bahrain until 1799 when those islands were occupied by the Imam of Muscat. Nine years later, Bahrain was recaptured by the combined forces of the Khalifah's and the Wahhabis', but the Wahhabis would not yield control to the Khalifahs. The latter then combined with the Anglo-Persian force and regained control of Bahrain.

In 1814, the British made their first direct contact with Bahrain and pledged their neutrality if the islands were attacked by the Iman of Muscat. There followed a period of 47 unsettled years—full of intrigue and attacks from pirates and threats from the Wahhabis—until 1861 when Muhammad, Ruler of Bahrain, signed a "Perpetual Treaty of Peace and Friendship" with Great Britain concerning such matters as slavery, maritime aggression and British trading in Bahrain.[77]

75. Belgrave, James H. D., *Welcome to Bahrain—A Guide for Tourists and Travlers,* Mark & Moody Ltd., K.B.E., Stourbridge England, 1953, p. 82.

76. According to Belgrave's *Welcome to Bahrain,* p. 82, the Khalifah family, along with the Sabah and Jalahama families belonging to the Bani Utbah clan are said to have given up their nomadic life and settled on the site of the present Town of Kuwait in 1716. The Sabah family remains the ruling family of Kuwait.

77. Belgrave, James H. D., *Welcome to Bahrain—A Guide For Tourists and Travelers,* Mark & Moody Ltd., K.B.E., Stourbridge England, 1953, p. 85.

Notwithstanding, the peace of the islands continued to be disturbed by attacks on Bahrain shipping by the Wahhabis. After six years of relative quiet, war again broke out between the Qataris and the Khalifahs, and as a result the British sent a man-of-war to Bahrain to settle matters. The British consulted with local notables and bade them choose their ruler from among the Khalifah family. "The choice fell upon 'Isa, son of 'Ali b. Khalifah, who was at the time residing at Qatar, and he was summoned to Bahrain and acclaimed as its ruler. He reigned for 54 years until his abdication in 1923.[78]

Shaikh 'Isa was succeeded by his son, Shaikh Hamed, who acted as deputy ruler for 12 years until his father's death, when he became Ruler in fact in 1935. Shaikh Hamed died in 1942 and was succeeded by his son, Shaikh Sulman bin Hamed al-Khalifah who remains the present ruler.

Having been instrumental in establishing political order in Bahrain in 1869, the British kept a protecting hand over Bharain's affairs. In 1870 and 1874, they rejected Turkish claims to sovereignty over Bahrain and further consolidated their power in Bahrain by the treaties of 1880 and 1892. These treaties were most important, as it later developed, in restricting foreign commercial interests from obtaining concessions in the islands. In 1902, a British Political Agent was posted in Bahrain, and in July 1913 the Ottoman Empire agreed with the British to recognize Bahrain's independence. Three years later, King Ibn Saud agreed with the British to refrain from acts of aggression agains Bahrain.

Hence, after centuries of strife and turmoil, Bahrain reached an era of peace and quiet from external sources and at long last was able to reform conditions in the pearling industry, improve

---

78. Belgrave, James H. D., *Welcome to Bahrain—A Guide For Tourists and Travelers,* Mark & Moody Ltd., K.B.E., Stourbridge, England. 1953, p. 86.

her limited agriculture, reopen her ports to world trade and arrange for the exploitation of her new found natural resource—petroleum.

MAJOR FRANK HOLMES AND HIS OIL CONCESSIONS

New Zealand born Frank Holmes, emerged during the First World War as a mining engineer serving with the British Armies in India and the Middle East. During those campaigns he won the rank of Major. After the war he stayed in the Persian Gulf area imbued with the economic potentialities which could flow from finding and unleashing whatever natural resources lay beneath the vast area of Arabian sands.

Primarily he was schooled to think in terms of minerals and metals. But having trekked and sailed up and down the coasts of the Red Sea, Arabian Sea and the Persian Gulf—during which he met and mingled with traders, desert chiefs and nomads—Holmes came to realize that to the Arab, fresh water and abundant fuel were considered to be more precious than gold or silver or pearls. His husky body, rugged features, brusk manner, bold approach and evident sincerity engendered confidence among the Arab peoples. They knew him as a man of his word and as a man interested in their well being.

For some years following the cessation of hostilities, Major Frank Holmes devoted much of his time, money and effort to roaming up and down the coasts of the shaikdoms and sultanates making up the Arabian peninsula, drilling wells in search of potable water and noting the occasional surface evidence of petroleum and natural gas. His ventures in fresh water finding were partially successful and, incidentally, were rewarded with Arab goodwill and promises that concessions would be granted to him to search the underground for liquid and gaseous fuel.

Such was the situation when Major Frank Holmes went to England in 1920 to win financial backing for further exploration of the Middle East's natural resources. His London quest was almost immediately successful. So convincing was Holmes, that a group of British investors in mining ventures in Africa and Asia, including Sir Edmund Davis and Percy Tarbutt, quickly organized the Eastern and General Syndicate, Ltd., and engaged Holmes to be their free lance agent.

The war had demonstrated the great importance of oil as fuel on land and sea and now that Persian oil was being produced in ever increasing quantities, Eastern and General Syndicate, Ltd., was easily persuaded by Holmes to include oil among the other minerals to which the company would dedicate its efforts to finding in the Middle East.

It so happened that Major Holmes' first assignment as free lance field agent was to scout for oil concessions in likely places along the fringe of the old Ottoman Empire. In his new role, Holmes loomed large on the Arab's horizon—he was recognized and welcomed by the people of the Middle East. His field appearance and actions are best told by the following quotation.

> Holmes was an unusual person, well suited to the rigors and peculiarities of the task assigned him. Middle aged, burly, amiable, loquacious and unpredictable, he cut a fantastic figure as he traveled on foot, ass, camel, and steamer along the coast of the comparatively unknown Arabian subcontinent and its environs. He was accompanied only by an interpreter (Holmes apparently knew very little Arabic) and a Somali servant; he wore, over conventional European clothes a thin 'aba,' which concealed nothing and over his cork helment, a red kerchief and 'ighal,' which made his head appear colossal. With chance acquaintances along the road he chattered expansively, but always he posed as one traveling for reasons of health.[79]

79. Moore, Frederick Lee, Jr., *Origin of American Oil Concessions,* Princeton University, 1948, p. 10.

For about three years, Major Holmes wandered around the Middle East, ingratiating himself with the local rulers and keeping an ever watchful eye out for oil indications. In the name of his company, he dickered for oil concessions with King Ibn Saud of Arabia, with the Ruler of Kuwait, with the Ruler of Qatar and with other rulers along the Trucial coast. He was particularly interested in the well-known oil seepages on the Farsan Islands in the Red Sea. During these exploratory travels, Holmes was unsuccessful in closing any deals—partly due to the evasion tactics of the British Colonial Office.

In September, 1922, Colonel H. R. P. Dickson, who had previously been Political Agent at Bahrain, was sent to Bahrain by Sir Percy Cox on a special mission—to persuade Ibn Saud to come down to 'Uqair on the coast for a conference on a frontier question. While in Bahrain, Colonel Dickson was requested to entertain, "A certain Major Frank Holmes, mining engineer and Dr. Mann, both of Eastern and General Syndicate, Ltd.,"[80] who were shortly due out.

Colonel Dickson was suspicious that Holmes knew of an oil seepage on the mainland near Qatif and that he might try to get a mining or oil concession out of Ibn Saud. However, Ibn Saud had sent for Holmes, hence Dickson could only facilitate his sojourn in Bahrain and his travels across the mainland desert.

> Major Holmes and Dr. Mann arrived by next up slow mail, and were duly brought around to our house by Qusaibi and made at home there. Two things greatly amused my wife and myself. The first was the appearance of Major Holmes. He carried a large white umbrella lined in green, wore a white helmet issued to French troops in Africa, and over his face and helment, a green gauze veil—quite like pictures one has seen of the tourist about to visit the Pyramids. The second was the amazing number of presents

80. Dickson, H. R. P., *Kuwait and Her Neighbours,* George Allen and Unwin, Ltd., London, 1956, p. 268.

Holmes had brought for Ibn Saud. There must have been over fifty cases, leather bags, boxes and guns.[81]

As the Holmes party was about to leave the Dicksons in Bahrain, Holmes was asked why he was journeying such a round about way to get to his destination on the mainland. At once Holmes became mysterious and replied:

"Dickson, I am a butterfly collector, and I have been told that a wonderful black variety, known nowhere else in the world, is to be found in the Qatif oasis. I have already called it the Black Admiral of Qatif, and am out to get a specimen. Then my name will be famous.[82]

This story was too good to be allowed to go unnoticed—Mrs. Dickson was quick to reply, "Major Holmes this is the first time I've heard of an oil seepage being called by the name of a butterfly."

Undaunted, Holmes is reported to have said, "My God, you are a wonderful woman—I shall telegraph today to the curator of the Zoological Gardens in London and ask that you be made a Fellow of the Zoo." Evidently Holmes did just that for shortly thereafter Mrs. Dickson was advised she had been duly elected fellow of the Zoological Society.

Sir Percy Cox had been delegated by his majesty's Government to endeavor to reach an agreement with Ibn Saud over a disputed frontier with Kuwait and Iraq. Finally, through Colonel Dickson's efforts, a meeting was arranged at 'Uqair[83] in late November, 1922, between Ibn Saud; Sir Percy Cox, representing the British government; the Political Agent[84] in Kuwait representing the Ruler, Shaikh Ahmed al Jabir al

---

81. Dickson, H. R. P., *Kuwait and Her Neighbours,* George Allen and Unwin, Ltd., London, 1956, p. 269.

82. Dickson, H. R. P., *Kuwait and her Neighbours,* George Allen and Unwin, Ltd., London, 1956, p. 270.

83. Frequently spelled "Ojair."

84. Major J. C. Moore.

Sabah; the Iraq Minister of Communications and Works and others interested in the boundary question. Unexpectedly, Holmes also appeared on the scene and pitched his tent between the retinue of Ibn Saud and the camp of the British. "The Anglo-Persian Oil Co., too, had its agents on hand at the Ojair Conference.[85]

That conference ended in establishing two neutral zones; the neutral zone of Kuwait in which the Kingdom of Ibn Saud and the Shaikhdom of Kuwait had undivided equal rights, and the neutral zone of Iraq in which the Kingdom of Ibn Saud and the government of Iraq had undivided equal rights. Those neutral zones remain today as defined in 1922.

The settlement of these frontier problems was a victory for Sir Percy Cox, but at the expense of Kuwait which lost two-thirds of its territory. This was a blow to Kuwait and to its young ruler. Major More, representing the Ruler of Kuwait, did nothing to protect the state to which he was the accredited Political Agent, against this ruthless steal of recognized territory.[86] As long as he lived Shaikh Sir Ahmed al Jabir al Subah (who died on January 29, 1950), never forgave the British for this breach of faith—in fact it may have been the compelling reason why he would not give the British an exclusive oil concession over his country.

At the close of the conference, Ibn Saud told Sir Percy Cox

85. Moore, Frederick Lee, Jr., *Origin of American Oil Concessions,* Princeton University, 1948, p. 12.

86. Dickson, H. R. P., *Kuwait and Her Neighbours,* George Allen and Unwin, Ltd. London, 1956, p. 276.
Colonel Dickson in his book *Kuwait and Her Neighbours* has this to say about the territorial deal. From p. 276: "The obvious end in view being expediency and desire to mollify the powerful and troublesome Ibn Saud, the southern boundary of the recognized territory of Kuwait was pushed back a hundred and fifty miles, reducing the Kingdom to an area of six thousand square miles. Throughout the talks, Major More, who was supposed to be watching the interests of the Shaikh of Kuwait, had said nothing."

that he favored giving Holmes' company an oil concession on Hasa (the eastern province of Arabia) and inquired if Britain had any objection. Sir Percy is alleged to have said, "Go ahead, but I warn you that Eastern and General Syndicate is not an oil company and will probably sell to others."[87]

It was not until May 6, 1923, that Ibn Saud granted an exclusive option for exploration and mining rights in the Province of al-Hasa to the Syndicate. However, in accepting this grant, Holmes wrote to Ibn Saud that, "The Syndicate shall not sell to the Anglo-Persian Oil Co., Ltd., either as to whole or part thereof, any oil or mineral concession or concessions that may be granted by Your Highness to Eastern and General Syndicate, Ltd."[88]

On May 17, 1924, Ibn Saud granted to Holmes' company, an option for an oil concession over Saudi Arabia's undivided half of the so-called, Kuwait Neutral Zone.

During his travels to and from Arabia over the period 1920-1923, Holmes had stopped over in Bahrain many times. He knew the island's geography thoroughly. He knew of its few oil seepages and its fresh water problems. While Bahrain had some wells of fresh water, they went brackish at times and never produced enough water for any considerable irrigation. Mostly, the Bahrainis relied on the offshore, undersea, fresh water springs for drinking and domestic purposes. Pearl divers gathered this under sea fresh water and brought it to land in boats.

However, the great storms of 1924 raised havoc in the Persian Gulf area. That year the Islands were hard put for water. It was then that Major Holmes offered to drill two water wells on Bahrain, "The price being naught if he should meet with failure

87. Dickson, H. R. P., *Kuwait and Her Neighbours,* George Allen and Unwin, Ltd. London, 1956, p. 277.
88. According to T. E. Ward's memorandum of April 4, 1948.

but $15,000 per well and consideration of his application for an oil concession if he should succeed.[89]

T. George Madgwick, professor of oil mining at Birmingham University was employed by Eastern and General Syndicate, Ltd., to geologize Bahrain and to make the location for the two water wells. The Syndicate also ordered to be sent out from England, the necessary well drilling equipment.

When the locations had been made for the two drill tests, Holmes took off for the Farsan Islands—chasing an oil concession there—leaving Professor Madgwich in charge of the drilling on Bahrain. As is usual in drilling a new area, difficulties were encountered which slowed up progress, so it was not until after mid-1925 that the wells reached their objective— potable water in quantity. Thus the drilling venture proved successful and Shaikh Hamed was so pleased that he granted Holmes' company a two-year option to acquire an exclusive oil exploration license over the Bahrain Islands. This license was dated December 2, 1925.

The water well drilling on Bahrain continued for some time after Major Holmes sailed for London to report his successful negotiations for oil concessions over Hasa, the Kuwait Neutral Zone and Bahrain. During all the first half of 1926, Holmes, acting for Eastern and General Syndicate, Ltd., attempted to sell these oil options to British investors and to British oil companies. Anglo-Persian seemed quite interested but the Royal Dutch Shell Group never got around to seriously considering dickering for these options.

The present day reader should bear in mind that in 1926 the only oil being produced in commercial quantities from Middle East countries was in Iran. The Iraq oil field at Baba Gurgur had not yet been discovered, and there were no oil seepages known in all the Arabian Peninsula except the Burgan oil im-

---

89. Moore, Frederick Lee, Jr., *Origin of American Oil Concessions,* Princeton University, 1948, p. 14.

pregnated sands in Kuwait, and the hard-to-find reported oil seep near the Qatif oasis in Hasa. Generally, the mainland of Arabia along the Persian Gulf was a vast desert of shifting sands. However, on the Island of Bahrain, country rocks of Eocene Age were exposed in bold relief and within the area rimmed by these rocky hills, were several seeps. Hence, although Bahrain was very small geographically compared to Hasa and the Neutral Zone, the prospects of finding oil with the drill appeared most promising.

At Major Holmes' request, Professor Madgwick had geologized Bahrain while supervising the water well drilling. He confirmed the report (1908) of Dr. Pilgrim of the Indian Geological Survey that the main island of the group was, in fact, an eroded elongated dome, which at depth should be favorable to the accumulation of oil in quantity. Actually, Bahrain was what geologists call a "picture book anticline," from which the crest had been worn away leaving only the rim rocks dipping away from the central axis.

"Upon Professor Madgwick's return to London from Bahrain he again urged consideration by the Syndicate of developing the Bahrain structure. He found the Syndicate's directors lukewarm to undertaking the risk of oil development on their own; they preferred to sell the concession."[90] Madgwick approached Cory Brothers and Co., wealthy British coal merchants, but they were unable to come to terms with the Syndicate. Independent investors were not interested in the great and expensive gamble of trying to find black gold—they were more interested in mining for the yellow metal in Africa.

The Royal Dutch and Anglo-Persian, both, were involved in trying to unscramble the international oil tangle over Iraq. Furthermore, the Persian government was pressing the Anglo-Persian Co. to speed up development of the oil fields in Persia.

90. Moore, Frederick Lee, Jr., *Origin of American Oil Concessions,* Princeton University, 1948, p. 22.

So, although Anglo-Persian considered all of the Syndicate's concessions, as lying within its "zone of influence," they apparently decided to evince no active interest. Maybe they felt that if the British oil companies refrained from taking up the Syndicates oil options, no one else in the oil industry would be interested and, in that case, they would eventually, in their own good time, be able to negotiate for new oil concessions over the same area on more favorable terms. But the British oil men did not reckon with the American oil companies' post war interest in acquiring foreign oil reserves.

Neither Major Holmes nor any of the Directors of Eastern and General Syndicate had had personal contacts with the top executives of those American oil companies that might be interested in Middle East oil. However, Professor Madgwick had been corresponding with Thomas E. Ward, President of the Oilfield Equipment Co. in New York, first about a possible opening for him as petroleum consultant for the Canadian Dominion government in Alberta,[91] and secondly about the Bahrain concession prospects.

On his way to Canada in August 1926, Madgwick called on Ward. The latter was impressed with Madgwick's account of Bahrain's geology and allowed as how he might be helpful to the Syndicate in putting them in touch with potentially interested oil company executives. Ward asked that he be furnished with a copy of Professor Madgwick's geological report and a copy of the oil option—furthermore that a member of the Syndicate come on to New York as soon as possible to start negotiations. In due course, Ward received from Madgwick, then in Calgary, a memorandum containing his written opinion on the oil prospects of Bahrain, and almost coincidentally, Ward

91. Mr. Ward had recommended Professor Madgwick to the Canadian government. Professor Madgwick received his appointment in the summer of 1926.

was advised by Major Frank Holmes that he would be arriving in New York shortly with a copy of the option agreement.

By this time, the two year oil option contracts entered into by Holmes with Ibn Saud over al-Hasa and the Kuwait Neutral Zone were, "Subject to forfeiture and cancellation, if not actually null and void,"[92] as the Syndicate had neither made the prescribed payments nor started any field operations.

"Contacts were made by Ward with leading American oil groups, including the Standard Oil Co. (New Jersey) and the Gulf Oil Corp., as well as with leading geologists and financiers. First reactions were not encouraging. The reasons were understandable, for oil companies are guided by expert advice of their own geologists, and there was a lack of convincing geological data available to Holmes and Ward. Even the aforementioned opinion of Professor Madgwick on Bahrain was guarded, and there were no geological reports in connection with Hasa, the Neutral Zone or Kuwait. In his opinion dated September 23, 1926, Madgwick could not make a bold statement on certainty as to the likehood of striking a worthwhile field in Bahrain but he did say, a deep test is warranted."[93]

Actually, when Holmes first came to New York he was more interested in selling others his hopes to acquire an oil concession over the Farsan and Kamaran Islands in the Red Sea—where there were reported to be several large oil seepages—than he appeared to be in disposing of the Syndicate's Bahrain option. Holmes had hardly initiated his discussions with the American companies regarding the Red Sea island prospects before he received word from London that the Royal Dutch Shell Group had been granted an oil concession over those islands. Holmes was very disappointed, and while in that frame of mind, re-

92. India, Foreign Department, *Collection of Treaties,* 1929, 5th Edition, Vol. XI, 1933, p. 98.

93. Moore, Frederick Lee, Jr., *Origin of American Oil Concessions in Bahrain, Kuwait and Saudi Arabia,* Princeton University, 1948, p. 24 and 25.

turned to London and left further negotiations of the Syndicate's oil options, on the American side, in the hands of Tommy Ward.

Ward continued to press the American companies to consider these several oil options in the Middle East, which Holmes had gotten. Especially, he pressed the merits of the Syndicate's concession on Gulf Oil Corp.[94] Largely on the strength of Gulf's New York geologist who reported negatively on Professor Madgwick's report and recommendations, Gulf turned down the Syndicate offer on Bahrain in November, 1926.

Early in 1927, T. E. Ward again sought to interest the Standard Oil Co. (New Jersey) through Captain C. Stuart Morgan who had a first hand knowledge of the Persian Gulf area. Among others, Ward talked with C. F. Bowen, chief geologist of Jersey-Standard and Norval Baker,[95] his assistant. However, in spite of Stuart Morgan's enthusiasm for the Bahrain prospects, little Bahrain appeared rather insignificant compared to the bigger prospects in Iraq. The formation of the American oil group in Iraq—known as the Near East Development Corp.—and the finalizing of America's share interest in the Turkish

94. From a note written to the author by Floyd W. Ohliger in April 1960. In 1926 Ohliger was with Gulf and did not become associated with Standard Oil Co. of California until sometime later.

"That morning in 1926 when Tom Ward and Major Holmes first came to the New York Office of Gulf, I, too, was in the anteroom. I had come over from Pittsburgh to deliver some geological maps and data on behalf of Dr. K. C. Heald. Being eager to do my job, as the Major was to get someone interested in Bahrain, I arrived in the office almost as early as the janitor. Tom Ward and the Major arrived shortly after, and early for their appointment. We shared the waiting room. I probably told them that I was from the Pittsburgh office—messenger that I was. We chatted and—as anyone might expect who knew the brusk effervescent Major—the Major proceeded to tell me all about Bahrain, and showed me a sketch map that he had, just as if I were somebody who might have a word in Gulf's decision.

"The foregoing incident has intrigued me down through the years in the light of the eventual developments of Bahrain and my closeness to it."

95. Norval E. Baker later became chief geologist for the Iraq Petroleum Co., a post he held from 1935 to 1953.

Petroleum Co. transcended Bahrain. Generally, the Americans felt that the area of Bahrain oil prospects were "too small."

During mid-summer 1927, Ward went over to London for direct talks with the Syndicate principals and Major Holmes. Terms of sale were agreed including a small overriding royalty to Ward if he was able to negotiate a sale. The Syndicate realized its options on Hasa and the Neutral Zone were probably forfeit for noncompliance but still it felt these options had some validity and might be of some aid and comfort to the purchaser should the purchaser later desire to revalidate those options or maybe negotiate for a new oil concession.

Ward returned to New York in September, 1927, and at once reopened discussions with Gulf. These discussions prospered. By November, the basis for a trade had been agreed. At Ward's suggestion, two contracts would be drawn, one for Bahrain and one for al-Hasa, the Neutral Zone and Kuwait.[96] On November 30, 1927, the two contracts were executed by T. E. Ward for Eastern and General Syndicate and by Frank A. Leovy for Eastern Gulf Oil Co.[97]

These contracts with Eastern Gulf Oil Co. were executed only three days before the Syndicate was due to make an option payment in Bahrain. The Syndicate took prompt steps to extend the Bahrain exploration license.

Gulf lost no time in sending a team of geologists out to Bahrain. Dr. Kenneth C. Heald, then chief geologist for the Gulf companies, nominated Ralph O. Rhoades[98] to be chief of the field party assisted by W. F. Eastman and C. F. Shalibo. They sailed from New York on December 24, 1927 for Beirut via Europe—from there the party planned to cross over the moun-

96. The Syndicate really had only the "promise," of concession over Kuwait.

97. Wholly owned subsidiary of Gulf Oil Corp.

98. Ralph O. Rhoades retired (late 1960) from active service as Chairman but remained on the board of Gulf Oil Corp. until his death in July, 1961.

tains of Lebanon and the desert of Syria and Iraq by bus, thence by rail to Makinah (for Basra) in Iraq and on to Bahrain by steamer. They were met in Bahrain by Major Holmes about mid-January 1928.

"The geological mapping was completed by Rhoades by the middle of 1928. His study revealed unmistakable evidence of a large anticline covering most of Bahrain Island, with details of large oil seepages occurring in the eroded crest of the structure, and his report stated that there were excellent prospects of finding oil in commercial quantity. On the map he marked locations for drilling of the first two wells.[99] Incidentally, this structure map of Rhoades hung in the executive offices of the successors to Gulf in Bahrain for many years.

Eight months after Gulf had signed the two agreements (one of which covered Bahrain) with Eastern and General Syndicate, the Near East Development Corp. was formalized. Because of the commitments involved in Gulf's becoming a member of Near East Development, Gulf was now faced with the dilemma of either relinquishing its 4¾ per cent interest in the Iraq concessions of Turkish Petroleum Co. in order to hold onto its option contract over Bahrain or to surrender the Bahrain option in order to maintain its position with Near East Development.

On the American side, all concerned were agreed that Gulf should first offer its Bahrain options to the Near East Development Corp., and should the parent company not approve such action, then the Bahrain options would be offered to the Turkish Petroleum Co. as an international group.

In October, 1928, Stuart Morgan put the American view to their British-French-Dutch counterparts in London. Even at the price of $50,000—approximately the cost to Gulf to date of the Bahrain option—the Turkish Petroleum Co. refused for themselves and likewise refused to allow Near East Development

99. Moore, Frederick Lee, Jr., *Origin of American Oil Concessions in Bahrain, Kuwait and Saudi Arabia*, Princeton University, 1948, p. 31.

to hold and operate the Bahrain concession. Under such circumstances Gulf entertained the idea of finding an eligible American oil company to take the Bahrain option over from them.

Major Holmes had come on to New York in October while Morgan was in London presenting the Bahrain case to the Iraq group. The situation was explained to Holmes who promptly returned to London to talk with his principals.

As a last resort, Gulf presented its case to Sir John Cadman, Chairman of Anglo-Persian Oil Co., Ltd., when he came over to America in November, 1928, to attend the American Petroleum Institute meetings. His answer was a flat "No."

Now it so happened that the President of Standard Oil Company of California, Kenneth R. Kingsbury, was also in Chicago to attend that same API convention. Knowing that California-Standard had no foreign entanglements, Gulf approached him in regard to Bahrain. Kingsbury was at once intrigued by the situation, as also the oil prospects and so instructed his company's Vice President, M. E. Lombardi, to confer with Gulf representatives and Ward in New York as soon as possible.

Lombardi came on to New York in early December and was very impressed by the Rhoades geological report on Bahrain as also the favorable terms Gulf was asking for its rights. He so reported to Kingsbury. On December 21, 1928 an agreement was executed in which Standard Oil Co. of California undertook the obligations and commitments set forth in the Bahrain option contract with Gulf, dated November 30, 1927. At the same time, Gulf offered to relinquish to California-Standard, any claims it might have to the option agreement for oil concessions over al-Hasa and the Kuwait Neutral Zone, but Standard declined.

Gulf received the nominal sum of $50,000 from California-Standard for its out-of-pocket expenditures but received no other cash consideration, retained no deferred payments out of oil and had no over-riding royalty interest whatever.

In closing this phase of the saga of Major Frank Holmes and his oil concessions, the author feels constrained to add a note about one of the peculiar and distinctive traits of this colorful character. His manner of smoking a cigarette while talking was a fascinating sight—never to be forgotten once seen. Holmes was a chain smoker. Always a cigarette dangeld from his lips. He seemed never to remove his smoke when talking or to be conscious that he had a cigarette in his mouth. Consequently, as the Major talked, and he was a loquacious fellow, his cigarette butt, whether long or short, bobbed up and down with the movement of his lips, for all the world like a long protruding loose tooth. When the Major was excited and talking, the rapid movement of the cigarette dangling, as if about to fall from his lips, had an almost hypnotic effect on his audience.

Bahrain Petroleum Company, Ltd.
(Bapco)

As noted in the foregoing, Standard Oil Co. of California had acquired all of Eastern Gulf Oil Co.'s rights in Eastern and General Syndicate's oil options over Bahrain by the agreement executed December 21, 1928. But now another hitch occurred, namely, the insistence of the British government that the acquisition of any concession in Bahrain by a foreign entity must be approved by the British Colonial office. This requirement stemmed from the British treaties with Bahrain of 1880 and 1892.

The British Colonial office insisted that only a British company would be permitted to operate in Bahrain. There ensued protracted discussions between California-Standard and the Colonial office and seemingly an impasse had been reached when T. E. Ward suggested that, by the Balfour Declaration of the British Commonwealth of Nations, a Canadian company would enjoy British status, hence, the registration of a Standard

subsidiary company in Ottawa under the laws of Canada[100]
should fulfill the British nationality requirements.

In 1929, California-Standard proceeded to form a wholly
owned subsidiary, The Bahrain Petroleum Co., Ltd., under the
laws of Canada, with domicile in Ottawa.

The State Department in Washington was duly informed of
the existence of The Bahrain Petroleum Co., Ltd., and was
requested by California-Standard to advise the British government through diplomatic channels that said Canadian company
was considered to qualify under the British nationality requirement and that the company now desired the formal approval
of the British Colonial office in order to proceed with the exploration and development of the Bahrain oil concession.

Some months elapsed before California-Standard obtained the
green light from London.

In May, 1930, the first of Bahrain Petroleum Company's
(now familiarly known as Bapco), representatives arrived in
the islands. Fred A. Davies was one of this group and was in
charge of exploratory work.[101] Major Holmes would continue
to act as agent for the Syndicate in the Middle East and as
liaison for Bapco.

On August 1, 1930, the oil concession was assigned by California-Standard to Bapco. By the original concession terms the
company enjoyed the exclusive oil rights to about 100,000 acres.
"Such are the politics of oil that it had taken five years for an
oil company to be formed to develop Bahrain oil and had it
not been for the enterprise of an American company, which
took up the concession after it had been refused by the British,
the oil of Bahrain might never have been exploited."[102]

100. The Company laws of Canada permit 100 per cent stock ownership
by American citizens.

101. A few years later, Fred A. Davies was assigned to the mainland
operations, first for Casco and then Aramco.

102. Belgrave, James H. D., *Welcome to Bahrain*, Mark & Moody, Ltd.,
Stourbridge, England, 1953, p. 44.

On June 1, 1932 the first Bapco well came in just south of Awali on Bahrain. It is still producing. In the desert around the Jebel ad-Dukhan the oil field was developed. At the end of 1961 there were 154 producing oil wells on Bahrain, all flowing and 5 gas wells. Since 1932, through 1961, the Bahrain concession (which Gulf sold for $50,000 in 1927) has produced an aggregate of 262,862,000 barrels of crude.

Much of the credit for the development of these oil fields can be attributed to the untiring and efficient effort of E. A. Skinner who was connected with those operations from 1931 until his semi-retirement in 1954. Skinner was no novice to foreign oil operations when he went to Bahrain, having previously had considerable field experience in the oil fields of South America, Europe and the Far East.[103]

In 1936, California-Standard, seeking nearby markets for the increasing production from its Bapco oil fields (as also the oil it hoped to develop from its Saudi Arabian concession on the mainland), sold a half interest in the Bahrain concession to The Texas Co. for a half share of the latter's wide spread market facilities east of Suez. The new joint company was registered in the Bahamas as the California-Texas Oil Company (Caltex).

Bapco built a refinery on Bahrain only eight miles from the producing field. It is now one of the largest in the Middle East (daily capacity of 205,000 barrels), and refines more than 100,000 barrels of crude daily from the Arabian American Oil Company's (Aramco) oil fields on the mainland as well as all of Bahrain's oil. From 1938 through 1961 Bapco has received

---

103. Edward A. Skinner passed away in New York City, November 23, 1956 at the age of 64. "Ed Skinner will long be remembered in Bahrain as a pioneer, a technician, an executive and a friend"—from the *Islander*, Bahrain, November 29, 1956. He was admired and respected throughout the oil industry, everywhere.

more than 870.2 million barrels of Aramco crude oil for refining. Nearby, on the close-in island of Sitra, Bapco built its tank farm and a steel drum plant.

The Ruler of Bahrain and Bapco signed a Supplemental Agreement in 1940 under which the company received a 55-year extension to its concession, including all lands, shoals, reefs, waters and submerged lands of "the present and future domains" of the Ruler of Bahrain—an area of some 1,644,000 acres.

Bapco currently employs 7,442 workers of which 5,628 are Bahrainis—the rest are British, American and other nationals.

The company provides commissaries, schools, hospitals, movies, swimming pools, churches and mosques, social and recreational clubs for its employees, as well as homes for married and single workmen—both the Bahrainis and the Europeans.

The original concession provided for a royalty payment to the Bahrain government of 3½ rupees per ton—before devaluation of the Indian rupee this royalty amounted to about 14 cents a barrel. The royalty was further increased to approximately 30 cents a barrel in 1950 by amicable agreement. Then the following year an additional annual lump sum was paid to the government by the company. Finally, on January 1, 1952, in line with what other oil companies were doing in the Middle East, Bapco entered into a 50-50 sharing of the profits agreement with the Ruler, H. H. Shaikh Sulman Bin Hamed al-Khalifah K.C.M.G., K.C.I.E.

"The oil industry today is the most important factor in Bahrain's economy and is recognized as such by the government and the people of the country,"[104] said James H. D. Belgrave, (son of Sir Charles Belgrave, K.B.E.—long-time adviser to the government, and Commandant, State Police) in 1953. It is even more true now.

104. Belgrave, James H. D., *Welcome to Bahrain*, Mark & Moody, Ltd., Stourbridge, England, 1953, p. 46.

Bahrain was the first all American oil venture in the Middle East.

During 1961, Bapco produced a total of 16,444,492 barrels. No drilling rigs were operating at the beginning of 1962.

Annual production for Bahrain by years since 1932 and the estimated proven oil reserves in the ground at the end of 1960 are shown in Appendix IV.

5

Saudi Arabia

To PROPERLY UNDERSTAND THE IMPORTANT ROLE of oil in Saudi Arabia, one should first take a brief look back over Arabia's history and economy before the Kingdom of Hejaz (Hijar) and Nejd (Najd) came into being—otherwise the influence and impact of Americans in Arabia may not be fully appreciated.

There is every reason to believe that the outer fringe of the great Arabian Peninsula was known to man as soon as he began to venture on the high seas. Thus it may be assumed that there have been some civilized inhabitants along coastal Arabia for at least 6,000 years. So far, however, archaeologists have only found evidence of the early Bronze Age—say 1,500 to 2,000 B.C. in the thousands of tumuli (burial mounds) on Bahrain and in the similar, but fewer, tumuli on the mainland opposite Bahrain.

Some 2,000 years ago, the ancient Greeks and Romans recorded on their maps, the existence of a fabulous city called, Gerra, in the al-Hasa of Arabia near the Persian Gulf. Some authorities claim ruins, identified as being Gerra, have been uncovered near the seaport of Oqair.[105] On the other hand, Colonel Dickson—who lived in and traveled extensively over Arabia for more than 40 years—says:

"Hufuf (oasis) may well be ancient Gerra, and that Jabal Qara is a survival of the old name. I suggest also that the modern port of 'Uqair (Little Q'ara) might have been the ancient port of Gerra, as Piraesus is to Athens."[106]

Gerra was reported by one of the old geographers to have been a Chaldean Colony, that is a colony of Babylon. Early writers refer to Gerra as one of the richest cities in the world. Apparently this city, on the edge of the Arabian desert, was not only a trade center through which passed the overland caravans, but was also a port of call for the deep-laden vessels from India and the Far East as they sailed up the Persian Gulf to the rich kingdoms which then flourished in the fertile valleys of the Tigris and Euphrates.

According to the Greek, Strabo, (quoting earlier writers):

"By the trade, both the Sabaens and Gerraei have become the richest of all tribes and possess a great quantity of wrought articles in gold and silver such as couches, tripods, basins, drinking vessels, to which we must add the costly magnificence of their houses; for the doors, walls and roofs are variegated with inlaid ivory, gold, silver and precious stones."[107]

Strabo also says:

"The merchants of Gerra generally carry the Arabian merchandise and aromatics by land; but, Aristobulus says on the contrary, that they frequently travel into Babylonia on rafts and

105. Also spelled, 'Uqair. This place is located some 50 miles south of Damman, the present terminus of the railroad from Riyadh.

106. Dickson, H. R. P., *Kuwait and Her Neighbours*, George Allen and Unwin, Ltd., London, 1956, p. 81.

107. Lebkicher, Roy, Renta, George, and Steineke, Max, *The Arabia of Ibn Saud*, revised edition, Russell F. Moore Co., Inc., New York, 1952, p. 26.

thence sail up the Euphrates with their cargoes, but afterwards carry them by land to all parts of the country."[108]

Sabeans were the people of Sheba (Saba) who once flourished somewhere to the north of Arabia. They are believed to have invaded southwestern Arabia and conquered the Minaens about 600 B.C. Sabeans also traversed eastern Arabia. In Philby's exploration of Arabia inland from the Red Sea, he found on one of his trips, an ancient stone-lined well, still with "plenty of water at four fathoms," some 36 miles southward from Raushan at an elevation estimated at well over 4,000 feet above sea. The wells of Bir ibn Sarrar belonged to the Bani Munaba section of Shahran.

Philby's guide said this well was built by elephants and this, according to Philby, dated it. He surmised, "The well, therefore, must have been at least 1,366 years old at this time, and may have dated even from the early days of the Queen of Sheba, who also used elephants to go to Solomon 3,000 years ago."[109]

According to Wendell Phillips, who made considerable explorations in southwestern Arabia, the Kingdom of Saba lay in the mountains and valleys of what is now known as Yemen (Yaman) and may have existed, judging by inscriptions, from the eighth century B.C. until the sixth century A.D. It is believed that for a time, Saba was joined with the Kingdom of Qataban, which had its center in the Hadhramaut (now part of the Aden Protectorates).[110]

From the Hadhramaut came the sacred frankincense and myrrh, also coffee. From the Yemen came metals and lush agricultural products. These commodities and pearls from the Persian Gulf and the Red Sea were the trade goods of Arabia

108. Lebkicher, Roy, Rentz, George, and Steineke, Max, *Aramco Handbook,* Arabian American Oil Company, revised edition, prepared in 1960.

109. Philby, H. St. J. B., *Arabian Highlands,* published for The Middle East Institute by Cornell University Press, Ithaca, N. Y., 1952, p. 119.

110. Phillips, Wendell, *Qataban and Sheba,* Victor Gollancz, Ltd., London, 1955.

for many long centuries. In fact, Arabia had little else to offer in the way of natural resources until oil was discovered along the Persian Gulf.

Thus, for thousands of years, the hinterland of Arabia was referred to as a vast inland sea of sand and rock, sparsely inhabited by nomadic tribes. Only the coastline fringe was known to traders and seagoing folks.

Then came the rise of Islam and the Arabian Empire. Mohammed (also spelled Muhammad) was born, according to tradition, about A.D. 570. At that time, the country, especially along the Red Sea coast, was in a state of anarchy. There were, "constant tribal feuds and fights and persecutions between the Jews and the Christians. The Jews had become particularly powerful in the western part of the country. The majority of the Arabs, however, still worshipped pagan gods. Mecca, even then, was a sacred city, the site of a temple, the Ka'ba, in the corner of which was fixed a black stone (perhaps a meteorite) worshiped as an idol and believed to have magical powers. Large pilgrimages were made to this stone, and at that time, as today, they were one of the chief sources of revenue of the residents of Mecca."[111]

Mohammed was middle-aged before he began to have his revelation. His first converts were members of his immediate family, then the poor people and slaves. Gradually, the new faith spread throughout Arabia. Mohammed died in A.D. 632. Before his death it is said that he, "Dispatched messages to the leading rulers of the world . . . calling upon them to acknowledge the one true God and to serve him."[112]

During the seventh and eighth centuries, the Arab Lords swept over all of the present day Middle East (except Turkey),

111. Lebkicher, Roy, Rentz, George, and Steineke, Max, *The Arabia of Ibn Saud*, Russell F. Moore Co., Inc., New York, 1952, p. 31.
112. Lebkicher, Roy, Rentz, George, and Steineke, Max, *The Arabia of Ibn Saud*, Russell F. Moore Co., Inc., New York, 1952, p. 32.

all across north Africa along the Mediterranean coast and overran, Spain, Portugal and part of France. In the year A.D. 750
the Omayyad dynasty, which centered in Damascus, fell to the
Abbasid dynasty who moved its capital to Baghdad where the
caliphate remained until devastated by the Mongols in A.D. 1258.

From that time until the rise of Ibn Saud in the early 1900's,
Arabia had no central government. It was really nothing more
than an adjunct of the Mamelukes in Egypt and later of the
Ottomans. Except for a few cities like Medina, Jeddah (also
spelled Jidda and Jiddah) Mecca, Hofuf and Riyadh, there
were relatively few towns and villages and these were to be
found principally along the coasts or hovered around oases in
the north central area. Mostly, the interior of Arabia was inhabited only by nomadic tribes, warring one with another for
control of watering places and pasturage when not engaged in
blood feuds. So, for nearly 700 years Arabia slept—her peoples
clinging to feudalistic customs and culture—unconscious, as it
were, of the changing world.

The beginning of Arabia's renaissance occurred in the mid-
eighteenth century when Shaikh Mohammed ibn Abdul Wahhab
(Wahab) started an Islamic revival. The followers of this
puritanical group were known as the Wahhabis. When unable
to peaceably convert, they fought to conquer. The House of
Saud became allied to the Wahhabis. Before the end of that
century, the Wahhabis controlled all of Nejd.

By the early 1800's, under the House of Saud the Wahhabi
expanded. Wahhabis invaded Iraq and controlled both the holy
cities as well as almost all of the Arabian Peninsula. They had
become a threat to the Ottoman.

The Sultan took forceful measures to put an end to Arab
disturbances. His Egyptian soldiers finally met the Wahhabis
and defeated these men of the desert. Coincidentally, the Wahhabis lost their leader (Saud) by death. For many years thereafter the Wahhabis were more or less disorganized, although

by 1834 they had regained control of Nejd and al-Hasa. The following 75 years were largely a period of civil war and feuds, within tribes and tribe against tribe. During this internal turmoil, the Turks gained control over al-Hasa in 1871 which they held until World War I.

The House of Rashid rose to power and forced the family of Saud to flee from Riyadh in 1891.

> Ibn Saud was about eleven years old when his family took flight. For a time they lived among the Bedouins on the edge of Rub' al Khali. Later, they moved to Qatar, then to Behrain, and finally, they were given refuge in Kuwait where they spent the better part of a decade . . . In Kuwait, he (Ibn Saud) also learned a great deal about the political forces of the Persian Gulf, particularly the powerful position of the British and of their rivalry with the Germans, Russians, and Turks for control of that important channel of commerce. Shaikh Mubarak of Kuwait was a great friend of Ibn Saud and his father.[113]

In 1896, Shaikh Mubarak's two brothers were killed, (both were weak characters and unwilling to oppose the Turks, who nominally dominated Kuwait) and Mubarak declared himself the ruler. He refused any honors from the Turks and sought the protection of the British. Such protection was refused at the time. Actually, it was not until 1899 that Her Majesty's Government acceded to enter into a treaty with Kuwait, making it a "protected state."[114]

In 1900, Adul Rahman ibn Faisal Al Saud and his four sons were still living in Kuwait as guests of Shaikh Mubarak. That fall, Mubarak led an invading force of his Kuwaitis into the

---

113. Lebkicher, Roy, Rentz, George, and Steineke, Max, *The Arabia of Ibn Saud,* Russell F. Moore Co., Inc., New York, 1952, p. 44. See also *Aramco Handbook,* by Roy Lebkicher, George Rentz and Max Steineke, revised edition prepared in 1960.
114. More will be said about this treaty later in Chapter 6, Kuwait.

very heart of Arabia. Early in 1901 Mubarak's men, (said to number 10,000) in the interest of the Saud family, engaged the al Rashid forces at Sarif, near Buraida. The severe fight came off badly for Mubarak—not only were his men defeated, but Mubarak lost two members of his family during the engagement.

Ibn Rashid planned to retaliate against Kuwait but hesitated because a British gunboat was anchored in Kuwait Bay. The Turks, likewise, were deterred from disciplining Kuwait for the same reason.

This impasse emboldened young Ibn Saud, then a lad of 20 years, to conceive of a sneak attack on Rijadh—where the palaces of al-Rashid were located—with a small select band of guerillas, recruited in Kuwait.[115] This band successfully evaded a Rashid force some 200 miles west of Kuwait and came secretly into Riyadh.

By night, 23 of Ibn Saud's small force quietly passed over the outer walls of the Palace court and gained access to the roof of one of the favorite wives of the Rashite governor, knowing that the governor was accustomed to visit her, "for a half hour or so after morning prayers each day."[116] Sure enough, at dawn the governor emerged from the fort for a rendevous with his lady. Half-way across the court he was attacked by Ibn Saud's men, and slain. Saud called on the garrison to surrender, which they did. In no time, Riyadh was controlled by Saud and was promptly put into a state of defense.

Ibn Rashid's main forces, quickly gathered around Riyadh. They were too many and too well armed to be repelled by Saud's men, so the latter withdrew into the desert again and finally made their stand in Qasim.

115. According to Colonel Dickson, this band consisted of only 40 men, "among whom were his younger brother Muhammed," and two of their kinsmen.

116. Dickson, H. R. P., *Kuwait and Her Neighbours*, George Allen and Unwin, Ltd., London, 1956, p. 138.

The news of this bold escapade spread like wildfire throughout Nejd and from all points of the compass armed Bedouins (Badu or Badawi) flocked to Saud's standard.

For the next several years, there were a number of engagements between the Saud and Rashid forces and generally Saud's guerillas came off best.

In May, 1904, Ibn Rashid again advanced on Saud's desert army at a place near Buraida. Rashid had augmented his forces with eight battalions of Turkish troops with artillery. The resulting day-long bloody battle was indecisive, although technically the Turks won. A second engagement took place later that summer between the same armies and this time it was the Rashid-Turk forces that were routed leaving behind great stores and a large sum of gold which fell into Ibn Saud's hands.[117]

In April, 1906, Ibn Rashid was killed in an engagement with Saud's men, again near Buraian, four years and three months after Saud's dramatic seizure of Riyadh. However, this defeat of Rashid did not end Saud's troubles. Other chieftains in the north and in the south rose up to challenge Saud's authority. As yet, Saud had not gained control over the Hejaz (the province in western Arabia along the Red Sea), or al-Hasa, (the province in northeastern Arabia along the Persian Gulf), although most of the tribes in the Nejd (the province of central Arabia north of the great sand sea known as the "Empty Quarter") recognized him as their leader.

Ibn Saud's second great coup came in April, 1913, when by stealth his men got control of the fort at Hofuf where the Turkish forces were garrisoned. The Turkish governor surrendered and soon the Turkish garrisons at Qatif and Oqair also

117. The author has noted considerable differences in detail in the story of the *Career of Ibn Sa'ud,* as told by Roy Lebkicher et al., in *The Arabia of Ibn Saud* (p. 44-50) with that related in H. R. P. Dickson's book, *Kuwait and Her Neighbours,* under the captions, "Ibn Saud Seizes Riyadh" and "Qasim occupied" (p. 138-139 and 141-142).

surrendered. A few months later, the Ottoman government signed a treaty of friendship with Ibn Saud, recognizing him as the Ruler of al-Hasa as well as central Nejd. Ibn Saud was then a young man of 33, but already old in political and military strategy in his country.

> After the outbreak of war (First World War), Britain be-
> gan a campaign almost immediately to wrest control of Mes-
> opotamia from the Turks. The Turks, on the other hand, had
> allies in Ibn Rashid and in some of the Arab leaders in
> southern Iraq, while the Hejaz was, of course, a Turkish
> province.[118]

The British realized that they needed Ibn Saud as an ally. Their first combined engagement against Rashid forces did not come off too well. During the fighting, Captain Shakespear, a British agent, was killed. This affair cooled off the British some- what, especially in the matter of a joint military effort. However, in December, 1915, Sir Percy Cox, British Political Resident in the Persian Gulf concluded a treaty of friendship with the Saud government, which in return for "protection" gave the British control over Saud's relations with other powers.[119]

As noted in Chapter 4 under the story of Bahrain, Sir Percy Cox again negotiated with Ibn Saud in 1922 for the adjudica- tion of Arabian frontier boundaries with Kuwait and Iraq, from which came the two Neutral Zones.

By 1923, Ibn Saud's domain was hemmed in by British pro- tected Shaikhdoms on the east and south, and the Hejaz on the west now controlled by the British puppet, King Husain. How- ever, the latter's high-handed rule and tyranny was his undoing.

118. Lebkicher, Roy, Rentz, George, and Steineke, Max, *The Arabia of Ibn Saud,* Russell F. Moore Co., Inc., New York, 1952, p. 56.

119. This treaty was annulled by the Treaty of Jeddah in 1927, *The Arabia of Ibn Saud,* Roy Lebkicher, George Rentz, and Max Steineke, Russell F. Moore Co., Inc., New York, 1952, p. 57.

The people of Hejaz rebelled and he was forced to flee with British help from Jeddah in October, 1924, with baggage and family, first to Jordan and thence to Cyprus, where he remained the rest of his life.

Ibn Saud entered Mecca in October, 1924, and in January, 1926, was proclaimed King of the Hejaz.

On May 20, 1927, the Treaty of Jeddah was signed with the British under the terms of which a new Arabian Kingdom was recognized as a sovereign state. However, it was not until 1932 that the Kingdom of Hejaz and Nejd were designated as the, "Kingdom of Saudi Arabia."

Thus, after 31 years of almost constant struggle with various tribes, with the Turks and with puppet governments within Arabia and, notwithstanding all sorts of international pressure from the outside, Ibn Saud—now a man of 52, emerged King of an empire, united under one political head for the first time in many centuries.

The author admits this history of Saudi Arabia is very sketchy and may be lacking in many significant facts. However, these few pages were prompted to highlight the important role of Ibn Saud in cementing the tribes of Arabia into a great empire, which in turn, enabled the renaissance of the Arab from feudalistic customs and cultures to the modern ideologies of government, economics and education.

Then Came Oil to Saudi Arabia

In Chapter 4 of this story of *Americans and Oil in the Middle East* has been related the story of how and when Major Frank Holmes for Eastern and General Syndicate, Ltd., secured options to acquire oil concessions over Bahrain, al-Hasa and the Kuwait Neutral Zone. These rights were all acquired by Eastern Gulf Oil Co., a subsidiary of Gulf Oil Corp., in November, 1927.

According to Frederick Lee Moore, Jr., who presented an

excellent thesis to the School of Politics and International Affairs
at Princeton in 1948 entitled, "Origin of American Oil Concessions in Bahrain, Kuwait and Saudi Arabia," Standard Oil Co.
of California was ripe for a Middle East oil venture. Moore says
in his thesis (p. 34):

> From 1920 to 1928, California-Standard had not been able
> to develop one barrel of foreign commercial production and is
> estimated to have spent approximately $50,000,000 on foreign
> exploration, concessions and drilling. Domestically, it was a
> strong and aggressive company, which obtained plenty of
> reserves and managed in marketing under the leadership of
> its Vice President, Harry D. Collier, who subsequently became
> president and later chairman, to keep its lead over all other
> companies on the west coast, in the midst of the fiercest type
> of competition. In 1928, the signs in one of its Venezuelan
> concessions were encouraging; the company by this time had
> reduced its foreign holdings to include land in only Colombia,
> Mexico and Venezuela. Considerable exploration activity was
> underway in the Dutch East Indies, where $75,000 had been
> expended on searching efforts by the company by the end of
> 1928. Standard Oil of California needed additional oil re-
> serves to expand its foreign markets, to avoid depletion of its
> California reserves, and to save the expense of long tanker
> hauls across the Pacific.

Thus it was that when California-Standard was approached
by Gulf in regard to its Bahrain options, it was immediately
interested and on December 21, 1928 entered into an agreement
with Gulf and the Syndicate whereby it assumed all the obligations and commitments under the contract of November 30,
1927. Coincidentally, Gulf offered to assign to California-
Standard its agreements with the Syndicate pertaining to al-Hasa
and the Kuwait Neutral Zone, notwithstanding that all concerned knew at the time that the Holmes' options on the main-

land were probably invalid by reason of the Syndicate's failure to make payments or to initiate any exploration work program.

However, California-Standard was not interested in these perhaps defunct mainland options, apparently feeling that Bahrain was enough of a gamble. Thus Gulf continued to hold these options until on April 15, 1932, when by mutual consent, it relinquished back to the Syndicate all rights pertaining to al-Hasa and the Kuwait Neutral Zone. Meanwhile, Gulf had decided to go all out with the Syndicate in an attempt to acquire a valid and exclusive oil concession over the territory of Kuwait State.

Even though California-Standard's management did not acquire Holmes' mainland options, they became aware, early in 1928, that some people believed the mainland of Arabia along the Persian Gulf had oil prospects. They may even have learned of the evidence of surface structure near Dammam and of the reported oil seepage near Qatif.

No doubt, California-Standard had in mind that if its exploration and drilling on Bahrain resulted in finding oil in commercial quantities, it would naturally indicate the possibility of finding oil on the mainland, only twenty-odd miles distant. Whatever Standard's reasoning at the time, it proceeded apace with the Bahrain program. The discovery well on Bahrain came in June 1, 1932.

Soon after the Bahrain discovery, Standard made a move toward the mainland. "The first step in approaching the Saudi government was made in early November, 1932, in the form of a telegram to the well-known author and explorer, H. St. John B. Philby, who was then in Jeddah. He was asked to propose to the government that the company make a preliminary geological examination of al-Hasa with a view toward negotiating a concession if conditions seemed to justify further exploration. The government, however, wanted to negotiate a concession before any geological work was commenced."[120]

According to K. S. Twitchell, some ten months prior to California-Standard's telegram to Philby, he (Twitchell) had discussed the oil prospects of al-Hasa with King Ibn Saud. At the time Twitchell was employed by the King to make explorations for water wells along pilgrim routes and to look into the possibility of reworking some of the old gold mining dumps. The King had asked Twitchell to visit Bahrain and report to him on the exploration under way there. Says Twitchell:

> I returned to Hofuf via Oqair on January 10, 1932. The King had returned from the Naja on the twelfth, and asked me to call for a discussion of the trip. As always, I had a most cordial interview with unexpected queries and subjects arising. Ibn-Saud asked me to arrange for oil geologists and oil-well drillers. I recommended strongly that the results of the Number 1 well at Bahrain be awaited before doing anything regarding oil. Since no evidence of faulting or difference geologically between Bahrain and the mainland of Hasa could be seen, and in view of the fact that oil well exploration and drilling is extremely expensive, and that if the Bahrain well did not strike commercial oil it would be unlikely that it would be found in Hasa, a definite wait-and-see policy was advocated. On the other hand, if the Bahrain well proved a success, it was logical that commercial oil would be found in Hasa, but in greater quantities, because of its much greater area. Furthermore, it seemed quite possible that American capital might be found to undertake the great expense of oil development in Hasa under conditions that would greatly benefit Saudi Arabia. After much deliberation, the King decided to follow this advice.[121]

120. Lebkicher, Roy, *Aramco and World Oil*, Russell F. Moore Co. Inc., New York 1952, p. 26.

121. Twitchell, K. S., *Saudi Arabia*, Princeton University Press, 2nd Edition, p. 145.

During these discussions, the King made reference to his former arrangement with Holmes and said in effect that he wanted nothing more to do with the British since they had not lived up to their agreement.

Some five months later—the same month as the discovery well came in on Bahrain—the King's representatives urged Twitchell to try to find American capital to carry on the work of developing mines, oil and roads in Saudi Arabia. Twitchell said he was an engineer and not a promoter but he would try to interest American capital on two conditions: first, that his sponsor, Charles R. Crane, be consulted and give his consent; and secondly, that the King authorize him by letter to undertake this project.

In due course, both conditions were met, whereupon Twitchell returned home and began his quest of capital. The mining companies, generally, considered Arabia too speculative to venture.

Twitchell met Terry Duce of The Texas Co., who later advised that his company was not interested and suggested he approach the Near East Development Corp. and the Standard Oil Co. of California. Twitchell then sought out Stuart Morgan and Norval E. Baker of Near East Development. They seemed intrigued by the al-Hasa prospect but said they could not consider the acquisition of such terrotory because of Near East Development's prior commitments to the Turkish Petroleum Co. When Twitchell approached Gulf he was advised that Gulf, too, was an interested party in Near East Development Co.[122]

Finally, Twitchell met with M. E. Lombardi of California-Standard, in New York and they made a deal. Lombardi gave Twitchell power of attorney to act for his company in Saudi Arabian matters.

122. For further reference to Twitchell's meetings with representatives of The Texas Co., Near East Development Co., Gulf Oil Corp. and Standard Oil Co. of California, see Twitchell, K. S., *Saudi Arabia*, Princeton University Press, 2nd Edition, p. 149-150.

Again to quote Twitchell:

> Accompanied by our son, Mrs. Twitchell and I sailed from
> New York on January 13, 1933 for London, where we were
> to meet Mr. and Mrs. Lombardi and Mr. and Mrs. Lloyd
> Hamilton. Mr. Hamilton was to write the terms of the oil
> agreement and take care of all legal technicalities, while I
> was to give advice on Saudi Arabia and local conditions. This
> arrangement proved entirely satisfactory. I defined the boun-
> daries on behalf of the oil company, while the Minister of
> Finance, Shakh Abdullah Suliaman Al Hamdan, signed on
> behalf of the Saudi Arabian government. The very able and
> simple form of agreement is outstanding and contributed to
> the reputation of Lloyd Hamilton, which is the highest in oil
> circles.[123]

The concession agreement was duly signed in the King's
small temporary encampment on the outskirts of Jedda, on
May 29, 1933.

During these negotiations between the Standard Oil Co. of
California and the Saudi Arabian government, competition
came on the scenes, namely, Stephen H. Longrigg for the Iraq
Petroleum Co. and Major Frank Holmes for the Eastern and
General Syndicate. Apparently, however, neither received any
encouragement in their respective interviews with the King—
possibly because they represented British companies but more
likely, because they could not commit their companies to a very
substantial cash payment in, "gold sovereigns." The concession
also provided that the Saudi Arabian government receive, free
of cost, a royalty of four shillings gold (or its equivalent in
sterling or dollars) per ton of crude oil produced and saved.
This gold clause caused the company considerable difficulties

123. Twitchell, K. S., *Saudi Arabia*, Princeton University Press, 2nd Edition, p. 150-151. (Note: Lloyd N. Hamilton, deceased in 1945 was unre-
lated to the author—they were, however, very good friends.)

later on—principally because of the scarcity of gold coin and gold bullion in which to effect payment—until rectified by mutual consent in revised concession agreement.

This original concession agreement included all of al-Hasa and adjacent lands, a total area, said to be, some 360,000 square miles—one of the largest oil grants in the world.

On May 31, 1939, six years after the signing of the original concession agreement and after oil in commercial quantities had been discovered in the Dammam field in al-Hasa, W. J. Lenahan, (California-Standard's representative to the Saudi Arab government, stationed at Jeddah) in spite of keen competition from other international groups—succeeded in executing a supplemental agreement with the Saudi government by which the concession area was further increased by 80,000 square miles, to make a total of 440,000 square miles (about the size of Texas and California combined). This supplemental agreement included, among other areas, the Saudi Arabian undivided one-half interest in the two Neutral Zones of Kuwait and Iraq.[124]

Standard of California began exploration on its mainland concessions in September, 1933, with two geologists borrowed from the Bahrain venture, aided by Twitchell for his knowledge of the country and the customs of its peoples. This first party quickly found surface evidence at Dammam[125] of domal structure of such size as to be considered favorable for the accumulation of oil in the underground.

In November, 1933, Standard of California assigned its Saudi Arabian oil concession to its wholly owned subsidiary, California

124. Subsequently, the company surrendered its rights in lands west of the 46th meridian (1947), its rights in the Kuwait Neutral Zone (1948) and its rights to a tract of 34,000 square miles in the southwestern part of the concession (1949) and in 1955 two tracts totaling about 34,800 square miles; thus at present Aramco's oil rights in Saudi Arabia include some 340,000 square miles.

125. Dammam is located almost directly on the Persian Gulf Coast, approximately 25 miles due west of the north tip of the Island of Bahrain.

Arabian Standard Oil Co., commonly referred to in industry as Casco.[126]

In 1934, it was decided to explore the Dammam dome by drilling. A camp site was chosen near the present Dhahran field headquarters and construction of the tent camp was begun in December of that year concurrently with the assembling of the drilling rig.

Guy S. Williams was named drilling superintendent and Floyd W. Ohliger the petroleum engineer.[127]

Dammam No. 1 well was spudded on April 30, 1935. This well did not find commercial production, in fact out of the first ten wells drilled on the Dammam structure only three were retained as small oil producers, one as a gas well, one as a water well, two were abandoned and three others were later deepened. It was one of these latter three wells—No. 7—that was completed in March, 1938, as a large oil producer from the "Arab" zone at a depth of 4,727 feet. Thus, the first major oil discovery on the mainland of Arabia occurred nearly five years after the original concession contract was signed.

Now that commercial production was assured, the company began the construction of a permanent headquarters camp at Dhahran and intensified its drilling activities in the proven area as also in wildcat areas.

The geologists were unable to find any significant surface evidence of structure except in the vicinity of Dammam, hence,

126. It was not until January, 1944, that the name of this company was changed to Arabian American Oil Co. or Aramco, its present name.

127. From Roy Lebkicher's, *Aramco and World Oil,* Russell F. Moore Co., Inc., New York, 1952, p. 32. "R. P. Miller (one of the two first geologists from Bahrain) became resident manager until he returned to the United States in the autumn of 1935. He was succeeded by F. A. Davies, who was in turn succeeded by F. W. Ohliger in the summer of 1937. Ohliger remained as manager, later as general manager, until he became a vice president, in charge of relations in 1947." Ohliger became a director of Aramco in 1951—he retired in 1958. Fred Davies became president in 1940 and Chairman of the Board from 1952 until his retirement in 1959.

geophysical parties began to explore the coastal area and hinterland of this vast oil domain. Aerial photography, and magnatometer, gravity and seismograph surveys were initiated in due course and with surprisingly excellent results, considering the climatic and terrain difficulties in this land of huge shifting sand dunes. According to Roy Leblicher, who has written the story of Aramco, "Aramco's geologists (and geophysicists) have to their credit nine oil fields out of a total of twelve wildcat tests" —a most remarkable record.

Since commercial oil was discovered at Dammam in 1938, Aramco has found and developed some eight additional oil fields—including Abqaiq, Ain Dar, Qatif, Fadhili, Abn Hadriya, Safaniya (offshore), Uthmanigah and Haradh. There is reason to believe that the underground reservoir of these latter two fields may be one and the same. If so, the combined Uthmanigah-Haradh field could be one of the longest and largest oil producing structures in the world.

In December, 1936, the Texas Co. paid California Arabian Standard Oil Co. (Casco) $3 million in cash and undertook to pay an additional $18 million out of oil produced in Saudi Arabia for a one-half interest in the Saudi Arabian oil concessions.[128]

In the pre-World War II days, after the Dammam discovery, plant facilities for storing and moving and processing oil had moved apace with the drilling of additional wells. Pipe lines were laid to the Persian Gulf port of Al-Khobar and oil began to move to Bahrain by barge. Ras Tanura was chosen as an oil loading terminal site and also for a refinery.

The first tanker was loaded with crude at Ras Tanura on May 1, 1939. This was the occasion for a three-day festival, attended by King Ibn Saud with other members of the royal fam-

128. Previously, (July, 1936), The Texas Co. had traded Casco a half interest in its marketing facilities east of Suez for a half interest in the Bahrain concession.

ily, ministers and many other Arabian dignitaries. The royal tent camp, the Arabs in their flowing robes, the banners, the music, the camels, the horses and the 400 Arab soldiers made a colorful and impressive spectacle.

A 3,000-barrel refinery—essentially for fuel oil and gasoline—was completed at Ras Tanura in the fall of 1940 but was shut down shortly thereafter for the duration of the war.

The American government pressed Casco to expand its production and delivery facilities all possible during World War II —and to that end, aided the company in getting the necessary technical men and plant equipment into the job. The early stages of the war were a serious drain on United States oil reserves and it was a long haul to move oil supplies from the Americas to the theater of action in Europe, Africa and the Far East.

It was also a long haul to move oil from the Persian Gulf by tanker to the Mediterranean through the Suez Canal.

In 1943, Harold L. Ickes, Petroleum Administrator for War, and Secretary of the Interior, was so impressed with the importance of Saudi Arabian oil to the national welfare of the United States and so much concerned over alleged British attempts to undermine the American oil companies' position in Arabia, he first moved to secure American lend-lease for Ibn Saud's government and then was instrumental in causing the Petroleum Reserves Corp. to be organized. With regard to the Petroleum Reserves Corp., Ickes said,

> It is suggested that the first order of business of the corporation should be the acquisition and managerial interest in the crude oil concessions now held in Saudi Arabia by an American Company. The potential crude oil reserves underlying this concession have been estimated at approximately 20,000,000,000 barrels—as large as the total current known crude oil reserves of the entire United States.
>
> Their acquisition will serve to meet an immediate demand

by the Army and Navy for large volumes of petroleum products in or near Arabia and will also serve to counteract certain known activities of a foreign power which presently are jeopardizing American interests in Arabian oil reserves.[129]

What Ickes was saying, in effect, was that the American government should acquire control of the American company owning the Arabian concessions just as the British government had done back in 1914 with respect to the British company owning the oil concessions in Persia.

The negotiations between the officers of Petroleum Reserves Corp. and for the purchase of the latter company's stock began in August, 1943, and went on by fits and starts into the fall months. With a willing buyer in sight, the oil company became increasingly reluctant to sell. Even when Petroleum Reserves Corp. backed off its insistence on buying 100 per cent of the company's stock and seemed content with only one-third interest, Casco maintained it was not interested.

Failing to persuade Casco in selling all or part of its interest in the Bahrain and Saudi Arabian oil concessions, the Petroleum Administrator for War canvassed ways and means to extend US government control over the promising oil prospects of Kuwait. The Kuwait oil concession was jointly held by Anglo-Iranian Oil Co., Ltd. (British) and Gulf Oil Corporation (American) and prior to the outbreak of World War II those companies had drilled several wells into the oil sands at Burgan. However, these wells had not been placed in production because of hostilities. When approached about Kuwait, Gulf advised Washington that it was not interested in selling out.

And so negotiations by the American government to buy stock in a private American oil company owning oil concessions in the Persian Gulf area, ground slowly to a halt—no sale!

129. Shwadran, Benjamin, *The Middle East, Oil and The Great Powers,* Frederick A. Praeger, New York, 1955, p. 311.

Prior to these discussions in 1943, Petroleum Reserve Corp. had sent to the Middle East a group of experts to report on developments and oil reserves. This mission was headed by E. L. DeGolyer, leading US oil geologist and oil reserve appraiser, W. E. Wrather, Director of the US Geological Survey and C. S. Snodgrass, Director of the Foreign Refining Division of the Petroleum Administration for War. This mission reported back that "The center of gravity of world oil production is shifting from the Gulf-Caribbean areas to the Middle East, to the Persian Gulf area, and is likely to continue to shift until it is firmly established in that area."[130]

On February 6, 1944, the Petroleum Administrator for War announced the conclusion of an agreement in principle between Petroleum Reserves Corp. and the presidents of the Standard Oil Co. of California and The Texas Co. (owners of the Arabian American Oil Co.). The government undertook to:

> Construct and to own and maintain a main trunk pipe line system, including requisite facilities for the transportation of crude petroleum from a point near the presently discovered oil fields of Saudi Arabia and Kuwait to a port at the eastern end of the Mediterranean Sea."[131]

The current press gave this announcement great publicity and even forecast that Petroleum Reserves Corp. would ask the companies to arrange for the construction of the pipe line and to manage its operation so that the government could have the first right and option to buy the total Arabian production of the companies. The companies in return would be required to tender a minimum quantity of crude each year for transport through the pipe line system at an agreed pipe line tariff.

130. Shwadran, Benjamin, *The Middle East, Oil and The Great Powers,* Frederick A. Praeger, New York, 1955, p. 319.

131. Feis, Herbert, *Seen From E. A.,* Alfred A. Knope, New York 1947, p. 140.

It was envisaged that such a pipe line project would stimulate production in Kuwait as well as Arabia and thereby considerably enhance American prestige in the Middle East.

However, this seemingly strategic and practical solution to the oil supply problem that was vexing all the Allies but more especially, the United States, became bogged down in politics and the upsurge of resentment from private enterprise in the American oil industry. As a way out, the Senate named a special committee to study and recommend a national oil policy—and thus the pipe line proposal died in mid-1944.

According to Feis, "All branches of the government now became alive to the fact that any action taken in regard to Middle Eastern oil would command great political interest."[132]

Out of this situation came the proposal from the American government to the British government to send experts to the United States to consider a possible petroleum agreement. The British accepted this invitation and sent over the heads of Anglo-Iranian and Royal Dutch Shell companies along with a battery of civil servants. The ensuing conferences dealt with a multitude of complex international problems incident to foreign oil finding and production but, notwithstanding, the discussions made progress rather quickly. On August 8, 1944, the international oil agreement was signed and shortly thereafter published. "It was to enter into effect upon reciprocal notice of the two governments of their readiness to have it do so."[133]

President Roosevelt sent this bipartisan agreement to the Senate on August 24 for approval.

Although this international oil agreement said nothing specifically about the Middle East or about the one-time proposed pipe line to the Mediterranean from Saudi-Arabia, it did provide

132. Feis, Herbert, *Seen From E. A.*, Alfred A. Knope, New York, 1947, p. 156.
133. Feis, Herbert, *Seen From E. A.*, Alfred A. Knope, New York, 1947, p. 158.

for an orderly development of oil reserves, quite apparently with the Middle East in mind. However, public reaction in the United States to this agreement was as violent as in the case of the proposed US government owned pipe line to the Mediterranean.

Groups within the American oil industry labeled the agreement the markings of a cartel system. The arguments for and against waxed furiously in Congress and in the press. On December 3, 1944, the *New York Times* quoted Senator Connelly, Chairman of the Senate Foreign Relations Committee, as having said the day before:

"It is my view that the treaty is unfair to the American oil industry and is not necessary for the general welfare. I have been opposed to ratification since it was first submitted to the Committee."

In January 1945, the oil agreement was returned to the President, unratified. Then a further effort was made to amend the agreement in accord with the objections of the majority of the American oil industry. On September 24, 1945, the revised Anglo-American oil agreement was signed by Harold L. Ickes for the United States and by Emanuel Shinwell, Minister of Fuel and Power, for Britain. On November 1, of that year, President Truman sent this signed document to the Senate for approval, but it did not come up for hearings until June of the next year. It was reported out of the Foreign Relations Committee in July, 1947, to the Senate body where it came to its final resting place—no action.

While the fireworks about the Anglo-American oil agreement was going on in the United States, Aramco was quietly proceeding with its aerial and land surveys preliminary to locating a trunk pipe line system—some 1,000 miles long—extending northeasterly from Dhahran across Arabia and Trans-Jordan to a terminus on the Mediterranean either in Palestine or Lebanon.

Also this company, acting for itself and in behalf of Bapco, had obtained material and equipment from American sources—even while the war was going on—to construct a 50,000-barrel-per-day refinery at Ras Tanura; to lay a 12-inch submarine pipe line from the main line to Bahrain; and to enlarge Bapco's refinery on the islands. The submarine line to Bahrain was put in operation in April, 1945, and the Ras Tanura refinery went on partial stream the following September. Such speed under war conditions would not have been possible without the companies having the benefit of material and equipment priorities from the American government and without the benefit of expert technical assistance of American construction companies, principally the International Bechtel McCone Co. (now International Bechtel, Inc.).

Even before the Ras Tanura refinery was on full stream it had been decided to increase and improve the refinery to a daily capacity of 140,000 barrels.

While these pipe line surveys and major plant construction were under way in Arabia, the principals of California-Standard and Texaco were discussing with officials of Gulf Oil Corp. the possibilities of a joint trunk pipe line system to the Mediterranean to handle both Arabian crude and Gulf's share of Kuwait crude. These discussions went on for many weeks in New York City but finally were terminated largely because of the difficulty in getting the consent of the Saudi Arabian government to allow Kuwait oil to pass through Arabia. There were also some other difficulties having to do with financing and allowed volume throughput from Kuwait but these were not considered insurmountable.

By 1945, three major oil fields in Arabia were in production, namely, Dammam, Abqaiq and Qatif. That year, these three fields produced an average of 58,000 barrels daily. In 1946, Arabian production averaged 164,000 barrels daily and the next year 246,000 barrels daily.

All these fields were connected by big-inch pipe lines one

with another and to the Ras Tanura tanker loading terminal, the submarine line to Bahrain and to the Ras Tanura refinery.

In December, 1946, plans were agreed upon for the building of a combination 30-inch and 31-inch trunk pipe line to the Mediterranean to be privately financed by the California and Texas companies. Shipments of this pipe from the United States began in November, 1947.

Construction of this major pipe line system, with its desert pumping station, which had to be supplied with water, housing for workmen and guards, commissaries, first aid and all utility services, was completed in September, 1950. The first tanker was loaded at Sidon in Lebanon on December 2, 1950.

This pipe line system is operated jointly by Aramco and Tapline (Trans-Arabian Pipeline Co.). The eastern end as far as the Qaisumah station is operated by Aramco (approximately 315 miles) and the balance of the line from Qaisumah to, and including, the 5 berth tanker loading at Sidon (a distance of 752.8 miles) by Tapline. When put into operation, this was the world's largest crude oil pipe line. This big-inch pipe line system is reported to have cost some $200 million.

About the end of 1946, Standard Oil Co. (New Jersey) and Socony-Vacuum,[134] the only remaining companies in the Near East Development Corp.—the corporate vehicle for holding the American shares in the Iraq Petroleum Co.—began to seek additional sources of Middle East crude to supply their expanding markets. They wanted a long time, large quantity, crude supply from the Anglo-Iranian Co., either from Iran or Kuwait or both in return for a loan with which to build a big-inch pipe line from Abadan and Kuwait to a site to be selected in the Mediterranean.

Such a trade was made on a cost plus basis shortly before the nationalization of Anglo-Iranian's concession and properties

134. Now Socony Mobil Oil Co.

in Iran. Because of the Iranian situation, the proposed Middle East pipe line from the head of the Persian Gulf to the Mediterranean was not built. However, Anglo-Iranian (now British Petroleum) continues to deliver these American companies substantial quantities from Kuwait.

At the same time, they (Standard of New Jersey and Socony) were also negotiating with Aramco for the purchase of crude oil, and even for the purchase of shares in that Company. Objections were raised by members of I.P.C. (Iraq Petroleum Company), on the grounds that the action of Standard of New Jersey and Socony-Vacuum were in violation of the Red Line Agreement, for Saudi Arabia was within the area of that agreement, and the case eventually came into the British Courts. Yet the negotiations between Aramco and the two companies were continued and in December, 1946, an agreement in principle was concluded. It provided for Standard of New Jersey to purchase 30 per cent of the Aramco stock and Socony-Vacuum 10 per cent, and the shares of Texas and California to be reduced to 30 per cent each. The purchase price was $102 million—$76.5 million for Standard's share and $25.5 million for Socony-Vacuum's share. However, until the deal could be concluded, pending the outcome of the litigations between those two companies and the I.P.C. members, a bank loan of $102 million was to be arranged and Standard of New Jersey and Socony-Vacuum were to guarantee it according to their shares. When acquisition of the Aramco stock had been completed, the bank loan was to be retired.[135]

That is not all, The two American companies now became the same percentage owners in Tapline and guaranteed their respective shares in a $125 million loan for the construction of the pipe line to the Mediterranean.

135. Shwadran, Benjamin, *The Middle East, Oil and The Great Powers,* Frederick A. Praeger, New York 155, p. 349.

In addition, Standard of New Jersey and Socony agreed to grant California-Standard and Texaco a prior claim on Aramco earnings. This, in effect, amounted to ten cents a barrel for each barrel of crude produced by Aramco until dividends based on the total production of 3 billion barrels (i.e., $300 million) had been paid. In other words, Standard of New Jersey and Socony agreed to pay California-Standard and Texaco for 40 per cent of Aramco and Tapline stock about $500 million.

This was one of the biggest oil deals of all time. However, the author believes it would be the consensus of the oil industry that Standard of New Jersey and Socony made a good deal—considering the vastness of the Saudi Arabian oil reserves. It also was a good deal for the California-Standard and Texaco for they at once obtained a substantial payment in cash and also a ready market for 40 per cent of their rapidly increasing Arabian production.

In the fall of 1948, Aramco surrendered back to the Saudi Arabian government, all its Kuwait Neutral Zone rights and obtained confirmation and clarification of its rights to the Saudi Arab offshore area. This move permitted the Saudi government to go ahead with its deal with the Pacific Western Oil Co. (Getty Interests) for the Saudi Arabian government's rights in the Kuwait Neutral Zone.

On November 3, 1948, the famous Iraq Petroleum Co. "Red Line" Agreement was, in effect, cancelled by mutual consent of the parties thereto, hence, Standard of New Jersey and Socony were now free to take delivery of their respective stock interest in Arabian American Oil Co. and Trans-Arabian Pipeline Co.

Even before 1950 the Saudi Arabian government had begun to press Aramco for an increase in its revenue from oil, notwithstanding the original concessions terms were specific and valid. The pros and cons were debated at length. In the fall of that year agreement between the company and state was amicably reached. In 1952, Roy Lebkicher reported on the new basis for determining the Saudi government revenues from oil as follows:

> In the autumn of 1950, the government for the first time imposed income taxes on corporations and individuals. By separate decree, taxes on petroleum producers were established as a rate which provides that the government shall receive, in taxes, rentals, per ton royalties and other levies, an amount equal to the petroleum producer's net income after all charges and taxes. Under the terms of its concession, Aramco was exempt from taxation, and other impositions except the payment of royalties and certain rentals. However, on December 30, 1950, an agreement was reached under which Aramco submitted to the imposition of income taxes.[136]

Thus, the 50-50 basis of sharing profits came into the oil industry of the Middle East.

What was the effect of equal sharing of profits on the Saudi Arabian government's revenue? Figures on the earnings of Aramco are not readily available to the public since the general public does not own any of Aramco stock and the stock is not listed on the big stock exchanges. However, one can glimpse the effect of the 50-50 from the statements made by Standard Oil Co. (New Jersey) in its report, "Joint Oil Producing Ventures in the Middle East," submitted December 31, 1953 to the Attorney General's National Committee to Study the Anti-trust Laws. On page 17 of that statement, this sentence appears: "Aggregate payments to the government by Aramco through taxes and royalties increased from $10,000,000 in 1946 to $37,-000,000 in 1950 and to $212,000,000 in 1952."

According to the testimony of Fred A. Davies, Chairman of the Aramco Board, before the subcommittee on Anti-Trust and

136. Lebkicher, Roy, *Aramco and World Oil,* Russell F. Moore Co., Inc., New York Revised 1952, p. 28.

Monopoly of the Senate Committee on the Judiciary, and before the subcommittee on Public Lands of the Senate Committee on Interior and Insular Affairs, meeting jointly in Washington, D.C. on March 20 and 21, 1957, Aramco's payments to the Saudi Government for taxes on income and for royalties and rentals aggregated $279,801,437 for the calendar year 1956.

Equating these payments in terms of barrels of oil produced and saved in those same years—using *World Oil* Magazine's estimates—the Saudi Arabian's government revenues from oil increased from about $16\frac{2}{3}$ cents a barrel, in 1946; to $36\frac{1}{2}$ cents a barrel, in 1950; to 70.2 cents a barrel, in 1952 and to 77.5 cents a barrel, in 1956.

THE KING DIES

On November 9, 1953, H. M. 'Abdul 'Aziz ibn Rahman ibn Faisal al Saud, King of Arabia, died and was succeeded by his son, Saud. Thus ended the historic career of an empire builder. A man who manifested throughout his adult life "enormous strength, boldness and vitality; magnetic personality; sound judgment; thorough integrity; the ability to forgive his enemies or to be harsh and even ruthless as the occasion demanded; above all, a solid faith in his religion, the precepts of which were ever his guide and inspiration."[137]

All of Arabia and neighboring states went into 20 day mourning for the great King.

Shaikh Abdullah al Mubarak, acting ruler of Kuwait at the time, said to Colonel H. R. P. Dickson, "The greatest King throughout the Islamic world, and one the Arabs have not seen the like for many centuries, has gone, but this is the way of all men and is God's will."

Kind Saud, upon the death of his father, ordered all prisoners

137. Roy Lebkicher, George Rentz, and Max Steineke, *Aramco Handbook*, Arabian American Oil Co., Revised edition, prepared in 1960.

awaiting trail, or under sentence of death or imprisonment throughout the land to be released unconditionally—also that all blood money compensation of whatever extent, due from any of his people, was to be forgiven them and paid for by the state— this as an offering to God. The people of Arabia understood what this order meant better than any Westerner.

OPERATIONS

Since commercial production was discovered at Dammam in 1938, Aramco has found and developed a dozen or more other oil fields of importance. These new fields include Safaniya (partly offshore), Manifa (entirely offshore), Abu Hadriya, Khursaniyah, Fadhili, Qatif, Abqaiq, Ghawar (embracing the Ain Dar, Shedgum, Uthmaniyah, Hawiyah, Haradh, and Fazran fields) and Khurais. All these fields were separate discoveries, although the large Ghawar structure is now believed to embrace what was originally thought to be six different oil fields.

The oil industry rates Ghawar fabulous for its size and thickness of oil column. Imagine a single structure some 150 miles in length believed to be productive over an area conservatively estimated at 900 square miles. The vertical oil column in places exceeds 1,000 feet. The gravity of the oil currently being produced from Ghawar ranges from 36° API in the north to 33° API in the south. Production from 87 wells on the Ghawar structure amounted to 257,517,305 barrels during 1961.

The Khursaniyah field, which lies roughly 70 miles northwest of Dammam and a few miles inland from the Persian Gulf, was put into production in October, 1960, at the average rate of 57,-000 barrels daily. This new field covers an area about 7 miles long by some 4.5 miles wide.

Abu Hadriya field was discovered some 20 years ago but because of its remoteness (100 miles northwest of Dhahran) its development was postponed in favor of more prolific shallow fields. However, now its estimated initial production of 50,000 bpd is scheduled to be on stream in 1962.

The newest of Aramco oil fields is called, Khurais. The area believed to be productive is some 30 miles long and about 8 miles wide. Khurais lies the farthest inland of all Aramco's discoveries—the field is approximately 157 miles southwest of Dammam and some 75 miles west of Ghawar. There are no immediate plans to place the Khurais field into production.

Aramco has completed 378 wells on the Arabian mainland and offshore. At the close of 1961 the status of the completed wells was as follows: 216 producing, 80 shut-in or standing, 34 observation, 19 injection, 19 suspended and 10 abandoned. In addition 3 wells were drilling.

"At the close of the year (1960) the company's proved recoverable reserves were estimated at about 45,600,000."[138]

In spite of Aramco's intensive exploration activity and wildcat drilling for many years past, not all the oil prospects in the Saudi Arabian oil concessions have been tested—not by any yardstick. The oil fields already proven are huge, but it is likely that several more—maybe many more—large reservoirs will yet be discovered.

Aramco's cumulative production through 1961 exceeded 4.764 billion barrels.

In 1961 gross production from all Aramco's Arabian fields amounted to 508,269,201 barrels (divided 420,190,103 barrels from mainland fields and 88,079,098 barrels from offshore fields) an average daily of 1,392,518 barrels, the highest daily average in 23 years. This 1961 production was distributed as follows:

To Tapline facilities at Qaisumah	115,523,355 barrels
To Bahrain via underwater pipe line	62,796,120 "

138. "1960 Report of Operations to the Saudi Arab Government," by the Arabian American Oil Co., p. 11.

To Ras Tanura refinery tankage   90,810,070 barrels
To Tankers at Ras Tanura   239,136,805   "
To field tankage or used in operations   2,851   "

The Ras Tanura refinery has a present rated capacity of 210,-000 barrels a day. During 1961 Aramco distributed to the Saudi Government and the public in Saudi Arabia 4,001,247 barrels of refined products.

At the end of 1961 Aramco had 14,063 employees in Saudi Arabia of whom 10,947 or 77.8 per cent were Saudi Arabs, 1,807 were Americans and 1,309 were of other nationalities.

EFFECT OF OIL AND ARAMCO ON SAUDI ARABIA

The size and population of the Saudi Arab Kingdom have been variously estimated. Several of its frontier boundaries have not yet been resolved and no census has been taken in modern times. The 1960 Almanac gives the area as 617,760 square miles and the estimated population as some 6 million people. These are probably as good guesses as any. Thus, we may assume that, geographically the size of Arabia is only slightly less than the combined area of California, Arizona, New Mexico and Texas and that its population is less than that of New York City. However, more than one-third of Arabia is considered uninhabitable except by the nomads.

In south central Arabia, is a great inland sea of sand—called by the Arabs, Rub al-Khali, and more commonly known to westerners as the Empty Quarter. In this vast area of some 250,000 square miles (its maximum dimensions are said to be about 400 miles north-south and about 750 miles east-west), there is no year-round supply of drinkable water, at least none known to Europeans, and it is believed there are no permanent inhabitants.

Notwithstanding, explorers report that the Al Murra tribe is virtually overlord of the Empty Quarter. Until recently, no one attempted to cross the Rub al-Khali without Murra guides. They are known to be trackers, second to none in all Arabia. According to Richard H. Sanger,[139] "They (the Murra) roam with great confidence over territory where Bedouins of the north would hesitate to go. Their tracking instinct is remarkable, an ability which has built itself up through the centuries. They can tell the spoor of a white camel from a black one, the footprint of a virgin from that of a wife, and warrior from that of a youth."

Philby and other explorers say the Al Murra are the most primitive of all the tribes of central Arabia. They train themselves to do without water. They believe in jinns (genii)—they say these jinns have eyes pointing up and down, not horizontal as in mortal man, and the Murra ascribe the, "singing sands," (a phenomenon noted by European explorers) to the work of the jinns.

Prior to 1948, only three Europeans are known to have successfully crossed the Empty Quarter, namely, Bertram Thomas in 1931, H.St.J.B. Philby in 1932, and Wilfred Thesiger in 1946-1948. All these intrepid explorers were Englishmen.[140]

Now it so happens, that much of the Empty Quarter lies within the area of Aramco oil concessions. Therefore, it had to be explored by geologists and geophysicists or else surrendered, with whatever hidden natural resources it might have, still unknown. Aramco undertook the challenge. The difficulties which the early explorers had encountered in their treks by camel, Aramco largely overcame with self-contained motorized caravans, air lifts and aerial photography. The ruins of Qaruya, the

139. Sanger, Richard H. *The Arabian Peninsula,* Cornell University Press, Ithaca, New York, 1954, p. 128.

140. For a brief, yet vivid account of these crossings, the author recommends Chapter X, "British Explorers of the Empty Quarter," in Richard H. Sanger's book entitled, *The Arabian Peninsula,* Cornell University Press, 1954, and also Wilfred Thesiger's book, *Arabian Sands,* New York, 1959.

lost fabled Sabean city, was found by Aramco's survey parties and then visited by Philby.[141]

Thus, the vast unknown Empty Quarter has been opened up —no longer are its singing sands, deserted oasis and lost cities the fascinating mysteries they once were. Now, motor trails cross the Rub al-Khali and at strategic places air strips have been laid out in this "inland sea of sand" to support Aramco's exploration activities and for use in emergencies.

All this has been made possible by the discovery of oil in Arabia and by American free enterprise.

The use of Arabia's first railroad, constructed by the Turks from Damascus to Medina in 1904-1908, was discontinued in 1924 and has not been operated since. However, Aramco completed the construction of a railroad for the Saudi Arabian government from Dammam to Riyadh via Abqaiq, Hofuf and Al Kharj—a distance of 350 miles—in October, 1951. In conjunction with this railroad project, Dammam was developed to be a deep seaport by the construction of a seven-mile pier out into the Persian Gulf at which ocean-going vessels can discharge overseas freight directly onto railway cars for inland movement. All this work was done by American contractors.

Before oil was discovered in Arabia, practically all travel was by camel, ass, or horse. Only in a few cities was there any motorized transport, and those cities were mostly located along the Red Sea side of Arabia. There was only one fairly good hardsurfaced road in all Arabia—the one between Jeddah and Mecca, constructed under the supervision of Egyptian engineers; travelers mostly followed the ancient caravan trails. Along these old trade and pilgrim routes, a series of stone birkas (cisterns) were built to catch water—these were spaced at intervals of a camel day's travel (about 20 miles).

Soon as commercial oil was assured, Aramco began to build

141. "Two Notes from Central Arabia—The Qaruya Ruin Field," by H. St. J. B. Philby, *Geographical Journal,* June, 1949.

oiled-sand and asphalt-topped roads in and around the oil fields. In addition, they improvised or procured motor equipment and tires which could navigate over loose, often shifting, sand. Busses and trucks, for long hauls, were air-conditioned. Thus, in a relatively few years, travel over the desert wastes of Arabia became comparatively rapid and comfortable, thanks to the pioneering of Aramco. In less than a decade, almost literally, the country went from camel to Cadillacs—especially for the Shaikhs, Chieftains, government officials, wealthy merchants and the royal family.

When the motor car was not fast enough, the Arab took to the airplane, perhaps even more nonchalantly than did westerners in their respective homelands. Aramco made this metamorphosis possible by establishing outlets for refined products in all the principal towns and villages throughout Arabia. As an example of this rapid conversion to motor transport, it is interesting to note that annual sales of refined products in Saudi Arabia jumped from 387,000 barrels in 1948 to 3,206,000 barrels in 1959.

Aramco at first had to import most of its technical staff and clerical help—there was no qualified Saudiis available for such work in the early stages of the oil operations. However, the oil company set about correcting this situation by establishing training schools and a training-on-the-job program for the erstwhile camel driver and shepherd from the desert and such skilled and semi-skilled labor as was available along the Persian Gulf. For the most part these latter were local shipbuilders, mud-brick masons and sailors.

From this motley uneducated manpower, Aramco fashioned truck drivers, tractor operators, electricians, plumbers, carpenters, competent masons, welders, shopmen (to operate all sorts of power tools), helpers for the drilling rigs, and many other skilled artisans, as well as clerks of all kinds. Most of these trainees had never had any schooling whatever—most of them could not read or write their own language. Many English words cannot be literally translated into Arabic and the names of most tools and equipment used in the oil operations have no Arabic equivalent. Hence, it was necessary to teach these boys from the desert and the seacoast a smattering of English before the training could, in fact, begin.[142] In addition, they must learn to read and write Arabic.

For a comprehensive picture of what Aramco is doing in its educational and training program, both inside and outside of Saudi Arabia, the following is quoted from the 1960 Aramco Report of Operations:

> In the 1960-1961 academic year, Aramco sent 29 Saudi Arab employees to colleges and universities outside the Kingdom for advanced, specialized training, 12 of them in Lebanon and 17 in the United States.
>
> Each of these student employees is following an educational program designed to give him thorough grounding in some technical phase of the oil industry, in modern business techniques, or in teaching, public health education, hospital administration or scientific agriculture.
>
> Earlier in the year, five Saudi Arab employees completed out-of-Kingdom training, two in the United States and three in Lebanon.
>
> Enrollment of employees in classes during working hours at the Industrial Training Centers averaged 4,531 each trimester during 1960. Almost one-third of these trainees studying academic and practical subjects related to their jobs were in secondary levels of instruction.
>
> In the voluntary program at the Training Centers for

142. The author has visited the training schools of the oil companies in Saudi Arabia and Kuwait several times and is always amazed at the quickness of the desert Arab to grasp the essentials of English and mathematics. He has observed Badu boys—with not a day's previous schooling—who, in only three to six weeks after getting out from behind the camel, have been able to do complex arithmetic problems on a blackboard in English when given the problem orally by his teacher.

those who study after working hours, an average of 4,212 employees attended classes each trimester.

In the industrial training shops which offer instruction in basic and specialized manual skills, 259 employees were enrolled in the last quarter of 1960, as compared with 185 at the close of 1959.

A total of 133 other employees received special job skill training in the Oil Operations and Medical organizations.

Supervisory training continued in all areas of the company's operations to help Saudi Arab employees qualify as mushrif (single work group supervisor) or muraqib (supervisor of several work groups).

Two new courses, "Essentials of Leadership" and "Your Company as a Business Enterprise" were added to this program. Classes in supervisory training were attended by 722 employees during the year. At the close of the year, 366 Saudi Arab employees had been promoted to mushrif or muraqib, and about 200 more were expected to qualify for such positions in the near future.

The eleventh elementary school built by the company for sons of Muslim and Arab employees was completed at Hofuf and accepted in September by the Saudi Arab Government Ministry of Education. The company has designed and built schools for 3,300 boys of elementary school age in the Eastern Province. Aramco maintains these schools and reimburses the Government for the cost of their operation, including salaries of teachers.

In addition, two intermediate schools were being built, one at Dammam and one at Hofuf. Each of these will accommodate 150 students.

With the opening of the 1960-61 academic year, Aramco inaugurated an Arab Refugee Scholarship Program to be administered by the United Nations Relief and Works Agency. Twenty-three qualified refugee students were selected for the first of these "Aramco Scholarships Through UNRWA," nine from Jordan, six from Gaza, five from Lebanon, and three from the northern region of the United Arab Republic.

They are attending institutions of higher learning in the U.A.R., Jordan and Lebanon.

Aramco has built housing for its local as well as foreign employees. At the end of 1960 more than 2,800 Saudi Arab employees had built or purchased their own homes under Aramco's Home Ownership Program and 200 more new homes were being built with company financing.

All Aramco employees have the privilege of buying all kind of local and imported merchandise in the company commissaries at subsidized prices—which, for some items, is below cost.

Hospitals, clinics and first aid stations have been constructed in strategic places to serve Aramco's employees and their families, regardless of race, color or creed. In addition, a program of preventive medicine has been established.

Protestant and Catholic churches and Muslim mosques have been built at the company's expense to serve its employees.

Wages have been increased over the years, employee thrift plans put into effect and service awards issued to all Aramco employees.

By such means Aramco has striven to integrate the Saudi into the oil business—to make the Arab a partner in the venture.

In recent years, Aramco has gone further in this program of integrating the Arab into the oil business by letting out as much work as possible to Arab contractors—many of whom were ex-employees that had been trained and supervised by the company until they were capable of fending for themselves. Now, practically all banking of people and material is done by contractors. Local contractors are used to fabricate most buildings and plant structures. Most of Aramco steel tank and pipe work is performed by Arab skilled, semi-skilled and common labor employed by contractors. Contractors have taken over many of the services—like ice, laundry and some merchandising. During

1960, 110 independent Saudi Arabian companies were paid the equivalent of $7,859,000 for services to Aramco.

The company has encouraged the local folk to go in for agriculture—where water is available—and for poultry raising.

These well-devised and well-executed programs of Relations, (Employee, Industrial, Government and Public) in Saudi Arabia, in varying degree, were under the general purview of Floyd W. Ohliger for many years, until he retired from active service with Aramco in 1958.

In concluding this story of Saudi Arabia, one finds that it is difficult to precisely evaluate the effect of oil on the country and its people. Certainly the economy of the Kingdom has benefited tremendously through the revenues from oil. So too, has benefited the social and cultural structure of the Kingdom. With the income from oil the King has established hundreds of schools and many hospitals for his people throughout the empire—all along American lines and standards. Public works, never before dreamed of, much less undertaken, have come into being. Motor vehicle travel and transport is now common throughout the land. Daily, local and international airplanes fly overhead on scheduled flights. There is now country-wide communication by radio and telegraph—the outside world news is currently received.

Health of a large segment of the urban population has improved. Water has been brought to the surface in the desert where there was no water before. All the people of Saudi Arabia have benefited in some measure, directly or indirectly by oil. All over the country, the standards of living have appreciably improved for the common man as well as the Shaikh.

The early American medical missionaries started, back in the early 1900's, what the American oil company has been able to intensify and expand many fold. A new concept of living has been born in Saudi Arabia during the last half century—in which the American way of life and American free enterprise has played no small part.

Dr. W. Harold Storm of the Arabian Mission, in his book *Wither Arabia,* commented at some length regarding the impact of the West upon Arabia and the Arab. Later, Colonel. H. R. P. Dickson expanded on the same subject in his book, *Kuwait and Her Neighbours.* Because the views of these two experienced scholars—though of different background and of different nationality—are so pertinent and still so timely, the complete text of Dickson's, "The Impact of the West, 1953," as it appears in his, *Kuwait and Her Neighbours* (pages 570-578) is reproduced in Appendix II.

6

Kuwait

THE ANCIENT HISTORY OF THE AREA, now designated as Kuwait, is very meager and somewhat hazy. In the many thousands of tumuli (tombs) found on Bahrain Island some 250 miles south of Kuwait, relics have been found that suggest the early Bronze Age—say 1500 to 2000 B.C., although some archaeologists suggest that the tombs date from the third century B.C., while still others suggest A.D. 200-600.

In Iraq, below Baghdad, are to be found the ruins of Babylonia and many other places referred to in the Bible. Across the Persian Gulf in Iran have been uncovered considerable monumental stone work and many sculptured pieces which evidently antedate Christ's time. But nothing which can be classified as ancient has been found on the mainland in Kuwait. This is difficult to understand, for Kuwait Bay is by far the best natural harbor in the Persian Gulf. One would think that Kuwait must have been on the ancient caravan routes from South Arabia as well as the port of entry for merchandise coming by boat from the Far East to be transhipped by camel overland to the eastern Mediterranean.

It seems likely that all the territory around the head of the

Persian Gulf was held successively by, "the Sumerians, Elamites, Kassites and Archaemenians but of their occupations nothing has, apparently, been recorded."[143]

Until recently, the oldest definite link with the past, uncovered in Kuwait, was a stone bearing a Greek inscription, the English of which reads: 'Sotel(s) An Athenian and Oistra to Zeus Saviour Poseidon Artom's the Saviours.' "It is thought to date between 400 and 100 B.C.[144] The stone was found in 1937 when a building was being demolished on the northwest coast of Failaka Island, which lies just off the entrance to Kuwait Bay. The shipwrecked sailors who carved this stone may have been members of one of Alexander the Great's expeditions, but no one knows for certain. (See footnote 145.)

Nothing further is definitely known about the historic past of Kuwait until that general area was incorporated in the Sasmian Empire of Persia (about A.D. 300).

> Sapur I (A.D. 309-379) is said to have caused a great ditch to be dug from Hit, on the Euphrates, to the northern shore of Kuwait Bay, in the vicinity of the site of the existing hamlet of Kazama, in order to prevent the predatory Arabs from making incursions into the Sawad, the fertile "black" lands of Mesopotamia (so called in order to distinguish them from the dim-colored desert wastes).[146]

143. Lockhart, Lawrence, *Outline of the History of Kuwait,* The Royal Central Asian Journal, London, July-October, 1947, p. 262.

144. Lockhart, Lawrence, *Outline of the History of Kuwait,* The Royal Central Asian Journal, London, July-October, 1947, p. 262. Some other authorities date this Greek stone as "circa 525 BC."

145. In 1960 the Danish Archaeological Mission, during its third season at the sites of Tel Saad and Tel Said on Failaka Island made some very remarkable and interesting discoveries. Those excavations have revealed a Hellenic Temple dedicated to Artemis, goddess of the Moon, a large Stele and many round seals—these latter dating back to the Akkadian dynasties (about 2500 BC).

146. Lockhart, Lawrence, *Outline of the History of Kuwait,* The Royal Central Asian Journal, July-October, 1947, London, p. 262.

According to the early historians it was some three centuries later, in A.D. 633, that the Arab General, Khalid ibnu'l-Walid marched to attack a Persian force near Kazama.

From the third to the sixteenth century, the name, "Bahrain" was applied to the whole coast of eastern Arabia from Kuwait to Qatar, while the main Bahrain Island was known as Awal, but since that date, the name, "Bahrain" has been applied to the Island.[147]

According to Abu'l-Fida (1273-1331) a famous historian and geographer of his day, Kazama in Kuwait was a well-known place.

Undoubtedly the Portugese who ventured into the Persian Gulf in the early 1500's, conquering Hormuz and establishing a trading post and fort on Bahrain also must have discovered Kuwait Bay as a safe anchorage. They are believed to have constructed a fort on the small low-lying island of al-Qurain (the Little Horn) known to early European mariners as Grane, located a short distance southwest of the present town of Kuwait —but if so, no trace of it remains today.

Modern historians generally agree that the factual beginning of Kuwait state was in A.D. 1716, when several of the clans of the great Anarza (Anizah) tribe of North Central Arabia settled down along the coast, in preference to their former nomadic life. According to Colonel Dickson,[148] who probably knew more about Kuwait and its people than any other European, during October 1710, a great drought drove the al-Sabah and the al-Khalifa families to migrate from the inner Najd to a place south of Wadi Duwasir and from thence to shores of the Persian Gulf in the Qatar Peninsula.

147. Belgrave, James H. D., *Welcome to Bahrain,* Mark & Moody, Ltd., Stourbridge, England, 1953, p. 77.
148. Dickson, Lt. Col. H.R.P., C.I.E., F.R.G.S., died in Kuwait June 14, 1959 at the age of 78.

Finding conditions there not much better than in the interior, the al-Sabah and the al-Khalifa families migrated slowly northward along the coast, with their camels, goats and sheep, until they came to Kuwait Bay where they found plenty of potable water in shallow wells. There they pitched their tent camps and settled down. However, for some reason not now known, the al-Khalifa family did not stay long in Kuwait but trekked back to Qatar. The al-Sabahs, nomads of the desert, took kindly to the sea and augmented their normal livelihood as shepherds by fishing, pearling and boat building.

Some 40 years after this migration, in 1756, Shaikh Sabah Abu Abdullah of Umm Qasr, a village on the west bank of the Khor Zubair (in present day Iraq, some 35 miles south of Basra) seized supreme power in Kuwait. The al-Sabah (Subah) have ever since then been the ruling family in Kuwait.

When a Danish explorer, Carsten Niebuhr, visited Kuwait a few years later, he reported the town had some 10,000 inhabitants and possessed 800 vessels and earned its living principally by pearling and fishing. During the summer months, most of the able bodied men of Kuwait were absent from their homes, either at sea or traveling with overland caravans to Baghdad and Aleppo.

About 1775, a Kuwaiti armed force descended upon Bahrain and cut off the Persian retreat from Qatar where they had enaged the "cousins" of the Sabahs in bitter fighting.

In 1776, Basra was captured by Karin Kahn of Persia. As a result of this invasion, many inhabitants of Basra and vicinity fled to Kuwait. Also, Kuwait gained considerable commercial advantages because of trade which now flowed into its port instead of to Basra, as formerly. This situation caused the English East Indian Co. to make Kuwait, instead of Basra, the southern end of its overland mail route to Aleppo.

The al-Khalifah family, which had come out of the Najd with the al-Sabah's remained largely in the Qatar Peninsula and settled down in and around the village of Zubara in order to be near the pearling banks. In 1783, an armed force of Shaikh Sabah from Kuwait assisted the Al-Khalifah in seizing the Bahrain Islands from Persia and established the al-Khalifah rule in Bahrain which, except for a brief intermission in the early 1800's has continued to this day. Thus, for more than 175 years, the governments of Bahrain and Kuwait have been staunch friends—the al-Khalifah's and the al-Sabah's are today as close as "blood brothers" (an Arab expression of trust, friendship and understanding).

The relationship between the British and the Kuawiti seemed to prosper and in 1792 the East India Co., being irked at the Turks' behavior, transferred its agency from Basra to Kuwait. Nearly 30 years later the British Residency at Basra was, for similar reasons, transferred to Kuwait.

Between 1750 and 1850, Kuwait was repeatedly threatened by the warlike Wahhabis from the interior of Arabia. However, so far as now known, Kuwait town was not actually invaded, perhaps because the Shaikh had a large cannon and also because the East India Co. had an armed cruiser anchored offshore and a small guard of Indian sepoys stationed at the British "factory."

According to Lawrence Lockhart, who wrote, *Outline of the History of Kuwait,* in those days the shipping of Kuwait, like that of other places in the Gulf, was often preyed upon by pirates . . . One of the most notorious free booters of all time in the Gulf was Rahmat ibn Jabir; he was a native of Kuwait, "and apparently did not preclude attacks on his own countrymen."

By the 1860's the skill and daring of Kuwaiti seamen was recognized all around the Persian Gulf.

About this time, Kuwait's natural harbor and good anchorage attracted the attention of European promoters, who envisaged the economic advantage (and profits) which might accrue from the construction of a railway extending from Kuwait by way of the Euphrates valley to the eastern shores of the Mediterranean. This was the famous scheme of General F. R. Chesney. The announced main purpose of this scheme was to strengthen and improve British communications and trade with India and the Far East. However, the scheme was attacked in England "as being unsound on both economic and political grounds," since most of the projected line would pass through territory dominated by the Turks, and the Ottomans had not been consulted. Finally, the building of the Suez Canal killed any chance of the British backing Chesney's brain child.

Meanwhile, Kuwait became a regular port of call for the ships of the British India Steam Navigation Co.

Soon it became evident that the Turks, the Russians and the Germans, as well as the British, were interested in the potentialities of Kuwait as a port and also as a possible railway terminus. At about the same time, the tribes of Ibn Rashid in central Arabia were showing signs of coveting control over Kuwait.

"Abdullah ibn Sabah al Sabah, Shaikh of Kuwait from 1866 until his death in 1892, had accepted from the Turks in 1871, the title of Qaimaqam," (Turkish name for governor of a sub-province).[149]

Abdullah was succeeded by his brother, Muhammad. He was even more subservient to the Turks than the previous Shaikh and it is said that his other full brother, Jarrah, was, if anything, more helpless and slothful than Muhammad. However, Mubarak, the half brother of Muhammad and Jarrah, was a strong man and had a fierce love of country. Finally, in desperation, lest Kuwait become a puppet of the Turks, Mubarak is alleged to have personally killed his two half brothers and seized the throne (1896).

149. Dickson, H.R.P., *Kuwait and Her Neighbours*, George Allen and Unwin Ltd., London, 1956, p. 136.

But Mubarak had international troubles at his door from the moment he seized power. The Turks appointed Mubarak their Qaimaqam[150] in January, 1897, and a month later, the Turks sent a quarantine official to Kuwait. This action of the Turks caused Mubarak to approach the British seeking protection. When, some months later, Mubarak got to talk with a representative of the British Political Resident in the Persian Gulf area, he intimated that unless the British could protect his state it would eventually become a vassel of the Turks.

The British then urged Mubarak to remain under Turkish suzerainty. Mubarak made a similar request for British protection a year later and was again given the same reply. Then in 1898, the Russians sought to obtain right to build a Kuwait-to-the Mediterranean railway and probably had eyes on Kuwait port as a coaling station. This Russian move caused the British to alter their views about protecting Kuwait from foreign intrusion and, as a result, a treaty was concluded on January 23, 1899 between Great Britain and the Shaikh of Kuwait.

Shaikh Mubarak then ruled Kuwait for some 20 years under the protection of Great Britain until his death on January 3, 1916. This little country and its ruler gave asylum to the Sa'uds of Arabia and, in fact, aided young Ibn Saud in his dare devil escapade to seize Riyadh from the Ibn Rashid forces (1900).

Because the terms of Kuwait-British treaty had such an important bearing on the future political and commercial development of Kuwait, it is here quoted in part, as follows:

> The said Shaikh Mubarak-ibn-Shaikh Subah, of his own free will and desire, does hereby pledge and bind himself, his heirs and successors, not to receive the agent or representatives of any Power or Government at Kuwait, or at any other place within the limits of his territory, without the previous

150. Colonel Dickson says Mubarak did not accept the "honor" while Lawrence Lockhart says he did accept the office.

sanction of the British Government; and he further binds himself, his heirs and successors, *not to cede, sell, lease, mortgage, or give his territory to the Government or subject of any other power without previous consent of Her Majesty's Government for these purposes.*[151]

Almost coincidentally with this treaty it became known that the Germans planned to make the southern terminus of their Berlin-to-Baghdad railway project, on the north side of Kuwait Bay. In 1900, German engineers arrived in Kuwait to survey and to negotiate for a terminal site. However, Shaikh Mubarak, mindful of his new protective agreement with Britain, refused, whereupon the Germans incited the Turkish government to seize Kuwait. The Turks acted at once by sending a warship, loaded with troops, into Kuwait harbor. But the Turks had not counted on the British. When the Turkish gunboat steamed into Kuwait Bay they found a British cruiser had preceded them. Thus stalemated, the Turks withdrew without making any attempt to land an armed force.

Next, Ibn Rashid set out to invade Kuwait but was deterred by trouble at home and by the presence of British troops in Kuwait.

Germany persisted. In 1902, she egged on the Turks to establish a military post on Bubuyan Island at Umm Qasr. It so happens that Bubuyan is very low lying, almost inundated at high tide. Whatever the reason, because of the bad location for a military post or because the British cruiser was still in the offing, this scheme did not come off.

As has been previously mentioned, the Saud family had fled Arabia and sought sanctuary in Kuwait, when Ibn Saud was a lad of ten or eleven. By 1901, Adul Aziz Saud was 21 and

151. The emphasis in italics in this treaty is the author's—this text later plagued the American company for six years in its attempts to secure an exclusive oil concession over all Kuwait.

eager to match men and wits with the Saud family's arch enemy in Arabia, the Rashids. That year, Shaikh Mubarak and young Saud took the field with a force said to number 10,000 men and met up with Rashid forces near Sarif in Arabia. In the ensuing fight, Mubarak and Saud's men sustained a crushing defeat.

After this set-back, Ibn Saud decided to make a soiree with a small band of selected men, 40 in all, against Riyadh—the old home of his father. It was a daring escapade, but succeeded. Thus, at long last, Ibn Saud—a boy in his early twenties—was launched on a career to conquer all his adversaries in Arabia. Eventually, Ibn Saud was successful, but it was not until 1932— 31 years after leaving Kuwait—that Ibn Saud was recognized as King over Hejaz and Nejd (Najd).

Lord Curzon, Viceroy of India, visited Kuwait in the late fall of 1903 while in the Persian Gulf area where he met with the assembled Shaikhs at Sharjah (Trucial Oman) to state Britain's policy with respect to "protected states." This was a very important statement of policy—one that made history. The gist of Lord Curzin's remarks to the assembled Arab chiefs was as follows:

> We saved you from extinction at the hands of your neighbors. We opened these seas to the ships of all nations and enabled their flags to fly in peace. We have not seized or held your territory. We have not destroyed your independence, but have preserved it. We are not going to throw away this century of costly and triumphant enterprise; we shall not wipe out the most unselfish page in history. The peace of these waters must still be maintained; your independence will continue to be upheld, and the influence of the British government will remain supreme.[152]

152. Freeth, Zahra, (daughter of Col. H. R. P. Dickson), *Kuwait Was My Home*, George Allen and Unwin Ltd., London, 1956, p. 24.

In June 1904, Britain appointed its first Political Agent to Kuwait.

In 1909, a branch of the Arabian Mission of the Reformed Church of America was established in Kuwait with the visits of Dr. C. Stanley Mylrea from Bahrain and later by Dr. Paul W. Harrison. However, it was not until January 1, 1912 that the Mission hospital got into full sway following the arrival of Eleanor T. Calverley, M.D., and her husband, Reverend Edwin Caverley. It proved to be a notable event in Kuwait history—far reaching in effect.

In 1913, Britain and Turkey negotiated a treaty which recognized the independence of Kuwait from Turkish suzerainty and the special treaty relationship between Kuwait and Great Britain. Soon thereafter, World War I broke out and the British occupied Fao in what is now Iraq, not far north of the Kuwait-Iraq frontier. This occupation was accomplished in cooperation with Shaikh Mubarak.

Now, for the first time, Kuwait adopted a national flag—having used for some years past, the Turkish emblem—a solid red banner on which the word, Kuwait, was emblazoned in white Arabic script.

Because of Mubarak's aid to the Allies in World War I, His Majesty's Government gave Kuwait a written promise that in the event of the Allies winning the war, they would grant the Kuwait ruler that:

"1. His five date gardens on the Shatt-al-Arab would be free of all taxes in perpetuity.

2. His title to such gardens would never be allowed to be challenged.

3. He and his heirs and successors would be maintained as

Shaikhs of Kuwait for all time by the British Government."[153]

Subsequently, after becoming independent, Iraq tried to tax the Ruler of Kuwait on the date garden property and even questioned the Ruler's title thereto but, as of now, the British have stood fast and kept faith with Kuwait.

Captain W. H. J. Shakespear was British Political Agent in Kuwait in 1914. He went on a mission for his government to Arabia and joined up with Ibn Saud against Ibn Rashid who had entered the war as an ally of the Turks. In the engagement which took place in January, 1915, between the two desert forces Shakespear was killed while manning a gun with the Najdi men. Saud's forces lost the skirmish.

In the fall of that year, Ibn Saud found himself besieged in Hofuf in al-Hasa by rebel Arabs. Mubarak sent a force of Kuwaitis to assist Saud and succeeded not only in lifting the siege but, in cooperation with Saud's men, they defeated the enemy near Qatif. With this Kuwaiti force were two future rulers of Kuwait, Shaikh Salim, Mubarak's second son and Shaikh Ahmad, Mubarak's grandson.

This victorious Kuwaiti force was still some days away from their homeland when they received word that Shaikh Mubarak had died (January 3, 1916) and that Shaikh Jabir, Mubarak's eldest son, had become Ruler.

Shaikh Jabir had ruled only a year when he died (February 5, 1917) and Shaikh Salim succeeded to the rulership. Unlike his father and his older brother, Salim tossed aside the traditional friendship of the Kuwaiti for the British and made known that he sided with Ibn Rashid—this move, in effect, gave notice to all concerned that he favored the Turks and had turned against Ibn Saud. Although Salim's army took no part in the

153. Dickson, H. R. P., *Kuwait and Her Neighbours*, George Allen and Unwin Ltd., London, 1956, p. 150.

conflict in Arabia, it is said that he did allow supplies for the Turks to pass through the Kuwait port. Finally, in February, 1918, the British blockaded Kuwait until the end of the war and warned Shaikh Salim of what would happen to him if he persisted in acting against the interests of His Majesty's Government.

Shaikh Salim continued to flout his former ally, Ibn Saud, as well as his British friends, by quarreling with the Sauds over some frontier questions. "The result was that Ibn Saud not only placed an embargo on all trade with Kuwait, but even went so far as to order his general Faisal ad-Darwish, to attack Kuwait with a body of the Ikhwan."[154]

The Ikhwan were fierce and fanatical Wahhabis allied with Ibn Saud. They were the current zealous warring desert puritans of Islam.

The Ikhwan forces moved on Jahara (Jahra), which lies at the western end of Kuwait Bay—a natural oasis. In October, 1920, a minor battle took place there between the Ikhwan and Salim's guards after which the latter withdrew to Kuwait 25 miles from the battleground. Although the Kuwaitis had won a victory of sorts over the invaders from Arabia,[155] Salim feared an attack on Kuwait. "The people of Kuwait so feared a further and more serious onslaught that they, in the short space of two months, surrounded their town on the landward side with the existing wall. It is four miles long, fourteen feet high and is pierced by four gates."[156]

154. Lockhart, Lawrence, *Outline of the History of Kuwait,* Royal Central Asian Journal, London, July-October, 1947, p. 272.
155. According to Colonel Dickson, the battle of Jahra was considered a very great victory for Kuwait—although the Ikhwan got off with considerable spoils they left some 800 dead on the field of battle while the Kuwaitis' loss of life was about 200 men in all.
156. From Lawrence Lockhart's, *Outline of the History of Kuwait,* p. 272. Author's note—In 1958 all this wall except the four gates was leveled to allow for the town's expansion.

Still feeling insecure against a mass attack from Ibn Saud's aroused followers, Al-Ikhwan, Shaikh Salim sent his young nephew, Ahmad ibn Jabir, on a mission of reconciliation to Ibn Saud, somewhere in Arabia. Shaikh Ahmad was accompanied on this mission by Chasib, the youngest son of the Shaikh of Muhammerah of Persia. The party left for Najd via Bahrain in February, 1921, and reached Ibn Saud's camp at Al Khafs, north of Riyadh, on March 2. Two days later the news of Shaikh Salim's death (on February 27, 1921 at Jahra) reached them and at once Ibn Saud said that he no longer had any quarrel with Kuwait. Whereupon Shaikh Ahmad and his group returned home.

With the death of Shaikh Salim, there came a most important change in the political life of Kuwait. During all the prior reign of the al-Sabah's in Kuwait, the power of the Ruler had been personal and autocratic, with only a minimum of delegation of authority. Under Shaikh Salim this feudal form of government had brought on an unnecessary war against the will of the people. Thus it came to pass that when the members of the al-Sabah family met to choose a successor to Shaikh Salim, it was decided that their next Ruler would be one who would assent to a council of advisers.

"The choice fell on Ahmad al Jabir al Sabah, the popular eldest son of the late Shaikh Jabir ibn Mubarak al Sabah and already a favorite of 'Abdul 'Aziz al Saud's," according to Colonel Dickson. On March 29, 1921, upon his return from Saudi Arabia, Shaikh Ahmad acceded to the rulership of Kuwait.

As soon as possible, Shaikh Ahmad put into effect the changes in government which the people of Kuwait had made known they wanted. Although the council of 12 members which was duly elected did not fully function, nevertheless a new regime in Kuwait was initiated—the first step in bringing about a more democratic society.

Shaikh Ahmad became Amir at the age of 36, and ruled his country with sternness tempered by justice and benevolence for 29 years until his peaceful death from a heart condition in his Dasman Palace in Kuwait on January 29, 1950.[157]

Early in Shaikh Ahmad's rule, the boundary disputes between Kuwait and Saudi Arabia were amicably settled at a meeting in 'Uqair Arabia between Sir Percy Cox for Britain, J. C. More, British Political Agent in Kuwait for the Ruler and Ibn Saud in person. This frontier agreement, signed on December 2, 1922, established the so-called Kuwait Neutral Zone in which Saudi Arabia and Kuwait were recognized as each holding an undivided one-half interest, politically and economically. However, this settlement was achieved at the expense of Kuwait which lost approximately two-thirds of the territory it had claimed. So far as the public records disclose, More (a British Political Agent) did not consult with Shaikh Ahmad before agreeing in the Ruler's name to relinquish these Kuwait territorial rights. It is said that Shaikh Ahmad never completely forgave the British for this seeming breach of faith.

Sometime during the next three years, Major Frank Holmes arrived in Kuwait and is believed to have drilled one or more shallow holes in or near the town of Kuwait in search of fresh water, at the request of the Ruler. While the water search was underway Holmes scouted the nearby areas for surface indications of oil. That reconnaissance brought to Holmes' attention

157. The author and his wife, along with C. A. P. Southwell, Managing Director of Kuwait Oil Co., Ltd., and S. A. Swensrud, President of Gulf Oil Corp., were Palace guests of Shaikh Ahmad from January 12 until January 18, 1950. The Ruler collapsed the day of their arrival at the Palace but insisted that his foreign guests remain notwithstanding his incapacity. It was only when his condition was reported as considerably improved that the visiting party left to continue its scheduled Middle East trek to Bahrain, Saudi Arabia and Persia. Unfortunately, 11 days after the party had left Kuwait, the Ruler's condition worsened rather unexpectedly, and he died.

the so-called "mud volcano" at Bahra north of Kuwait Bay and the Burgan oil impregated sands south of Kuwait town. The Burgan natural sand-asphalt was excavated during World War I for use by the allied forces and also to surface a road leading from the town to the Ruler's Dasman Palace.

Although the wells drilled by Holmes did not encounter any appreciable fresh water, nevertheless the Ruler was very pleased with Holmes' effort and readily agreed to give him an option to acquire the oil and gas rights over all Kuwait. This option agreement was a promise rather than a legal document. However, it has long been a tradition in the Middle East that an Arab's word is as good as his bond.

Subsequent developments in the Kuwait oil concession negotiations demonstrated that Shaikh Ahmad kept his word with Holmes insofar as he could with the approval of His Majestys Government's Colonial Office.

From 1925 through 1934, except for the interest aroused locally in Holmes' water venture, followed by rumors of a possible grant of an oil concession to either an American company or a British company and the later flurry occasioned by the arrival in the country of geologists and other representatives of those companies, the way of life in Kuwait continued much the same as in former years. Pearling, shipbuilding and trading remained the principal source of income. For the most part, during this period, Kuwait prospered—quietly but nevertheless persistently.

Then came the seekers after oil. Almost overnight, a new day dawned in Kuwait's economic life, when on December 23, 1934, H. H. Shaikh Ahmad al Jabir al Sabah granted to Kuwait Oil Co., Ltd., an exclusive oil concession over his entire Shaikhdom, including the territorial waters in the Persian Gulf. The Kuwait

Oil Co., Ltd., was then jointly owned by D'Arcy Exploration Co. and Gulf Exploration Co.[158]

Although oil was discovered in Kuwait prior to the beginning of World War, II, the wells drilled had not been put into production before hostilities broke out in the Middle East. All concerned felt it was advisable to suspend exploitation for the duration.

Thus it was not until mid-1946 that exploitation began, and the resulting royalty payments began to flow into Kuwait's exchequer. These royalties soon exceeded the prescribed "annual payments."

When the oil revenues began to soar, Shaikh Ahmad put in motion long range plans for Kuwait's future. He sought advice from British financial and engineering experts as to ways and means of insuring the welfare of his people against the day when oil revenues might be curtailed, for whatever reason, or cease altogether. With the help of his froeign advisers, and his own Kuwaiti council, Shaikh Ahmad initiated plans for a new city with all modern conveniences, including a local dependable supply of potable water. These plans encompassed the bulding of many schools, hospitals and low cost housing. But equally important, was his far-sighted decision to invest a sizeable portion of the annual revenue from oil in gilt-edged British bonds and other securities.

Shaikh Ahmad always spoke of the Kuwait Oil Co. as "his company."

With the demise of H. H. Shaikh Ahmad al Jabir al Sabah, the elders of the al-Sabah family met and chose Shaikh Abdullah al Salim al Sabah to be their Amir. At the time of Shaikh Ahmad's death, his cousin Shaikh Abdullah was Kuwait's

158. For the story of the negotiations which culminated in the granting of the Kuwait Oil concession, see the following text: "Americans Tangle With British For Oil."

Minister of Finance and it so happened that he was out of the country when chosen to be the new Ruler.

As soon as Shaikh Abdullah became the head of his State, he at once cautiously and with wisdom, proceeded to delegate authority to other qualified members of the al-Sabah family, to liberalize, somewhat further, the patriarchal form of government, and to implement and expand the welfare plans set in motion by his predecessor.

We are indebted to an article in *The Times* (London), issue of March 4, 1952 entitled, "Kuwait's Burden of Wealth—A New Oil Center in Arabia," for a splendid word picture of Kuwait of that day. Because this story not only portrays the then existing situation in Kuwait but so accurately forecasts its future under the benevolent leadership of Shaikh Abdullah, the entire text of that article is quoted in Appendix II.

Ever since oil began to be produced from Kuwait wells in quantity, there has been a revolution—however peaceful—in that little Shaikhdom's political, social, economic and cultural life. The great pearling fleet that used to number many hundreds of Kuwaiti manned vessels became reduced to a few score. Kuwait's famous shipbuilding industry that flourished for nearly two centuries has dwindled to insignificant proportions.

The almost daily parade of camel caravans, loaded with trade goods, entering and leaving the city's four gates are now rarely seen—in their place, huge trucks dash across the roadless desert. Where once in Kuwait town were narrow dirt streets ambling through lanes of one-story and sometimes two-story adobe homes and places of business, there are now asphalt boulevards—with 'roundabouts as in England—lined by modern multistory office buildings and concrete block homes.

Kuwait now has its own postage—no longer are the surcharged stamps of England used. Also Kuwait has adopted its own currency—the Dinar, equivalent to one pound sterling—hence the Indian rupee is no longer legal.

Kuwait is now a full member of the Arab League and soon will establish its embassies and consulates throughout the world. Early in 1962, it was reported that the Kuwait government would soon establish a fund to help finance development projects in Arab countries. Since June, 1961, Kuwait has been recognized by the Western World as an independent sovereign state.

The metamorphosis is not yet complete but what, so far, has been accomplished during Shaikh Abdullah's 12-year leadership, reads like a fairy story.[159]

AMERICANS TANGLE WITH BRITISH FOR OIL

This heading may be a bit misleading, since no one knew for sure that oil underlay the desert of Kuwait when an American oil company first became interested in trying to acquire an exclusive oil concession over all of Kuwait territory, including its islands offshore.

However, when Major Frank Holmes and T. E. Ward, in behalf of Eastern General Syndicate, Ltd., first approached the Gulf Companies in late 1926, with a collection of oil options and promises of concessions over Bahrain, al-Hasa, the Kuwait Neutral Zone and Kuwait, it was stated by Holmes that he had seen surface manifestations of oil in Kuwait. He had reference to a "mud volcano" across the bay from Kuwait town and an area called Burgan, some 28 miles south of Kuwait town, where there was a spot of oil impregnated sand.

After completing arrangements with Standard Oil Co. of California to take over the Bahrain concession in November, 1927, Gulf did not press the Syndicate to further its interests in al-Hasa or the Kuwait Neutral Zone but did urge Major Holmes to endeavor to acquire valid oil rights in Kuwait in

159. For more about the Kuwait of today, see the following text: "Kuwait—After Oil."

behalf of the Syndicate and Gulf. Holmes, in due course, arrived in Kuwait and advised the Amir (Shaikh Ahmad) that he now had an American client who could give any desired guarantees in respect to development.

When the Syndicate had first acquired the four so-called Holmes' oil options these had been offered to Anglo-Persian Oil Co. In March, 1926, Anglo-Persian advised the Syndicate, "We are disposed to consider accepting the transfer simultaneously and collectively of the four concessions." However, a month later, Anglo-Persian reconsidered and this time advised the Syndicate that, "In view of the opinion of our geologists on the spot . . . (we are) . . . now unfavorable to the proposal."

In spite of the apparent British company's disinterest, no sooner had Major Holmes made known the purpose of his return to Kuwait in 1928, than J. C. More, the British Political Agent in Kuwait, advised Holmes by letter of a clause which he said, "It is now desired to have included in any oil agreement with the Shaikh of Kuwait." That clause read:

> The Company shall at all times be and remain a British company registered in Great Britain or a British Colony, and having its principal place of business within His Majesty's Dominions, the Chairman and Managing Director (if any) and a majority of the other Directors of which shall at all times be British subjects, and neither the company nor the premises, liberties, powers or privileges hereby granted and devised, nor any land occupied for any of the purposes of this lease, shall at any time be or become directly or indirectly controlled or managed by a foreigner or foreigners of any foreign corporation or corporations, and the local General Manager of the Company, and as large a percentage of the local staff employed by them as circumstances may permit, shall at all times be British subjects or subjects of the Shaikh.
>
> In this clause the expression "foreigner" means any person who is neither a British subject nor a subject of the Shaikh,

and the expression "foreign corporation," means any corporation other than a corporation established under and subject to the laws of some part of His Majesty's Dominions and having its principal place of business in those Dominions.

This is the famous, "Nationality Clause," which plagued the American interests in Bahrain and now raised its head in Kuwait.

Furthermore, the treaty of 1899 between Britain and Shaikh Mubarak of Kuwait made it impossible for the Ruler to make any concessions or grants to a foreign entity without the prior knowledge and consent of Her Majesty's Government.[160] During those days, matters pertaining to the protected States were handled by the British Colonial office—but have since been transferred to the British Foreign Office.

In March, 1929, the Gulf Oil companies brought to the attention of the State Department these British political measures which effectively prevented American interests, as such, from doing business in the Persian Gulf area. Whereupon the State Department directed the Charge d'Affairs in London to make proper inquiries of His Majesty's Government.

The following May, the British Foreign Office advised the US Charge d'Affairs in London—in regard to Bahrain, particularly—"that His Majesty's Government is prepared in principle to consent to the participation of United States interests in this concession, subject to . . ." While Kuwait was not mentioned by name in this communication, American interests were of the opinion that the position stated as a prerequisite for Bahrain, would apply also to other protected states in the Persian Gulf, of which Kuwait was one of several.

Throughout the balance of 1929 and all of 1930, Major Holmes in behalf of the Eastern and General Syndicate and The Gulf Companies continued to press the Shaikh of Kuwait

160. For the pertinent part of this treaty see pp. 178 and 179 of this text.

and the Colonial Office authorities for an exclusive oil concession over Kuwait territory. Concession terms satisfactory to Shaikh Ahmad had been negotiated by Major Holmes but the Colonial Office stood firm on the necessity of including the Nationality Clause in the proposed agreement—as they said, "Arising out of the Shaikh of Kuwait's insistence."

Colonel H. R. P. Dickson was designated Political Agent for the British Government in 1929, which post he held until 1936, when the age limit forced his relinquishment of this post. Colonel Dickson was a close friend of Shaikh Ahmad and many members of the ruling family, also he was experienced in Arab procedure, customs, culture and language. Hence, his appointment as Political Agent in Kuwait was an important move for his government.

In early May, 1931, Holmes furnished the Council of State in Kuwait with a copy of the proposed concession agreement and at the request of Colonel Dickson furnished the Political Agent's office with another copy. On May 23, Major Holmes cabled his principals in London of what he had done and included in his message this statement: "Am informed by the Council of State that the Shaikh of Kuwait told the Political Resident of Persian Gulf and Colonel Dickson, Political Agent, Kuwait, verbally, that he had promised Frank Holmes the Kuwait oil concession and that he intended to keep his promise . . ."

Mulla Saleh, Secretary of the Kuwait Council of State, is alleged to have told Major Holmes about this time that the Ruler would not have Anglo-Persian as concessionaries in Kuwait as it was felt locally the British interests were seeking more than oil rights. At any rate, in November, 1931, Holmes advised his principals that the Shaikh, the Council and the people were all behind the Syndicate.

In February, 1932, Anglo-Persian geologists arrived in Kuwait and began exploration. Incidentally, this was nearly six years after Anglo-Persian had advised the Syndicate that its geologists had turned down the oil prospects of the four Major Holmes concessions agreements and promises.

The following March, in answer to repeated representation by the American government protesting the exclusion of American interests in obtaining rights to operate in protected states, the Foreign Office said in substance,

> Britain will agree to the omission from any oil concession, which the Shaikh may grant, of a clause confining it to British interests. Hence, if the Syndicate will renew its application to the Shaikh of Kuwait for a concession which it will subsequently transfer to the Gulf companies, H.M.G. will raise no objection to the application being taken into consideration with any other applications of others which may be forthcoming.

This declaration of policy aroused considerable hopes in the minds of the Syndicate and its American client.

During the interval 1927-1932, Gulf had released the Syndicate to deal with the Standard Oil Co. of California regarding Bahrain and had surrendered its rights to the options on al-Hasa and the Neutral Zone. Thus in May, 1932, Gulf retained only its rights to Kuwait under the agreements executed with the Syndicate on November 30, 1927.

In the late spring of 1932, Major Holmes submitted to the Shaikh of Kuwait and the British Political Agents, copies of the Syndicate's revised concession proposal. Shortly thereafter, Anglo-Persian also submitted a proposed oil concession agreement to the Kuwait authorities.

During the fall of that year and the early spring of 1933, it may be presumed that British authorities were examining the drafts of oil concession agreement submitted by the Syndicate and Anglo-Persian. At any rate, for about six months nothing happened in Kuwait on the oil concession matter.

In May of 1933, William T. Wallace, Vice President of Gulf Exploration Co., visited London where he had talks with Sir John Cadman and William Fraser, then Chairman and Deputy Chairman respectively of the Anglo-Persian Oil Co. Anglo-Persian made it quite clear to Wallace that an American company would not succeed in obtaining an exclusive oil concession in Kuwait over their opposition. However, they would have no objection to Gulf as a joint partner in a Kuwait concession.

Anglo-Persian further stipulated that it was unwilling to assume any set joint development program and would not, under any circumstances, deal with the Syndicate nor recognize any overriding royalty to the Syndicate. This statement was most significant in the light of the facts—namely, that the Shaikh of Kuwait apparently was reluctant to grant an exclusive oil concession over all his territory to the British and the Colonial Office of His Majesty's Goverment was in a position to refuse acquiescence to any grant of an exclusive oil concession over all of Kuwait to American interests. It was a stalemate.

In November, 1933, Gulf made a mutually satisfactory agreement with the Syndicate, under the terms of which the Syndicate transferred to the Gulf companies all its rights, title and interest in any Kuwait oil concession. Bear in mind this step was taken some seven years after Major Holmes and T. E. Ward had first approached Gulf in New York with the Syndicate's oil options over four different places in the Persian Gulf area.

Gulf continued to discuss with Anglo-Persian the possibility for a joint venture in Kuwait and in a matter of months the parties reached an amicable agreement.

The Kuwait Oil Co., Ltd. was incorporated February 2, 1934,[161] jointly owned by D'Arcy Exploration Co. (subsidiary

161. Shortly after Kuwait Oil Co., Ltd. was incorporated, Gulf divested itself of any interest in the Iraq Petroleum Co. by sale of its stock in the Near East Development Corp. to the only two remaining American companies in that corporation, i.e., Standard Oil Co. (New Jersey) and Socony-Vacuum Oil Co.

of Anglo-Persian) and Gulf Exploration Company. Promptly thereafter, Anglo-Persian appointed A. H. T. Chisholm as its negotiator and Gulf appointed Major Frank Holmes as its negotiator. Chisholm and Holmes were jointly instructed to proceed to Kuwait and attempt to work out a satisfactory oil concession agreement with the Ruler in behalf of Kuwait Oil Co., Ltd. These negotiations prospered—since, no longer was there any objection from the Colonial Office.

On December 23, 1934, the oil concession contract was executed between the Kuwait Oil Co., Ltd. and the Shaikh of Kuwait for an exclusive oil and gas concession covering all the Kuwait territory on the mainland, certain islands claimed by Kuwait offshore and a three-mile strip alongshore of territorial waters—for a term of 75 years. In early 1935, the company began intensive field exploration in Kuwait.

Shaikh Ahmad was so pleased with Major Frank Holmes and his efforts to open the Persian Gulf areas to foreign interests that he was chosen to be Kuwait's London commercial representative—a position which he occupied until his death in 1947.

As mentioned elsewhere, Colonel H. R. P. Dickson was the British Political Agent in Kuwait when Shaikh Ahmad signed the oil concession agreement with Kuwait Oil Co. in December, 1934. In fact he signed this agreement as Britain's representative. In 1936, when Colonel Dickson retired from government service because of age, Shaikh Ahmad appointed him to be his Chief Local Representative—a liaison post having to do with Arab relations between the oil company, the local government and the people of Kuwait. Both Colonel Dickson and his wife had long resided in the Middle East and both spoke Arabic idiomatically and fluently. Colonel Dickson, in his dual role as Chief Local Representative and interpreter, was generally present at any meeting between the Amir or other members of the ruling family and European representatives of the oil companies. His intimate knowledge of the Arab and Arab culture, customs and etiquette, his close association with Kuwait Oil Co.'s staff, as well as his close acquaintance with the visiting representatives of the Anglo-American owners, were invaluable in keeping relations on a friendly and personal basis for more than 20 years. Until his death in June, 1959, Colonel Dickson retained this post at the insistence of two Amirs, Shaikh Ahmad, and his successor, Shaikh Abdullah.

The terms of the Kuwait concession agreement of 1934 were generally similar to others which obtained in the Middle East. However, World War II caused a cessation of development in the newly discovered oil fields in Kuwait, while in Iran, Iraq and Saudi Arabia drilling, development and oil production were accelerated during the war years. Actually, it was not until mid-1946 that crude oil in tanker lots began to move from Kuwait.[162]

Thus, due to the war and other circumstances beyond the control of the oil companies, oil development in Kuwait lagged years behind similar development in the neighboring countries and as a result, Kuwait's oil revenues were seemingly slow to generate. Although from 1946 onward, Kuwait's oil production and oil revenues were accelerated at rates greater than those obtaining elsewhere in the Middle East countries, nevertheless the annual income to the Kuwait State from oil continued to be less than some of its neighbors for eight years more.

The year 1950 was both critical and historic in the Middle East oil producing countries. On January 29 of that year, Shaikh Ahmad al Jabir, Amir of Kuwait, died and was succeeded by Shaikh Abdullah al Salim. As the year progressed, it was evident that the situation between the Iranian government and the Anglo-Iranian Oil Co. was worsening and that nationalization of the oil properties in Iran loomed as a proba-

162. For the year 1946, Kuwait is credited with a total crude oil production of just under 6 million barrels, as compared with some 147 million barrels for Iran, almost 90 million barrels for Saudi Arabia and nearly 36 million for Iraq.

bility and not a mere possibility. Meanwhile, it was rumored that the American oil companies in Saudi Arabia were seriously considering to voluntarily submit themselves to a 50-50 income tax. In Iraq also, there were indications the government wanted its oil revenues increased. Coincidentally, oil production in Kuwait still lagged behind the annual oil production of both Iran and Saudi Arabia, though Kuwait's production in 1950 exceeded that of Iraq by an average of more than 200,000 barrels daily.

The threat of nationalization of oil in Iran, the prospects of a 50-50 income tax being imposed upon the oil companies in Saudi Arabia and the existing unbalance in oil revenues as between the several neighboring countries combined to confuse and unsettle the relations between the new Ruler in Kuwait and the Kuwait Oil Co., Ltd.

The news that Saudi Arabia had imposed a 50-50 income tax on Aramco, by agreement dated December 30, 1950, spread like wildfire throughout the Middle East. The Iraq government was quick to take steps to impose a similar income tax on the Iraq Petroleum Co., Ltd. and Shaikh Abdullah al Salim promptly instructed his London agent, H. T. Kemp, to demand of "his company," (Kuwait Oil Co., Ltd.), that Kuwait must have parity treatment in the matter of oil revenues with that enjoyed by his neighbors—more particularly Saudi Arabia.

In making these demands for parity with his neighbors, the Amir admitted that "his company" had meticulously lived up to prior agreements with Kuwait and that he had no fault to find with the company's operations or personnel. The Amir did not threaten to cancel the original contract or to contest its validity but rather, he stoutly insisted Kuwait must be treated similarly as her neighbors and he did not care how it was done.

Both the Foreign Office in London and the State Department in Washington were duly advised by Anglo-Iranian and Gulf of Kuwait's demands but neither government could or would offer any solution to the difficult problems confronting the companies. Both governments replied, in effect, that this is a commercial matter—do not come to us unless your properties and oil rights are nationalized or expropriated.

Kuwait had no general income tax laws at the time and by the terms of the original oil concession contract Kuwait Oil Co. was excused from payment of any and all taxes by reason of a payment of 4 annas* per ton of crude oil produced. This situation was further complicated by the fact that the concession had been granted in 1934 to the Kuwait Oil Co., Ltd.—a British company jointly owned by Anglo-Iranian and Gulf. However, the owners of Kuwait Oil Co. were agreed that they —without resorting to an International Court and without inviting pressure from their respective governments—should make every reasonable effort to satisfy Kuwait's request for treatment similar to her neighbors.

By mid-1951, it became obvious to Anglo-Iranian and Gulf that Kuwait oil revenues could only properly and legally achieve parity with those in Saudi Arabia provided: (1) all concerned would consent to a reorganization of the holding company structure which would result in the concession rights being directly vested in the respective owning companies; (2) the Kuwait government would enact a general income tax law, and (3) the companies would submit to the application of a 50-50 income tax law, when imposed. The governments of Britain, United States and Kuwait were duly informed of the companies' proposal and the approval of all concerned was sought.

Vigorous discussions were carried on throughout most of the last half of 1951, between the companies and governments involved. However, it was not until late in November of that year that agreement and consent of all concerned was obtained.

Shortly before the year end the Amir of Kuwait decreed the

---

* Author's Note: At the time of the agreement, 4 annas was equal to $.36 (US). At the present rate of exchange, 4 annas equals $.6½ (US).

50-50 income tax law and granted a new oil concession to D'Arcy and Gulf—those companies having agreed to submit to the imposition of an income tax law, when decreed. Under the terms of the new oil concessions the life of that contract was extended for an additional 17 years (to the year 2026) and the territorial rights over-water were redefined to cover a six-mile strip alongshore, instead of the former three-mile strip.

In return for these additional rights of both time and area, the companies relinquished all rights and claims they might have had to the offshore islands of Kubr, Qaru and Umm al Maradim in the Persian Gulf and furthermore, the companies agreed that the new oil concession did not embrace Kuwait's continental shelf outside the six-mile strip along shore.

Thus did Kuwait achieve parity of treatment with her neighbors and greatly increased oil revenues.

It was in the autumn of 1954 that the consortium reached agreement with the National Iranian Oil Co. and the Iranian government as to the ownership and operation of the former Anglo-Iranian's 100,000 square mile oil concession in Iran. That settlement was made along the general lines of the 50-50 income tax pattern previously adopted in Saudi Arabia and Kuwait, with one important exception, namely, that for the purpose of determining the oil companies' revenues subject to income tax, all sales of oil were to be booked at posted prices.[163]

Since Anglo-Iranian had a 40 per cent interest in the consortium and Gulf had a 7 per cent interest, it was not unexpected that Shaikh al Salim al Sabah, Amir of Kuwait, would

163. Crude and refined oil is traditionally sold in the United States at "posted prices," however, such postings are those made by the buyer and not by the seller. Exactly the contrary is the practice in Venezuela and certain other foreign countries—there the seller posts the price, principally for spot cargo sales, notwithstanding most overseas sales are made for large quantities of oil to be delivered over a long term of years.

request, sooner or later, similar treatment as that accorded to Iran in the matter of pricing Kuwait oil.

So, once again in 1955 the representatives of British Petroleum Co., Ltd.,[164] and Gulf sat down with Kuwait representatives in London, in Kuwait and in Beirut to thresh out this request for the posted price basis for determining revenue from oil sales f.o.b. Kuwait.

This problem was particularly difficult to resolve because of the effect the posted price basis would have on both BP's and Gulf's long-term sale customers. This latter problem was further complicated by the fact that some of these long-term sale customers were British. The creditability of foreign taxes paid by a British company is not the same as the creditability of foreign taxes by an American company under the respective existing British and United States income tax provisions.

During April and May these complex and knotty problems from the companies' standpoint were discussed. The Ruler's request was simple, namely, he wanted to be treated like his neighbor, Saudi Arabia, including posted price for all sales and a lump sum payment in respect of past years.

After clearing with British authorities and certain long-term sales customers in London, the negotiating team set out once again for the Middle East. Actually, there were two places where negotiating sessions took place, one in Kuwait and the second in Beirut. In between these sessions the British and American negotiators returned to their home offices for instructions.

It was on May 14, 1955 in Beirut, Lebanon, that the new agreement between the oil companies and Kuwait was signed. Under this new contract between the oil companies (D'Arcy and Gulf) and Kuwait, no change was proposed or made in the income tax law decreed by the Amir in 1950—the only new factors involved in accounting procedure thereunder being the

164. Formerly Anglo-Iranian Oil Co. Ltd.

provision for making all f.o.b. oil sales at not less than posted prices, except for certain discounts when applicable.

The agreed discounts—off posted prices—to be allowed the producing companies in Kuwait were: (1), a 2 per cent deduction for "selling expense" for the life of the concession and (2), a volume discount approximating 7 per cent for three years. The "posted prices" are the prices individually established and published from time to time, by each of the companies involved, as the prices at which the company will sell the oil, until further notice, to any person desiring to purchase it.

Both the 2 per cent selling discount and the volume discount have since been discontinued.

Notwithstanding that within recent years Japanese and other oil interests have offered fantastic cash payments and a local government participation amounting to somewhat more than 50 per cent of net profits on oil delivered on board tankers at Persian Gulf Ports, the Kuwait government has not raised the question of any further revision of the oil concession agreements with the British-American oil interests operating on the Kuwait mainland and *in sha'llah* (God's willing), it may never be an issue.

KUWAIT OIL COMPANY, LTD.

ORGANIZATION AND DEVELOPMENT

As soon as Shaikh Ahmad, Amir of Kuwait, had signed the oil concession grant in December, 1934, Kuwait Oil Co. began to make plans and take steps to initiate geological and geophysical surveys of the residual gravel and windblown sands which make up most of the desert terrain of Kuwait. The principal exposure of rock was a limey-sandstone escarpment found at the extreme western end of Kuwait Bay, stretching from near the Jahra oasis on the south for a few miles to the northward before dying out into the oblivion of the desert.

The first exploration parties were Americans. Field work began in March, 1935. All supplies and equipment, not only for the technical work but for living and transport as well, had to be imported. None of such things were then available in Kuwait town. Tents were used for housing, with fly tops for double protection against the heat of the desert. Desert water bags were hung in the tents to afford further relief from the heat, which in the summer often soars up to and sometimes over 120° Fahrenheit in the shade.

The exploration party's motor vehicles were among the first ever seen in Kuwait.   .

As noted earlier in this Chapter, there were only two known surfaces indications of oil in Kuwait. A so-called small mud volcano (a mound of earth caused by gas blowing or bubbling up through soft wet mud) in the flat just north of Kuwait Bay and almost directly across from Kuwait town, and the oil impregnated sands in the area called, "Burgan," located some 28 miles south of Kuwait town and about 15 miles inland from the Persian Gulf.

Thirty years ago, there were no man-made roads anywhere in the territory outside of Kuwait town and the few coastal villages. However, the desert was crisscrossed by caravan trails, some worn deep by the plodding feet of camels and donkeys. For the most part there are but few sizable sand dunes in Kuwait. The terrain, except in a few spots, looks flat but actually is a series of gentle broad swells and shallow depressions. Much of the surface is covered by a sandy clay with pebbles, forming a crust over the loose sands below. Under these terrain conditions the exploration parties soon found they could drive their motor vehicles practically anywhere across country, away from the tidal flats. One had only to set his objective and high tail for it on a beeline.

There are no rivers or lakes in Kuwait—in fact no fresh water, except in shallow wells in surface depressions where water from occasional rains collects. All the deep wells yield brackish water, which, although the Arab and livestock will drink, is generally so high in mineral salts as to act like a purge on Europeans. For centuries the people of Kuwait town had brought in sweet water from the Shatt-al-Arab by sailboats for local domestic purposes. So too, the pioneer oil explorers used imported sweet water for drinking and cooking.

The first exploratory well was located at Bahra north of Kuwait Bay, near the so-called mud volcano. Drilling was started on May 30, 1936. Shaikh Ahmad and a large retinue attended the spudding-in ceremony. This well was carried to 7,950 feet but failed to encounter any encouraging signs of oil or gas. It was abandoned April 14, 1937.

In the interim, geophysical surveys had proceeded over much of the coastal area south of Kuwait town. A sub-surface "high" was indicated just north of Burgan and a site for the second exploratory well was chosen. It was called Burgan No. 1. Drilling on this well began on October 16, 1937 and the following April, at a depth of only 3,675 feet, a high pressure oil and gas sand was encountered. On May 14, 1938, the discovery well was completed at a total depth of 3,692 feet. And what a discovery this proved to be—one of the largest oil fields, in terms of recoverable oil, in all the world.

Between 1938 and 1942, eight additional wells were drilled in what is now known as the Burgan field. During that interval another exploratory test was also drilled—at Madaniyat.

With the discovery of oil in commercial quantities, so far as possible, tents were discarded for housing the drilling crews and clerical force. More permanent huts of adobe and corrugated iron were substituted—however, even these quarters were primitive compared to the mobile and permanent air conditioned houses and offices now used.

All materials were unloaded from vessels at Shuwaikh, a suburb of Kuwait town, and for the most part stored there until needed in the field.

Because of the possibility of enemy attack during the hostilities of the World War II—and because necessary flow stations, steel tankage, pipelines and loading facilities had not yet been installed and also because priorities for all steel products were hard to get from either Britain or America, drilling operations were suspended on July 13, 1942 by order of His Majesty's Government. All the oil wells were plugged with cement as a precautionary measure.

During the war, this set-back in oil development, was at least partially offset by the increased revenue derived by Kuwait ship owners in handling most of the carrying trade between the ports of Basra and Abadan on the Shatt-al-Arab and India.

The American interests in the Kuwait Oil Company were able to somewhat alleviate the economic stress of war on Kuwait by prosecuting exploration work on a sulphur concession granted by the Amir to the Eastern Gulf Oil Co. in 1944. The American government gave priority for the necessary equipment and supplies for this exploration. Although the exploration results did not indicate that sulphur in commercial quantities could be profitably recovered in Kuwait by the Frasch method (commonly employed in the sulphur workings in the Gulf Coast of the United States) and the concession was eventually surrendered, nevertheless, the payments made by the company to the Kuwait Government and the expenditures incurred in Kuwait were a welcome boon to Kuwait economy during the War.

As soon as the war was ended plans were rapidly developed to reactivate operations in Kuwait. A scheme was agreed by the owning companies and their respective governments to develop Kuwait crude at the daily rate of 30,000 barrels. This first development scheme provided that all wells in the proven area would be located on a primary grid of 600 meters (i.e. wells spaced at least 1,800 feet apart) ; that the producing wells would flow into gas separators at strategically located gathering centers, then to tankage from where the degassed crude would be pumped to the main storage tank farm. From this tank farm (located on a rise of ground 390 feet above sea level and approximately 4 miles inland from the coast) the crude could flow by gravity through big-inch pipe lines on land and through submarine pipe lines into tankers nearly a mile offshore.[165]

On June 30, 1946, the Amir of Kuwait, Shaikh Ahmad al Jabir al Sabah, turned a silver wheel which opened the valve to start the loading of the *S.S. British Fusilier* with the first cargo of Kuwait crude oil. Besides the local company staff and Kuwaiti dignitaries, C. A. P. Southwell, Managing Director of Kuwait Oil Co. (now Sir Philip Southwell) was present. He ended his excellent speech with these words:

> The success that has, so happily, crowned our efforts would never have been possible without Your Highness' unfailing patience, loyal friendship and close collaboration, the excellent work of our Kuwait personnel, and the technical skill and large resources of this company, in which British and American interests and personnel are so happily blended.

Since that date through 1961, Kuwait has produced more than 4,847 million barrels of crude petroleum. The bulk of this production has come from the Burgan field which is now said to be proven over an area of some 135 square miles.

During 1961, Kuwait's crude oil production averaged 1,644,-

165. This was the first all-gravity loading tanker terminal in the Middle East and is today—after installation of more and bigger gravity lines, loading docks, etc., the largest gravity loading oil terminal in the world. Through 1961 more than 4 billion barrels of crude oil has been loaded onto tankers by gravity at Mina al-Ahmadi. American oil companies pioneered in creating the first major gravity oil loading facilities—first at Paraguana in western Venezuela in 1925 and second at Puerta La Cruz in eastern Venezuela in 1939.

455 barrels a day of which the bulk came from the Burgan area. However, by the end of 1961 an average of about 160,000 barrels per day was being pumped from the North Kuwait fields to Ahmadi.

At the end of 1961, Kuwait was credited with 379 connected wells—all flowing, and 27 other wells either abandoned, unconnected or used for injection or observation.

The Magwa field and the so-called Ahmadi field lie close to Burgan on the north and east respectively—for all practical purposes they may be considered as part of Burgan.

North of Kuwait Bay, the wells drilled in the Raudhatain field (discovered in 1955) were put on stream during April, 1960. By the end of 1961 there were 25 producing wells at Raudhatain. This oil is pumped through a 30-inch line south and around the west end of Kuwait Bay to the North Tank Farm at Ahmadi—a distance of some 63 miles.

Other exploratory wells have been drilled north of Kuwait Bay—namely at Sabriya (about 10 miles southeast of the discovery well at Raudhatain) and at Bahra. In each of these areas one well has been connected to the Raudhatain gathering center, making a total of 27 producing wells in North Kuwait at the close of 1961.

Test drilling at Minagish, some 25 miles west of Burgan field encountered commercial oil at depths of nearly 10,000 feet. Since the discovery well was completed in May, 1959, more holes have been drilled on a step-out pattern and all have encountered pay sand. In mid-1960, Minagish oil came on stream, using temporary facilities (at a rate of some 10,000 barrels a day) pending construction of permanent flow stations and a big-inch pipe line to the Ahmadi tank farm.

During the past two years deep hole exploration was carried on in northwest Kuwait at Mutriba and in West Kuwait at Mityaha.

Collectively, these Kuwait oil fields indicate one of the largest proven oil reserves known anywhere. But as a matter of fact no one really knows exactly how much oil there is, except maybe a few "long haired" boys (scientists) and even they could be wrong. However, it may be assumed that the Kuwait oil reserves are really large—possibly larger than the combined oil reserves of all the North and South American countries.

During the past 16 years, Kuwait Oil Co., Ltd. had expanded all its production and delivery facilities in the oil fields, the residential and operating headquarters at Ahmadi and the ports at Mina al-Ahmadi, until now with its many gathering centers, its big battery of mammoth steel storage tanks, its multiple big-inch gravity lines from those storage tanks to tanker berth and its two enormous piers built out in the Persian Gulf nearly a mile offshore, supplemented by several submarine pipe lines for delivery of fuel and refined products, make it possible to deliver on board tankers at berth well over two million barrels of oil daily. The present day oil production and delivery facilities in Kuwait are a far cry from the 30,000 barrels scheme initiated in 1945.

TANKER LOADING FACILITIES

No sooner had Kuwait oil began to be exported (1946) than it was realized the increased demands for Middle East oil would necessitate stepping up the drilling activity in the Burgan area and also a considerable expansion in delivery facilities. While submarine pipe lines had proven effective in delivering oil to tankers anchored off shore, so much tanker time was lost due to rough waters and storms—when loading had to be suspended for safety—that the Kuwait Oil Co. began to contemplate the possibility of steel-concrete loading pier at which tankers could remain tied up in all normal weather conditions.

Engineering experts were consulted in both Britain and America. After exhaustive study, including test borings out in the Persian Gulf, the company decided to build a "flexible" pier. The plans called for an all-welded steel structure—with a road-way approach 4,140 feet eastward from shore to the open sea at the end of which would be a 'T' head, 105 feet wide and extending northward 2,805 feet, providing 6 tanker loading berths. Another extension, 100 feet wide, would run southward 1,077 feet and would provide two berths—either for use in un-loading cargo vessels or for loading oil into tankers.

On the approach and along the 'T' head were to be con-structed eight 24-inch crude oil lines, a 16-inch line for fuel oil for ships' bunkers and a 12-inch line for diesel oil, as well as smaller pipe lines for fresh water, sea water for fire fighting services and compressed air.

This pier was bold in concept and novel in type of construc-tion. Because of the corrosive effect of the Persian Gulf waters on steel, a positive cathodic system was devised and installed. During this stage in the planning, many pessimists in the in-dustry held that such a steel structure could not last long—be-tween corrosion and the buffeting of tankers, winds and waves. However, the pessimists to the contrary, the dock still is in daily operation with only normal maintenance and no major struc-tural replacements.

The pier was designed to handle an estimated maximum of 600,000 barrels daily onto tankers, but with some subsequent minor installations there has actually been delivered to tankers at berth at this pier as much as 1,500,000 barrels in a single day. One of the super tankers, not long ago, was loaded with a cargo of 195,000 barrels of crude oil in 6½ hours—or that is, at the rate of about 30,000 barrels per hour.

One of the great problems in the design of such a mammoth steel pier in water depths of 45 to 50 feet at low tide, is how to provide sufficient rigidity to carry the load on the superstructure and yet be sufficiently flexible to give enough with the shock of tanker impact to avoid failure (breakage) of the structure.

Bear in mind, that to achieve a bottom penetration of say, 20 to 30 feet, it was necessary to use steel piles 90 feet long. Out of war experience, the engineers came up with a likly solution namely, the use of the so-called "Baker" fender. Each of such fender units consists of three steel cylinders filled with concrete —each 6 feet in diameter, 21 feet, 3 inches high and weighing 43 tons—suspended at the top and bottom on links between trunnions which enabled the unit as a whole to swing both inward and upward on the impact of a vessel. Forty-four such "Baker" fenders were installed along the face of the original dock. So successful have these fenders proved over the years that the records show the main dock structure and the many pipe lines on the dock deck have never been seriously damaged because of a tanker crashing into the pier.[166]

In addition to pipe lines, valves, fire-fighting equipment, hose derricks and other necessary equipment on the Mina al-Ahmadi oil pier superstructure, there are also buildings for storage, pump stations, office buildings for the staff in charge of loading and for administrative work, as well as a recreation room for officers and crews of vessels at the dock.

Nearly 24,000 tankers have taken cargo at the Mina al-Ahmadi South Pier since it was commissioned in November, 1949. It is interesting to note that in 1946 the average crude oil cargo per tanker loading at Mina al-Ahmadi was 93,000 barrels, whereas in 1961 the average crude oil cargo per tanker loading at that port was 246,000 barrels. Tankers of 700,000-bbl cargo capacity arriving at Mina al-Ahmadi to take crude oil are no longer a novelty.

Even with the great oil loading pier and several submarine

166. For the information of those unfamiliar with the docking of tankers coming in to load, it perhaps should be mentioned the bow of a large empty tanker rises up from 40 to 50 feet above the surface of the water and consequently presents a large surface to both wind and wave either of which can cause the vessel to swing out of control of the helm.

lines at Mina al-Ahmadi, the port's loading facilities were taxed to their capacity by 1956. Also, a new field had been discovered in northern Kuwait which, in due course, would be put into production. Logically, that oil, too, would need adequate delivery facilities at the port of loading. Furthermore, it was planned that the company's refining capacity would be increased by more than six times its original daily output. Thus, additional delivery facilities would soon be required for the increased volume of refined oil going abroad.

After careful engineering study, the owning companies and the management of Kuwait Oil Co. decided to build a new oil loading pier—designed especially to handle the largest super tankers, drawing 50 feet or more when fully loaded—some four miles north of the original pier. Generally, this new pier would be of similar construction as the original pier, except for using a somewhat different type of steel pile and heavier "Baker" fender. It was designed to have an estimated delivery capacity of one million barrels daily. Work began on this second oil loading pier (known as the North Pier) in November, 1957, and the pier was completed and commissioned in June, 1959.

As previously noted, the original layout for the delivery of crude oil from the south tank farm at Ahmadi to tankers off-shore—some five miles distant—was a gravity system. This gravity scheme was extended to include a North Tank Farm to serve the new North Pier. Each of the three super tanker berths at this new pier are fed with crude oil by gravity through three 38-40 inch diameter pipe lines and each of the berths is capable of loading a tanker at a rate up to 47,000 barrels an hour. The gravity system is still employed today for all crude oil deliveries to tankers at the Mina al-Ahmadi port. Only refined oils are pumped aboard tankers.

From mid-1946 through 1961, a total of 30,031 oil tankers were loaded at Mina al-Ahmadi, initially by submarine lines, then by both submarine lines and over dock side. Currently, all tankers receiving either crude or refined oils are loaded alongside the two piers.

REFINERY AND LOCAL MARKETING

Kuwait Oil Co., Ltd., put its first refinery on stream in 1949. It was a simple refinery of some 30,000 barrels capacity, producing motor gasoline, kerosene and gas oil for local consumption as well as bunker oil and diesel oil to fuel ships calling at Mina al-Almadi. In 1956, it realized that this refinery capacity would need to be increased substantially to take care of the demands of both local and overseas trade. The new refinery extension program agreed upon by the owners provided for the installation of two crude still units, each capable of topping 80,000 barrels daily.

Coincidentally, more tankage, more pipe lines and more service equipment were needed to take care of the increased volume of crude and refined oils to be handled by the new refining units at site, as well as extentions and alterations to the tanker delivery system. This enlarged refinery—now with a capacity of 190,000 barrels daily—went on stream in 1958. During 1961 the average daily thruput at Kuwait Oil's Mina al-Ahmadi refinery was 171,000 barrels.

The company also has had in operation since 1953, a small asphalt plant for the production of asphalt for the Kuwait state road construction program as well as for company use.

Until very recently all local sales to consumers in Kuwait of asphalt, motor gasoline, diesel, kerosene, gas, oil and lubricants were made by Kuwait Oil Co., Ltd. Bulk deliveries were made in Kuwait Oil tank trucks and by pipe line. Refined products were delivered to the customers at modern service stations erected by Kuwait Oil Co. at strategic locations in and around Kuwait town and its suburbs. However, some time ago the oil companies (Gulf and BP) voluntarily offered to sell all Kuwait

Oil Co's retail distribution facilities in Kuwait to the State, and to sell petroleum products to the State without profit. The sale became effective on June 1, 1961. The State appointed the Kuwait National Petroleum Co. (which had been established at the end of 1960 and in which it held a considerable interest, the remainder being held by Kuwaiti nationals), as its agent to handle local distribution of products.

Total local consumption of petroleum products in 1961 was approximately 2 million barrels; of this 1.3 million barrels were gasoline (of which about three-quarters is premium grade); 280,000 barrels kerosene; 500,000 barrels gas oil; and 9,000 barrels fuel oil.

GAS INJECTION

A gas injection plant designed to return 100 million cubic feet of gas to the underground daily was commissioned in the Burgan area early in 1961. Periodically, surplus distillate, benzine and gas oil from the Mina al-Ahmadi refinery have been put into the lower Burgan foundations via four injection wells.

LPG PLANT

Construction of a 6,500 barrel-per-day LPG (liquified petroleum gas) plant was begun during the fall of 1960. It was completed at the end of 1961. This plant compresses and liquifies gas from several gathering centers in the Burgan field. Condensate is pumped to the Mina-al Ahmadi refinery where a deethanizer, depropanizer, debutanizer and other facilities are installed. Low temperature storage facilities have been erected at the shipping port and the first bulk shipment (reported to have been 105,708 barrels of propane and 89,030 barrels of butane) in a tanker especially designed to carry LPG was made from Mina al-Ahmadi in March, 1962.

PERSONNEL

When Kuwait Oil Co. started operations in Kuwait, there were virtually no qualified Kuwaitis available for either technical or clerical work. Hence, it was necessary to import large numbers of Americans and British staff as well as skilled artisans and clerks from Iran, Iraq, Pakistan and India. Unskilled Kuwaiti labor was also limited. Thus it was that in the boom days of development after World War II, at one time, the Kuwait Oil Co. total local payroll involved more than 15,000 men.

With the completion of the initial major construction program, it was possible to whittle down the labor and technical staff until the permanent staff became more or less static at about 8,000—the majority being Kuwaitis and other Arabs from nearby countries.

The Arab has now largely replaced all foreign skilled artisans through the training program which the company has had in effect for many years in the Company Training Center at Magwa. The relatively short time required to train these, mostly unschooled, Arab lads from the desert and town to be skilled welders, plumbers, electricians, carpenters, masons, truck and tractor drivers, lathe operators, etc., is nothing short of amazing.

From driving a camel to driving a bulldozer in three months has actually happened. And, what is more important, these trained Arab boys not only have learned a new skill quickly and well, but they have become dependable employees and better citizens, filled with the honest pride of accomplishment.

Quite a number of Kuwaitis now hold supervisory jobs on the company staff. More and more, the local Arab, as his ability and skill permits, is integrated into the staff.

The pay for all the company staff has kept pace with the wage scale of the Kuwait State as also the neighboring countries. There has never been a strike of company employees. The company has instigated a thrift scheme and leaving benefit scheme for its payroll employees. Other benefits include a weekly paid rest day, housing allowance, special allowances for shift workers, annual paid vacations, paid pilgrimage leave for all Muslims with four years of service, once during their service with the company, subsidized meals in the company's canteens, and free medical treatment.

Married payroll employees with families domiciled in Kuwait, and single payroll employees of Kuwait nationality who are the sole support of legal dependents, receive a daily living allowance varying according to job grade from 94 cents to $1.54, while all other single payroll employees receive from 52 cents to 88 cents. Rents charged by the company for company built housing are kept within the limits of these living allowances.

All company employees of whatever nationality, color or creed are provided with recreation facilities, swimming pools and clubs. Furthermore, Kuwait Oil Co. has built several Muslim mosques, a Catholic and a Protestant church at Ahmadi for its employees and their families.

While on the subject of personnel, it seems advisable to say a few words about the British and American numbers which make up the local staff of the Company in Kuwait. Before the war, the General Manager of Kuwait Oil Co. was British and so were most of the department heads except in the geological and drilling department—and there was no particular friction between the international groups. After the war, the owning companies urged, and the Ruler agreed, that the operating company should be headed up by an American.

Accordingly, Thomas Patrick, a big-handed, country-boy type of petroleum engineer from Texas was chosen to be General Manager. Also, the drilling superintendent, the chief geologist and most of the well drillers were Americans, but the bulk of the European expatriates were British. When Patrick died in 1947, he was succeeded by another American (born in Texas, but with a lot of administrative experience in Venezuela), namely, Leland T. Jordan.[167] Under his direction most of Kuwait Oil local development has occurred.

The Americans in the Kuwait Oil local organization probably today number less than 40 against some 700 British. However, the staff work is very harmonious, all things considered, and the ruler is apparently pleased to have at least token American representation in the top staff of "his company."

HOUSING AND AMENITIES

After World War II, when oil operations were again resumed in Kuwait, the company was faced with the necessity of selecting a site for a permanent camp and of laying out a township plan for the location of employees homes of several categories, recreational centers, office buildings, hospitals, schools, churches, mosques, commissaries, bakeries, cinemas, industrial shops, warehouses and material yards, ice plants, laundries, fire stations, and in fact every facility customarily found in a small western city

167. "The General Manager of the Kuwait Oil Co. is L. T. Jordan from Texas. He commands the love, trust and admiration of every Arab in Kuwait, from the ruler down to the humblest Badawi in the land. The straightest man in the country they call him." From *Kuwait and Her Neighbours* by Colonel H. R. P. Dickson, George Allen and Unwin Ltd., London, 1956, p. 579.

In 1958, Sir Bernard Burrows, K.C.M.G., British Political Resident for the Persian Gulf, in the name of Her Majesty, presented L. T. Jordan in Kuwait with the Honorary C.B.E.—a very unusual and distinguished honor to be accorded to an American.

On October 16, 1961, in the British Embassy in Kuwait, the British Charge d'Affaires, A. K. Rothnie, in the presence of His Highness Shaikh Abdullah al Salim al Sabah— Amir of the State of Kuwait—officially advised Leland T. Jordan that Her Majesty, The Queen of England, had appointed him "Honorary Knight Commander of the Most Excellent Order of the British Empire," in recognition of his services in Kuwait.

L. T. Jordan retired from active service with Kuwait Oil Co. in Kuwait in November, 1961.

of say, 25,000 population. This was a major project requiring considerable imagination and foresight.

The only asset available to this township scheme was an almost unlimited area of treeless, unpopulated, sandy desert situated on a ridge rising up to an elevation of nearly 400 feet. So gradual was this rise from the Persian Gulf four miles distant, that the intervening area appears almost flat.

The site chosen for the company's headquarters and general camp was on this ridge some 22 miles south of Kuwait town and about six miles from the oil fields at Burgan and Magwa, lying to the west and north respectively. This site was named Ahmadi in honor of the then Ruler Shaikh Ahmadi.

The oil port to the east of Ahmadi was originally called Fahahil, after a little village on the nearby coast, but later the name of the port was changed to Mina al-Ahmadi (Ahmad's port), also in honor of the Ruler.

Other than space, elevation and convenient location with respect to the oil fields, the oil port and to Kuwait town, there was nothing else to commend this town site. No water (either fresh or brackish), no electricity, no sewerage, no telephone or telegraph, no grass or trees, no interesting topography, no roads to anywhere, no people—nothing but a lovely view of the sparkling blue waters of the Persian Gulf to the east.

Ahmadi today is a desert show place with broad, paved, tree-lined streets, and all the conveniences of a modern small city in the plains area of the United States. There are homes with lawns and gardens for the families of the British and American staff, homes for the families of the Indian and Pakistan staff and homes for Arab workers and their families. These latter homes are mostly built of brick. All are supplied with electricity, gas, water and fans and all have excellent bathing and washing facilities.

Most of the homes for the staff employees are cooled in the

summer months and heated in the winter months by circulating waters from a central system.

All homes at Ahmadi are within walking distances of shopping centers, movies, schools, mosques and churches, post office, commissary, clinics and offices and industrial buildings. However, because of the climate, company cars and busses are available to carry the employees from their homes to and from their places of work and to carry the children to and from the several schools.

Ahmadi is a tribute to the combined skills and thinking of the mixed international oil group, from management on down to the common laborer. Ahmadi has been built in the best Arab tradition, tailored to modern concept.

In the last few years, the Company has encouraged its Kuwaiti staff to build its own homes. To further this aim a Home Ownership Scheme has been introduced to assist its Arab employees in building houses to their own specifications and in areas of their choosing. The company assists through long term, low interest financing for 50 per cent of the cost. The balance of the cost is absorbed by the company when the employee has repaid his loan.

As respects the expatriate employees:

The Company provides modern facilities designed to make life pleasant in the heat and humidity of the Gulf climate. The houses are attractive in appearance and design, and equipped with all modern requirements. A supply of brackish water is provided for the irrigation of gardens which surround the houses, and which bloom with oleanders and other flowering shrubs and many varieties of annual flowers in the winter and early spring. What was formerly a monotonous desert has now been transformed into an attractive settlement of white walled bungalows, treelined avenues, and gay gardens on a rising slope overlooking the sea.[168]

In addition, the company provides well-equipped co-educational schools for the children of its expatriate employees, including the Indian—Pakistani group. In 1954, schools for Arab boys and girls, staffed and administered by the State Educational Department, were opened in buildings provided by the company.

Kuwait Oil Co.'s medical service for all its employees and their families was initiated in 1947 in Kuwait town. In July, 1948, the hospital was moved from town to Magwa, closer to the company's development in the Burgan area. The Magwa hospital grew to 254 beds and 26 childrens' cots—complete with a families annex, isolation block, maternity unit, two surgical theaters, X-ray, physiotherapy and eye departments, a pathological laboratory, administrative offices and two kitchens.

Coincidently with the growth of the Magwa medical service, field clinics were established at Wara, Mina-al-Ahmadi and at Ahmadi. But eventually these facilities were outgrown and in 1957 Kuwait Oil Co. decided to construct a thoroughly modern hospital at Ahmadi, where the company's main office and shops were located and where the bulk of the employees were housed with their families.

The new 200-bed "Southwell Hospital," dedicated on April 27, 1960 by Sir Philip Southwell (Managing Director of Kuwait Oil Co., Ltd., 1946-1959), is located in an enclosed area of about 40 acres, near the company's administrative building at Ahmadi. This completely air-conditioned hospital is the last word in design, architecture and facilities. The Southwell Hospital and the several company out-clinics are presently staffed by

168. From *The Story of Kuwait* by Kuwait Oil Company Ltd., London, January 1957, p. 46.

205 doctors, nurses and other trained personnel.[169] Twenty-four hour air-conditioned ambulance service is maintained by the company between the field operations and Ahmadi.

The company also maintains an Industrial Health Division— preventative medicine, food inspection, pest control, check ups for industrial hazards and the like.

BUSINESS INTEGRATION

As previously mentioned, Kuwait Oil Co., Ltd. is jointly owned by British Petroleum Co. and Gulf Oil Corp. Both of these companies have had long years of experience in foreign oil operations—the British side more particularly in Iran and Iraq and the American side principally in Mexico and South America. These international oil companies are conscious of the necessity of providing their overseas workmen with decent houses and modern amenities, medical care and school facilities, as well as a sound wage scale with fringe benefits to encourage thrift and savings, pension plans and the like. In addition, they also realize it is important to make the nonemployee citizen of the country in which the company is operating, feel that he, too, has a stake in the industry's future.

In Kuwait the Anglo-American oil interests have already taken some steps in the direction of integrating the Kuwaitis into the business of the local oil industry. This policy of business integration in Kuwait is so new and novel that there is no definite pattern of approach, or of how far the oil company can go without running afoul of private enterprise or state policies.

At the onset of oil development in Kuwait, there were no locally competent contractors capable of financing or executing any major construction program. Consequently, foreign contractors with foreign technicians were employed to build build-

169. *Southwell Hospital*, An account of Kuwait Oil Company's hospital and the planning and construction of the Southwell Hospital opened on April 27, 1960 published by Kuwait Oil Co., London, 1960.

ings, steel tankage, gathering centers, roads, pipe lines, etc. But the company has persisted in training personnel and has encouraged the Arab to organize and to equip for contract work in all fields of construction. Progress was made from the start, largely by trial and error. Now, practically all construction of all kinds in the oil fields and camps in Kuwait is performed, expeditiously and well, by private Arab contractors.

For the most part, transportation and trucking has also now been contracted to Kuwaiti contractors—sometimes initially financed by the oil company. In some cases, these contractors were former company employees.

Another step in this integration policy was to farm-out under contract to nonemployees, some of the services provided by the Company. This farm-out system includes laundry, ice, garbage disposal, and some retail shops—many of these facilities were originally built by the Company on Company property.

Home ownership for its Arab employees is now being pressed by the Kuwait Oil Co. This is another move in the direction of avoiding patronage.

One Kuwaiti-owned company has built several oil tank ships which are now chartered by the oil companies operating in Kuwait.

It has been the practice of the local Kuwait Oil Co. management for several years past to hold get-togethers with these Arab contractors at a company dinner at least once a year. These meetings have been productive of considerable good will and better understanding.

Kuwait Oil Co. had felt for some years past that this policy of business integration would be materially enhanced by disposing of its retail oil products distribution stations in Kuwait to the State or the Kuwaiti public. The proposal was made to the ruler but was not immediately acted upon. However, as discussed earlier under "Refinery and Local Marketing," Kuwait Oil Co.'s retail distribution facilities in Kuwait were transferred to the

Kuwait National Petroleum Co.—the stock of which is presently held 60 per cent by the State and the balance by Kuwait nationals.

There are presently two Kuwaiti Directors on the Board of the Kuwait Oil Co., Ltd., namely Feisel Mansour Mazidi and Mahmoud Khalid al Adassani.

"As a result of the Company's integration policy no less than $47 million (47.6 million dollars) was injected into the local economy in 1958. This considerable sum was made up as follows:

	Pounds Sterling	Dollar Equivalent
Wages and Salaries	£ 5,813,000	$16,276,400
Payments to Contractors	6,422,000	17,981,600
Purchase of Local Supplies	2,872,000	8,041,600
Other Expenditures	1,957,000	5,479,600
	£17,064,000	$47,779,200

It should be emphasized that this considerable sum is over and above the oil revenues which accrue direct to the state."[170]

In a small country such as Kuwait, where oil is the predominant source of national income as well as the principle source of livelihood for such a large number of Kuwaitis, directly and indirectly, the people generally understand that anything which tends to work a hardship on their indigenous oil industry will eventually, if not at once, work a hardship on their pocketbook.

KUWAIT'S WATER

From the very beginning, the Kuwait Oil Co. was conscious that an indigenous, ample supply of potable water was con-

170. *An Outline of the Activities of the Kuwait Oil Company*, by Kuwait Oil Co. Ltd., London, December, 1959, p. 7. (The author has inserted the Dollar Equivalents in this quotation).

sidered more important than oil by the Kuwaiti of both town and desert. Except for a meager supply of potable water from a relatively few shallow wells of rain water which collected in natural depressions, water for domestic purposes was brought in wooden tanks by sailboal from the Shatt-al-Arab in Iraq and delivered into cisterns and tanks on shore near the docks in Kuwait town.

For this impelling reason the company embarked on a systematic and intensive search for an underground source of potable water very shortly after it started drilling for oil. Water experts were brought in from the United States. These experts combed the entire country, aided by the company geologists and geophysicists. In every potential area, sites were selected for water well drilling. Soon the program of water well drilling got under way with special imported equipment.

Since 1945, more than 70 water wells have been drilled— almost all at the oil company's expense. Exploratory borings were scattered all over the Shaikhdom of Kuwait. Most of these tests found only brackish water—too full of mineral salts for consumption by either man or beast. However, at Abduliyah, roughly 16 miles west of the Burgan oil field, there was found to be a supply of brackish water sufficiently low in mineral salts to be potable for sheep, goats and camels. Even the nomads smacked their lips over this water, but the town folks and Europeans could only take it when diluted with either distilled water or water from the Shatt-al-Arab. Thus, at Abduliyah, a State operated water station was established.

There are now some 26 water wells at this station, with steel tankage for storage and open troughs for the nomad and his flocks. The wells are about 550 feet deep, each equipped with an electro-submersible centrifugal pump. Water from this station is pumped through pipe lines to the oil camps at Ahmadi and on to Shuwaikh where the State stores and dispenses this water to the public in Kuwait town.

A smaller supply of semipotable brackish water was found at Salabiyah, some eight miles southwest of Kuwait town where four wells are currently producing. This water also is piped into Shuwaikh.

Another supply of semipotable brackish water—suitable for use in rotary oil well drilling, has been found in recent years in the Raudhatain area in northern Kuwait. As yet this water is not being delivered into Kuwait town.

The sequel to this story of the search for potable water in Kuwait is also interesting. Kuwait Oil Co. found it both difficult and costly to transport Shatt al-Arab water to Ahmadi— the main oil camp and general office of the company—in quantities necessary to satisfy its staff and their families. This problem was overcome by installing at Mina al-Ahmadi, a sea water distillation plant with a daily capacity of 800,000 imperial gallons daily. This proved to be an entirely satisfactory and low cost operation, since there was readily available a more than adequate supply of fuel in the form of waste gas from the oil field separators. According to the engineers, this water installation at Mina al-Ahmadi was one of the largest plants of its kind in the world when put into operation.

For some time the company furnished a considerable amount of this water to Kuwait town by pipe line—gratis—until the State's own distillation plant could be designed and installed at Shuwaikh. Now, the State's water distillation plant near Kuwait town is by far the biggest installation of its kind in the world.[171] This great plant and the huge electric power plant alongside— both State built and operated—are fueled with waste gas from the oil fields some 25 miles to the south.

Because the Amir has felt that his town people should not become too accustomed to the use of distilled water for their

171. The state's water distillation plant now has a daily capacity of more than five million gallons. Plans are being considered to increase the capacity still further.

drinking and cooking, he insisted that the distilled water be mixed with the brackish water from the inland wells, before being distributed to the public. Furthermore, in order to discourage the flagrant waste of this mixed potable water, the Ruler decided against immediately piping this water into the homes, shops and offices throughout Kuwait town. Instead, for the most part, the water has been piped to large elevated steel tanks erected at various places in town, from where the water is carted by tank trucks to many central watering points and from there it is dispensed to the people in tins and goat skins by donkeys and hand carts.

During 1960, pipes were laid in two areas of Kuwait town for direct delivery of water to homes and other buildings. No doubt this delivery scheme will be further extended in due course.

No longer is Shatt al-Arab water imported. There is now even enough of the local supply of mixed brackish and fresh water to irrigate small flower and vegetable gardens in and around Kuwait town. Some of the gardens are quite beautiful with all sorts of flowers, shrubs, vines, trees and in a few places, lawns, during the cool months. Fresh water has changed the looks of the entire community, both the landscape and the people.

The Kuwaitis' inspiration to make gardens did not stem entirely from having a supply of sweet water. Arabs love color, flowers, trees and vegetables. For centuries, whenever the infrequent light rains fell, the Arab attempted to grow things in the desert sands. Around the oasis, where there is a water supply of sorts the year around, the Arab has lifted water from his wells in goat skins—usually brought to the surface by camels or donkeys pulling on the ropes running over shrieking wood pulleys hung on a crossbar. This water was allowed to run off in shallow ditches to irrigate tiny fields of grain and vegetables. At the west end of Kuwait Bay, Jahra is the principal oasis in Kuwait. However, in this modern age, the gasoline motor has largely replaced camel and donkey power for lifting water from hand-dug wells.

As soon as the oil company's supply of brackish water became adequate, it established an experimental garden and nursery at Ahmadi. There it was demonstrated that with adequate fertilizer and brackish water, flowers and fruit trees, palms and Australian pines could grow and flourish in Kuwait during the cool months and would even carry over through the intense heat of the summer months.

This Ahmadi garden became a show place for the people of Kuwait as well as the company staff. Thousands of Kuwaitis flocked to this garden to see the color, smell the fragrance and bask in the cool shade of the trees on every feast day and Fridays, (the Muslim day of rest). It was a practical demonstration which the Arab could understand and which he could duplicate. And the Kuwaiti did just that—in town and village and palace—wherever there was a patch of ground that could be protected from the searing desert wind-blown sands and where semipotable water and fertilizer were available.

Thus, Anglo-American ingenuity and know-how brought to Kuwait in addition to oil, two of the great necessities of desert life—water and natural beauty—from a seemingly sterile soil.

Kuwait—Before and After Oil

Nowhere else in this world has so much revenue from a natural resource accrued to such a small State with so small a population in so few years. Such is the situation in Kuwait, Arabia—a country of only some 6,000 square miles of territory, with less than 322,000 population of all nationalities, with revenues from oil now currently said to be in the order of $450 million annually. The story of Kuwait's rebirth since oil was discovered beneath her desert sands, reads like a fairy tale.

Before

Less than 30 years ago life in Kuwait town and the villages in the oasis and along the shore of the Bay and Persian Gulf went on much as it had for centuries past. In the 1930's the population of Kuwait town numbered about 60,000.

In the winter months when the meager rains came, Kuwaiti nomads and their nomad neighbors from the north roamed the hinterland seeking pasturage for their flocks. In town, the merchants bartered and sold their imported goods for the caravans heading into the interior or Arabia while the shipbuilders' guild was busy building booms, bagalas and sambuks (staunch wooden sailboats sometimes collectively called by Europeans, "dhows").

In the summer months, as the waters of the Gulf warmed up, the great Kuwait pearling fleet, numbering as many as 600 vessels put to sea with divers to seek the famous Persian Gulf natural pearls to be found off the banks of the Bahrain Islands.

During all seasons of the year there were always a score or more boats casting their nets or line-fishing in the bay or out in the Gulf for the excellent eating fish of that area.

Five times a day all work stopped while the devote Muslim said his prayers wherever he might be.

During the midday, winter and summer, the town folks and villagers kept indoors as much as possible. Shops closed and dogs slept in the dirt streets. During the early morning and late afternoon folks bargained for foodstuffs and garments in the Suq (bazaar), while lazy donkeys plodded back and forth with dripping goat skins of water hung over their backs. Camels ambled down the thoroughfare or sprawled lazily, chewing their cuds.

At dusk the flocks of goats and sheep, which had been out nibbling at the tracery of green stuff in the desert, were driven back into town. As the flocks made their way down the main street, one or several animals would turn off to their master's house without any visible signal or audible sound. This was always an interesting sight to watch.

As night fell, kerosene lamps and candles were lit. Soon all business suspended for the day. Shutters were put up on many of the shops and the merchants wended their way through the black night to their adobe dwellings and their families. By nine in the evening the city streets were dark and deserted. The only sounds of life came muted onto the air from behind closed doors and high mud walls—the sound of babies crying, adults laughing, sheep softly bleating, a donkey braying, camels hissing and grunting, maybe dogs barking, a string instrument twanging or perhaps the discordant sound of a radio or gramaphone—all blending into a harmony of peaceful living.

In Kuwait town there were no paved streets before 1946 except one lane, less than two miles long, stretching from the edge of town across vacant lands to Dasman Palace on the bay front where the Amir lived. This piece of highway had been surfaced with natural oil-impregnated sands from Burgan. All the other streets of the town were dirt, dry and dusty most of the year, but a muddy morass when a heavy rain came, which was seldom. The streets were narrow and lined with low, flat-topped buildings, for the most part constructed of mud bricks on coral foundations. The only stone or cement stucco buildings were a few business houses, several government buildings and the homes of various members of the ruling family.

As in most Arab communities, family life in Kuwait was lived behind walls and closed doors. Such homes had no windows on the street side and no visible gardens. The passer-by saw only bare walls with closed doors. Only in the market place were there any sidewalks, street windows or awnings.

On a cold day, the men from the desert often squatted with their backs against the sunny side of a wall for warmth, their woolen abbas bundled up to their eyes, or they might sit beside a brazier of coals in the coffee shop or bazaar, smoking their bubbling water pipes or gossiping with friends.

Fuel for heating and cooking was either kerosene, camel dung, or so-called camel thorn.[172]

In those "before oil" days, the only Arab schools in Kuwait were those in which boys were taught to read and study the Quran (Koran). There were no schools for girls. The American Arabian Mission had established a small hospital in Kuwait town in 1911 and 20 years later, Shaikh Ahmad had set up a State hospital. Even two hospitals, such as they were, could not begin to cope with the health, disease and accident problems of this growing community.

No unveiled women are to be seen on the streets of Kuwait. Thirty years ago a European man never saw an unveiled Kuwaiti woman, not even in the house of his closest Arab friend. When a Kuwaiti woman went outside the harem to shop in town, she was covered from the crown of her head to the ground by a thin black woolen or cotton garment—she could see through but her features could not be seen. Only the young Muslim girls, not yet in purdah, were to be seen in public unveiled.

In those days, the water front of Kuwait town was a thrilling

172. Camel thorn is a perennial thorny bush found over a large area of coastal Arabia. Usually, it grows in isolated clumps, seldom over two feet high. This bush has long woody roots. It is gathered in bundles and brought into town on donkeys or camels. It is amusing to see a small donkey laden down with camel thorn headed across the desert toward town—the viewer first sees an Arab alongside a mound of brush, then on closer inspection one can see the man is walking and the brush heap is also moving and finally, when close up, one sees four tiny feet plodding along under the brush and possibly also glimpses a bit of an animal's nose. Otherwise, the little donkey is completely enveloped by camel thorn. In cutting this brush, the gatherer usually pulls or digs out the roots and takes the whole plant. As a result, over the years the top soil—which is a thin clay-sand mixture along coastal Kuwait—becomes disturbed and allows the loose sand below to become wind-borne.

sight and a medley of sound. Sailing ships anchored offshore, lightening their cargoes of timber, spices, cloth, foodstuff and miscellanea. Fishing boats going and coming. Vessels beached for caulking and cleaning, new dhows being shaped on crude ways in front of the boat builder's yard. Arab porters, grunting and cursing and staggering under the mountain of goods piled on their backs as they made their way from the quay to the master's shop. Among this motley of nationalities were many black men from Africa—many of whom had been brought to Kuwait as slaves and while now ostensibly free—remained in this bustling port, the biggest and best anchorage anywhere on the Arabian mainland.

Motor cars and trucks were a rarity. The sight of one in Kuwait town would immediately draw a crowd. Even four-wheeled carts, carriages and wagons were seldom seen. Virtually all goods were transported in town on the backs of camels, donkeys and men. The bazaar streets, between shops, were so narrow that no wheeled vehicle could possibly get through the throng, much less pass another vehicle.

The suq (bazaar) covered many square blocks. Literally, it was a maze of alleys wandering past the shops of the tailor, iron monger, pearl dealer, sandal maker, silver and gold smiths, brass and copper workers, tanner, spice and herb merchants, vegetable and grain mart; dealers in colorful cloth for women; spinners of cotton, wool and metallic thread, shops vending saddlery for camels and donkeys, and many other stalls offering all manner of things necessary and luxurious to Arab living.

In one section, trained falcons were for sale. In another section, one could buy fish, poultry and mutton. The Badu (Badawi, Bedouin or Beduin) from the desert, jostled the city dweller as they thronged through the market place. It was a place of color and odors—never to be forgotten by the European.

Kuwait town of the 1930's was entirely enclosed on the land side with a 14-foot wall, pierced by four huge gates. This wall, some four and one-half miles long was built in 1919 as a defense against the warring Ikhwan from Arabia. It stretched in an arc from coast to coast. Close in to the city wall nestled the suburb of Shuwaikh—elsewhere on the land side was only the desert.

After

By 1937, it is estimated that the population of Kuwait was about 75,000.

No sooner had Kuwait's oil revenues begun to assume sizeable proportions—say along in 1947-1948—than the Amir, Shaikh Ahmad al Jabir, began to make plans for public improvements in the town and country for the benefit of the people.

The oil development boomed construction of all kinds and, since there was a paucity of skilled labor and not even enough common labor, foreigners of all nationalities flocked in. As the result, the city's population doubled almost overnight. The town was bursting at the seams. There were no hotels for non-Arabs, no living quarters for Europeans, insufficient medical facilities, and no restaurant serving food except Arab cooking.

The local government was reorganized to provide for setting up finance, education, public works, security, courts, customs and post office as separate departments each headed by members of the Ruling Family and each with its staff of foreign experts and advisers. Out of the council of ministers came the idea of a welfare state—the state would plow back some of the oil revenues for the benefit of the people and at the same time, would invest part of the oil revenues in British bonds for the benefit of posterity.

Shaikh Abdullah al Salim, who was chosen to succeed Shaikh Ahmad as Amir upon the latter's death in 1950, effectively put into motion the various steps necessary to implement this bold and unusual (certainly unusual in Arab tradition) Welfare State.

What has been done in Kuwait generally and in Kuwait

town in particular during the elapsed ten years has amazed the world. Nothing like it has happened elsewhere in our time.

The town planners laid out a whole new city to rise on the foundation of the old. Bulldozers plowed off the fronts of the mud brick buildings lining the main streets and road graders hacked out four-lane divided boulevards through town in several directions. New broad avenues circles the city inside the city wall. All streets in due course were paved with asphalt. Traffic lights and traffic police were installed at intersections. Trees were planted along some of the streets. In the center of town was created a great circle—sort of commons.

An ordinance required all new buildings to be constructed of stone, brick or cement block. Stores with huge plate glass windows appeared where only little shops had been before.

With the advent of new business, pearling and shipbuilding waned—all skilled and semiskilled Kuwaiti labor was needed for the state's construction program.

The long range city plan which had been envisaged and set in motion by Shaikh Ahmad and then further implemented by Shaikh Abdullah, may be roughly divided into three major schemes—the first, to convert the old town within the walls into a modern commercial city; the second, to create eight self-contained residential sections for some 50,000 people outside the walls (demolished in 1958, except for the memorable gates) each with their own mosques, primary schools, clinics, light industries, shop and civic centers, with two secondary schools for each four neighborhood sections (this housing scheme included a State project to build some 2,500 homes for people of limited means and to distribute to Kuwaitis another 4,000 plots on which they can build their own homes).

The third phase consisted of a new port with adequate piers at which medium draught freight vessels could dock, also Port Administration buildings, transit sheds and covered storage at dockside. In addition, areas outside the old walls were allocated to industrial purposes and public utilities. By 1962, much of this ambitious city plan had been accomplished.

Coincidentally, more than 300 miles of paved roads have been constructed by the State inside and outside of Kuwait town. New trunk roads circle the town and extend along the coast—connecting all the important villages as far south as Mina al-Ahmadi and west about 20 miles to Jahra (the latter road is being extended 75 miles northward to the Iraq border). This State road system connects with the paved highways into the interior, originally constructed by the oil company.

Since 1946, the number of motor vehicles operating in Kuwait has increased from a few score to well over 30,000. It is becoming increasingly rare to see a camel caravan inside the "old" city and, in fact, caravans are now seldom seen in the nearby desert.

Kuwait is justly proud of its educational program and the number and perfection of design and equipment of its schools. There are 76 State Schools in Kuwait where education is provided free of charge for boys and girls from the kindergarten to the secondary level. School meals, served from a central kitchen,[173] and clothing are also provided free. Altogether the number of pupils is approximately 31,000, of whom 20,000 are boys and 11,000 girls. The total number of teachers is 1,048 male and 660 female, including Kuwaitis, Palestinians, Egyptians and Iraqis.

173. In February, 1959, the author and his wife visited this central kitchen in Kuwait town where meals—hot and cold—are prepared. It was designed by Lyons of London. We were told that this kitchen currently prepares and distributes in insulated containers more than 70,000 meals each school day to 74 schools. The 400-employee kitchen bakery turns out 2,500 loaves of bread daily for sandwiches and butchers 50 to 60 sheep daily for meat. The Political Agent in Kuwait told the author that the cost to Kuwait State per student per year for all school services was presently $2,240.

All boys who pass the secondary level are entitled to free university training or its equivalent outside Kuwait, either in Egyptian or Lebanese universities or in the U.K. or U.S.A. The number of boys and girls receiving higher education abroad is at present 400, of whom 180 are in the U.K. and 60 in the U.S.A. The State also maintains primary schools at Bombay and Karachi, and at Sharjah and Ras al Khaima in the Gulf.

Especially noteworthy is the Secondary School at Shuwaikh—the future University of Kuwait. At present it provides education for 855 boys between 14 and 18 years old. There is nothing like it elsewhere in the Middle East. Set on spacious grounds, fronting on Kuwait Bay, this magnificent monument to the future generations rises up both grand and bold. The many buildings of pleasing design are all of the most modern construction—spacious, airy, well-lighted and appropriate. Included in this superb layout is a main central classroom block, with a fine assembly theater seating 2,000, six boarding houses (each designed for 200 boys), some 50 fine homes for the faculty, a beautiful mosque, a library and study hall, dining hall, laboratories, art school, gymnasium, stadium, large swimming pools, tennis courts and a football ground. Students from other Arab countries are welcome and some have enrolled from as far away as Morocco.

Among the many new State Schools is the "Shuwaikh Technical School" for boys desiring to study engineering and technical subjects, a Commercial School for 1,025 pupils in Kuwait town, also schools for blind boys and girls and a religious institute with 500 students.

Kuwait is also famous for its comprehensive and up-to-date medical services. Treatment is free to all the population whether Arabs or foreigners. There are at present two general hospitals, a T.B. sanatorium and mental hospitals.

Construction has started on a new 500-bed hospital (the Sabah Hospital) at Shuwaikh, which will cost £3 million ($8,400,000). A second T.B. sanatorium of 300 beds and a hospital for infectious diseases are also planned. There are 21 State clinics, with emergency beds, in Kuwait town and outlying villages.

The State employs a large staff of doctors including Palestinian, British, Iraqi and Egyptian. There are also doctors in private practice in the U.K. and elsewhere.[174]

In addition to the State's several hospitals and extensive medical service there is also in Kuwait town the 65-bed American Mission hospital and at Ahmadi the Kuwait Oil Co.'s new modern 200-bed Southwell Hospital with its outlying clinics.

Kuwait is now the medical center of the Middle East—that is, east of Cairo and Beirut.

As mentioned, the State has made available to its people such a supply of distilled (5 million gallons daily) and brackish (200,000 gallons daily) water that it is no longer necessary to import potable water from the Shatt al-Arab. However, the present supply of potable water is not adequate for any extensive or general irrigation purposes or even for unlimited domestic purposes either in Kuwait town or its environs. To alleviate this situation, a scheme has been under consideration for some time for bringing water to Kuwait from the Shatt al-Arab or near Basra—a distance of around 150 miles—by either big-inch pipe line or canal or a combination of both. Although the first survey was made in 1954, the project has not yet been started because agreement remains to be secured with Iraq. It is estimated it will cost about $6 million to deliver 75 million gallons onto the desert lands of Kuwait.

174. "The Story of Kuwait," by Kuwait Oil Company, Ltd., revised edition, London, December, 1959, p. 68, 69 and 70.

Construction started in 1960 on a new international airport on a site about seven miles south of Kuwait town adjoining the Kuwait-Ahmadi road. This airport will be complete in every way and will be capable of handling the biggest commercial aircraft.

In addition to all the State plans for the betterment of Kuwait and her people, private enterprise has done much to improve the local economy and living standards. Kuwaiti capital, either alone or in conjunction with some partial State financing has built up a large soft drink industry (nine plants), created a gas utilization company, built and put in service a large oil-tank vessel, set up tile making and precast concrete plants, oxygen plants, laundries, wrought iron and furniture works, motor engineering shops, and three new movies each seating 2,000. It has also established the well organized Kuwait National Bank, and has constructed many new modern steel-concrete office buildings and mercantile buildings, as well as hundreds of private family homes.[175]

During the last 10 years, not only has Kuwait taken on a new look physically both in town and outside but so, too, has the outlook of the people changed. The customs and culture of the Kuwaiti have suddenly felt the impact of the Western World. No longer does Kuwaiti life depend upon camels, sheep, pearls, shipbuilding and merchandising. Now, the Kuwaiti import the very best of the outside world's products, see how other people live, either on the TV screen or by travel, and witness first-hand the evolution of business and society stemming from education, better health and general prosperity. All this since oil.

According to the first official census which was taken in 1957, the population of Kuwait was recorded at 206,117. However,

175. During 1960 the Kuwait Commercial Bank was authorized.

the census taken in the spring of 1961 records a total population of 321,621 of which 96,860 live in Kuwait town. The population in the "suburbs" has increased from 86,705 in 1957 to 130,374 in 1961. About 100,000 Kuwait folk live in small villages along the coast, in the Mina-al-Ahmadi area, in Ahmadi, in and around the drilling camps and in the desert. Perhaps some two-thirds or more are Kuwaitis and the rest foreigners—Pakistanis, Palestineans, Arabs, Syrians, Iraqis, Persians, Egyptians (mostly teachers in the schools), several hundred Europeans (some employed by the state or working for private enterprise on construction work and some working for the oil company) and probably less than 75 Americans, all told, including the staff of the American Consulate, the staff of the Arabian Mission and the staff of the oil companies.

The Kuwait government has not officially released figures as to its annual revenue from oil; however, an estimate made by a staff writer to the Economist Intelligence Unit and published in the *Petroleum Times* (London), December 1 and 15, 1961, gave the Kuwait oil income in 1960 as $440 million. It may be guessed that it was somewhat more than that in 1961.

For some years past the Kuwait authorities have been investing a portion of these revenues and other income overseas. At the end of 1961 it was estimated that Kuwait's overseas holdings would approximate $672 million. Such investments are held in Britain, the United States, Japan, Norway, Switzerland, Germany, Egypt, the Lebanon and Jordan—probably the biggest portion is in sterling.

An investment committee of Kuwait's Ministry of Finance controls the disposition of these overseas investments. The current annual income from Kuwaits overseas holdings is believed to be about $33.6 million.

Kuwait's annual revenue from oil and other income is believed to be the biggest per capita of any country in the world.

COVETED KUWAIT—A POSTSCRIPT[177]

Premier Abdul Karim Kassem's announcement to the press in Baghdad on June 25, 1961, that Kuwait was considered an "intregal part" of Iraq, shocked the Middle East and the world. That public announcement was all the more startling since it came only six days after Britain had relinquished her 62-year-old "protection agreement" with Kuwait, and officially recognized Kuwait's full independence and sovereignty.

Premier Kassem claims that Kuwait was part of the Province of Basra when Iraq was a component of the Turkish Empire and that Shaikh Mubarak's signature on the treaty of protection, executed with the British January 23, 1899, had been "forged." On this premise, Kassem further stated that a decree would be issued shortly appointing the present Ruler of Kuwait, H. H. Shaikh Sir Abdulla al Salim al Sabah, as Governor of the Kuwait district of Iraq.

Although the Iraq government denied that it would use military force to enforce its jurisdictional claims over Kuwait territory, there were persistent rumors that Iraqi troops were mobilizing along the Kuwait frontier. The possibility of war loomed ominously in the Persian Gulf area. Obviously Kuwait's few-hundred-strong police force and border guards would be no match for the well armed, well trained, (70,000-80,000) Iraqi troops.

Against this possible threat of force from Iraq the Amir of Kuwait promptly sought help from Britain under the provision of the new "letters of friendship" exchanged by the British and Kuwait authorities on June 19, 1961—the day the 1899 protection agreement was annulled. The British responded at once to Kuwait's plea for help. On July 1, an advance contingent of

177. Because of the considerable world wide newspaper coverage devoted to the Iraq-Kuwait affair during this past summer the author is constrained to add this personal postscript to the foregoing Kuwait text.

British soldiers landed in Kuwait, preceded by a wing of Royal Air Force fighter planes. Several British naval units were reported enroute. Some troops from friendly Saudi Arabia also arrived at Kuwait's request.

Coincidentally with Shaikh Abdullah's call on Britain and Saudi Arabia for military aid, the Kuwait government sent emissaries to Cairo in order to further Kuwait's petition for full membership in the Arab League and also dispatched a mission to New York City to plead its case before the United Nations.

On July 7, "The Soviet Union vetoed a British resolution aimed at winning United Nations recognition of Kuwait's new independence and deterring Iraq from claiming the neighboring state. A few seconds later, the Security Council rejected a rival resolution calling for the immediate withdrawal of British military forces from Kuwait. This proposal was sponsored by the United Arab Republic and supported by the Soviet Union and Iraq."[178] Many well informed persons consider that the UN's double negative action in the Iraq-Kuwait matter was, in fact, a diplomatic victory for Kuwait.

On July 20, the Arab League admitted Kuwait to full membership after the Iraqi delegation had walked out of the League's council. Shortly thereafter the League moved to organize an Arab force to replace the British troops in Kuwait.

By October 1, 1961, Arab League armed forces, said to number 4,000 had arrived in Kuwait and British troops were withdrawn as Britain had said they would be.

Within a matter of four months after Kuwait had been recognized by Britain as a fully independent and sovereign State, it had emerged free and strong from a barrage of publicity and diplomacy, such as few new nations have ever encountered and lived. However, it still remains to be seen whether

178. From article by Kathleen Teltsch, captioned "Soviet Veto Bars British UN Plan to Shield Kuwait," New York Times, July 8, 1961.

or not and when, Iraq will again press its jurisdictional claims over Kuwait territory.

Although not so stated by Kassem, it is generally believed that Iraq covets Kuwait primarily because of Kuwait's wealth in current assets, its enormous underground reserves of "liquid gold" and its splendid port facilities. Maybe Iraq wanted to stake out its claim to Kuwait before other contenders could move in. Whatever may have motivated Kassem to publicly declare Iraq's claim to Kuwait's territory at this time it will be of interest to some to examine the historic record with respect to certain aspects of Iraq's claim.

One noted English historian had this to say as respects the situation which obtained in the Persian Gulf area during most of the 19th century.

> Kuwait like other small states on the fringe of the far-flung Turkish Empire, often paid only nominal allegiance to the Sultan—the Shaikh sometimes recognized Turkish suzerainty by the payment of tribute, but there were times when these payments were discontinued and independence was almost complete.[179]

So far as now can be ascertained, Kuwait was never administered by the Turks—definitely not during the present century —although the Turkish flag was sometimes used before Kuwait adopted its own standard in 1913.

It was because of Shaikh Mubarak's fear of the Turks and other foreign agressors that he, as Ruler of Kuwait, signed the "protection agreement" with Great Britain on January 23, 1899. Kuwait history discloses that, Shaikh Mubarak had asked Great Britain for a protective agreement several times over a period of several years before he got it. But for that

179. Lockhart, Laurence, *Outline of the History of Kuwait*, Royal Central Asian Journal, Londan, July-October, 1947, p. 266.

treaty, there probably would be no Kuwait State today. For
more than 60 years the British stood firmly by that agreement
and successively repulsed the Turks, Russians, Germans and
other would-be aggressors in every attempt to gain control of
Kuwait's fine harbor—the best natural anchorage in the Persian
Gulf—and also discouraged the desert tribes of Arabia from
seizing Kuwait territory.

It is a matter of fact that on July 29, 1913, Great Britain
and Turkey concluded a convention which provided, inter alia:

> (1) recognition by Turkey of Great Britain's special treaty
> relationship with Kuwait; (2) the territories of the Shaikh,
> although nominally forming part of the Province of Baghdad,
> were to be autonomous; (3) the Shaikh was to have direct
> control over a limited area surrounding his capital and a
> sphere of influence extending some distance beyond its bor-
> ders; (4) Turkey would not extend the Baghdad Railway
> to the south of Basra without first obtaining Great Britain's
> consent.[180]

Owing to the outbreak of World War I this convention was
never ratified.

However valid may have been the Turks claim to Kuwait
before World War I, it does not necessarily follow that Iraq
has the same or similar claim.

The Germans and their Turkish allies lost World War I and
as a result the Turkish Empire was dismembered. Eventually
(San Remo, 1920) Mesopotamia was mandated to the British.
Soon thereafter Britain declared its intention to establish a
national government for this mandated territory. A plebiscite
was arranged, following the results of which Emir Feisal of
Syria was declared King of Iraq in mid-1921. The Kingdom of

---

180. Lockhart, Laurence, *Outline of the History of Kuwait,* Royal Central Asian Journal, London, July-October, 1947, p. 270.

Iraq, as then defined, did not embrace the present territory of Kuwait.

Seven years later Calouste Gulbenkian, sometimes referred to as the father of the Turkish Petroleum Co. (now the Iraq Petroleum Co.), insisted that his international corporate partners in Turkish Petroleum refrain from individual effort within the old Ottoman Empire territory as he knew it. This Ottoman Empire, as demarked by Gulbenkian with a "red line" on a large map of the Middle East, excluded Kuwait—but embraced all of the rest of the Arabian Peninsula, including Bahrain, all of Mesopotamia, the Levant States, Palestine and Transjordan. As Gulbenkian said in 1928, when he drew the red line,

That was the Ottoman Empire which I knew in 1914. And I ought to know. I was born in it, lived in it and served in it.[181]

It is significant that Gulbenkian—noted for his uncanny ability in international finance and politics and his "nose" for oil—should have excluded Kuwait from his recollection of the old Ottoman Empire, if, indeed, it was not a fact generally recognized.

The Kuwait of today—with its vast underground resources and its fine harbor—is truly an economic "pearl" of great price. But this tiny new state is presently defenseless against power politics and aggression unless protected from the covetous by its Western friends, the Arab League and the United Nations.

In closing this story about Kuwait, the author wishes to publicly acknowledge his great esteem and personal friendship for H. H. Shaikh Abdullah al Salim al Sabah, Amir of Kuwait, whose guiding hand and wisdom have brought a new era of peace and prosperity to his country and to his people.

181. Hewins, Ralph, *Mr. Five Per Cent*, Rinehart and Company, Inc., New York, 1958, p. 141.

7

Kuwait Neutral Zone

THE LANDWARD BOUNDARIES of the Shaikhdoms and Sultanates facing on the Persian Gulf, Gulf of Oman and Arabian Sea, for centuries past, were ill-defined and unmarked. It was not until the turn of this century that the great foreign powers began to interest themselves in the frontier problems of these small principalities. In fact, it was not until Ibn Saud began to consolidate, under one ruling head, the many tribes and nomadic clans of the Arabian Peninsula that these frontires' questions achieved more than local attention.

As of now, there still remain several disputed boundaries along the fringe of the Kingdom of Saudi Arabia.

It was in 1922 that Britain used her offices to determine, by amicable agreement, the boundaries of certain areas under dispute with Saudi Arabia along the frontiers of Iraq and Kuwait. At Uqair in Arabia a conference between Ibn Saud and representatives of Iraq and Kuwait met and compromised their differences—mostly at the expense of Kuwait. However, that agreement was duly signed (December 2, 1922) by the parties concerned and witnessed by Sir Percy Cox for the British government. Two politically Neutral Zones were established, one between Najd and Iraq, comprising approximately 1,500 square miles, and one between Najd and Kuwait, comprising about

2,000 square miles. These are known as the Iraq Neutral Zone and the Kuwait Neutral Zone, respectively. In each zone, Najd (now Saudi Arabia) had an undivided political and economic one-half interest. Nomadic tribes from both sides were to be permitted free access to these neutralized areas for grazing their flocks. Caravans were to be permitted to cross at will and none of the contracting parties was to erect forts within these zones. In this Uqair agreement Kuwait also lost a large slice of desert on its western front to the Najd.

For some years after this frontier arrangement Shaikh Ahmad still considered the whole of the Kuwait Neutral Zone to be part of his territory. He is said to have told Colonel H. R. P. Dickson, when Dickson was Political Agent in Kuwait, that, "He would never consent to go half shares with Ibn Saud in the granting of any oil concession."

On May 17, 1924, Ibn Saud granted to Eastern and General Syndicate, Ltd., an option for an oil concession over Saudi Arabia's undivided half of the Kuwait Neutral Zone. However, the Syndicate defaulted in its payments and did no work on the ground, so in due course, Ibn Saud declared the concession null and void—presumably this was after the Gulf companies had relinquished to the Syndicate its option rights to al-Hasa and the Kuwait Neutral Zone in 1932.

Ibn Saud granted his oil rights in the Kuwait and Iraq Neutral Zones to California Arabian Oil Co. on May 31, 1939, along with other areas in Arabia (being extensions to the original grant in 1933). However, the American company surrendered back to Saudi Arabia its Neutral Zone rights in 1948, in exchange for other oil concessions offshore.

The Burgan oil field in Kuwait had been put into production in mid-1946 and step-out drilling in that field rather indicated that the Burgan high or a similar up-fold logically might be expected in the underground of the Neutral Zone to the south. The interest of the oil fraternity was aroused over such prospects, and by 1947 approaches were being made to the respective owners—Kuwait and Saudi Arabia—by several internatonal oil companies. Among these interested companies were Amerada (with Seaboard and Continental), Superior, Sinclair, Shell and Gulf. Some of these companies were only interested in negotiating for the undivided half accruing to Kuwait; others, only in the undivided half accruing to Saudi Arabia and others appeared interested in both. For some reason, neither the Iraq Petroleum Co. nor Anglo-Iranian were openly interested and so far as known, did not actively compete for oil concession grants, either from Kuwait or Saudi Arabia.

Shaikh Ahmad of Kuwait in the spring of 1947, announced he would award an oil grant over his portion of the Neutral Zone mainland to the highest bidder. In July of that year, a new group of American oil companies, previously inexperienced in foreign operations, got together and organized the American Independent Oil Co. (subsequently better known as Aiminoil), under the sponsorship of Ralph K. Davies.[182] The original group consisted of Ashland Oil and Refining Co., Allied Oil Co., J. S. Abercrombie Co., Deep Rock Corp., Globe Oil and Refining Co., Hancock Oil Co., Signal Oil and Gas Co., Sunray Oil Co., Phillips Petroleum Co. and R. K. Davies—ten entities in all.

This group outbid all other parties who had been interested in acquiring Kuwait's undivided half interest in the mainland oil rights of the Kuwait Neutral Zone. Aiminoil was awarded this concession on June 28, 1948.

Aiminoil's concession terms were generally more favorable to the granting country than any which had been negotiated in the Middle East up to that time. The royalty was fixed at $2.50 per ton (about 35 cents a barrel), the down payment

182. Ralph K. Davies, formerly Vice President of Standard Oil Co. of California. During World War II, Ralph K. Davies was the able Deputy Petroleum Administrator for War, under the Secretary of the Interior, Harold L. Ickes.

was reported to be $7.5 million and an annual payment thereafter of $625,000. Furthermore, the Ruler of Kuwait retained the right to one-eighth of locally made profits arising from producing and refining operations.

The following February (1949), King Ibn Saud executed a concession agreement with the Pacific Western Oil Co. for Saudi Arabia's undivided one-half of the mainland oil rights in the Kuwait Neutral Zone.[183] The terms of this contract were even more severe on the oil companies than were the terms of the Aiminoil contract. The initial payment amounted to $9.5 million, the annual payment $1 million and the royalty per barrel was fixed at 55 cents. Also, the government was to receive one-eighth of local production profits and one-quarter of local refining profits.

Both Aiminoil and Pacific Western lost no time in entering into a working arrangement—but as separate entities and not as a joint company.

Prospecting for the joint account of the two American oil company groups, began in the Kuwait Neutral Zone area the latter part of 1949. The early exploration and drilling activities were conducted on land from a floating base camp—a war landing craft anchored near shore. The only structures on land were the drilling rigs and equipment.

James MacPherson, formerly Vice President for Aramco in Saudi Arabia, was engaged by the two groups to direct the Neutral Zone operations. Under his able supervision, the pioneer geophysical surveys and exploratory drilling were pressed, expeditiously and economically. However, as so often happens in wildcat drilling, even when the wells are located on "geophysical highs," all the wells drilled in 1950, 1951 and 1952 failed to find merchantable oil in commercial quantities. After drilling

---

183. Pacific Western Oil Co., owned 84 per cent by J. Paul Getty, the remaining interest being owned by Tidewater Associated Oil Co. and Skelly Oil Co.

five "dusters" and expending for all operations in excess of $30 million,[184] finally, on April 13, 1953, the discovery well was completed, namely Wafra Number 4—rated at 2,500 barrels daily of 31° API gravity at a depth of 3,800 feet in the so-called "first Burgan Sand."

The first shipment of Kuwait Neutral Zone oil was loaded onto a tanker bound for Japan on January 5, 1954.

By the end of 1960 Aiminoil and Getty Oil together had drilled 280 wells in the Neutral Zone—of these, 248 are capable of producing and 197 were producing at that time.

During 1961 the Kuwait Neutral Zone mainland produced 57,405,445 barrels of crude oil. The cumulative production from these mainland fields approximates 229 million barrels through 1961.

Aiminoil's production is piped northward over the Kuwait Neutral Zone frontier and is delivered on board tankers at Mina Abdullah through sealoading lines at a terminal on the Kuwait coast of the Persian Gulf a few miles south of Kuwait Oil Co.'s Mina al-Ahmadi terminal.

Western Pacific's production is moved south, through a pipe line system, independent of Aiminoil, where it is loaded onto tankers at its Persian Gulf terminal, Mina Saud, on the coast of the Neutral Zone.

Both Aiminoil and Pacific Western have constructed crude stabilization and small topping plants at their respective Persian Gulf terminals.

During the fall months of 1961 a new royalty-tax agreement was agreed between the Kuwait government and Aiminoil whereby Aiminoil, from January 1, 1961, will pay taxes at the rate of 57 per cent on net profits on a realized basis or 50 per cent based on posted prices, whichever is greater. Presumably this agreement cancels the original agreement made in 1948.

---

184. Fanning, Leonard M., *Foreign Oil and the Free World*, McGraw-Hill Book Co. Inc., New York, 1954, p. 238.

8

Turkey, Israel, Syria
And Other Country Ventures

THIS STORY OF OIL in Iran, Iraq, Qatar, Bahrain,
Saudi Arabia, Kuwait and the Neutral Zone has been presented
in considerable detail. From these seven political units there
has been produced more than 18 billion barrels of crude petroleum through 1961, whereas all other areas in the Middle East
are only credited with a cumulative total production of some
20 million barrels.

Some commercial oil production has been developed in Israel
and Turkey, but so far these oil fields appear to be of only
local significance. Indication of commercial production is reported to have been encountered in wells drilled in northeast
Syria, however, this oil has not yet been exploited. In 1959,
a well drilled in the Shaikhdom of Abu Dhabi (Trucial Coast)
found encouraging indications of commercial production. Still
more recently, drilling offshore in the Persian Gulf has en-

Author's note: The Middle East as herein considered does not include
Egypt, Pakistan or India.

countered exciting oil indications—these may be oil fields of major importance.

For the sake of brevity the author has omitted any historical sketch from the following text relating to Israel, Lebanon, Transjordan, Syria, Turkey, the onshore fringe area of the Arabian Peninsula and the offshore development areas in the Persian Gulf. Concession acquisition and prior exploration activity for the most part, has been mentioned by reference only.

ARABIAN PENINSULA—THE ONSHORE FRINGE

Cities Service entered the Middle East scene in 1953, when it obtained an exclusive oil concession over all the province of Dhofar (approximately 32,000 square miles) in the Sultanate of Muscat and Oman, which lies along the south fringe of Saudi Arabia on the Arabian Sea. Subsequently, a half interest in this grant was assigned to Richfield Oil Corp. By the end of 1960, Cities Service Petroleum Corp., had completed six dry holes aggregating 40,340 feet of hole in the Dhofar concession without having discovered oil in commercial quantities. Operations are now reported suspended.

Petroleum Development (Trucial Coast) Ltd., and Petroleum Development (Oman) Ltd., associates of Iraq Petroleum Co., Ltd., hold oil concessions over the onshore area from the northern-most tip of Oman to the base of the Qatar Peninsula. These concessions were acquired between 1937 and 1945. In 1959, a well known as Murban No. 2 discovered what gives promise of being the first oil field in the Trucial Coast, Shaikhdom of Abu Dhabi. This well encountered 41° to 43° gravity API, oil, flowing at the rate of some 2,000 barrels per day, from a depth of more than 10,400 feet.

Subsidiaries of Iraq Petroleum Co. have drilled deep exploratory wells in the Trucial Coast Shaikhdoms of Dubai and Sharjah without finding oil in commercial quantities.

Associates of Iraq Petroleum Co. have also drilled two deep exploratory wells in the Sultanates of Oman and Muscat—200 miles south of the Trucial Coast. Both these tests were reported dry.

During 1960 three of the four main corporate partners withdrew from Iraq Petroleum's associated company, Petroleum Development (Oman) Ltd. Exploration of the Oman is now continued by the Royal Dutch Shell Group as majority stockholder and operator.

Petroleum Development (Western Arabia) Ltd., an affiliate of Iraq Petroleum interests, obtained an oil concession over the Farsan Islands in the Red Sea and a strip along the Red Sea coast. Test drilling done in 1937-1938 was negative and the concession was abandoned in 1941.

The same company also obtained limited exploration rights from the Iman of the Yemen in 1937 but the geologists reported unfavorably on the oil prospects.

About 1958, American Overseas Investment Corp. (100 per cent American) obtained a 5-year exploration concession over some 10,000 square miles of Yemen along the Red Sea coast.

John W. Mecom, an independent oil operator from Texas, now holds a concession over the same area as the American Overseas group did formerly. By June, 1961, Mecom had assembled four drilling rigs and other exploration equipment and shipped same to Yemen. Yemen's first wildcat well was spudded on July 19, 1961. In January, 1962, Mecom was reported to be drilling his fourth wildcat test in Yemen after three failures. Geologists have long believed from surface evidence that salt dome structures will be found along the Red Sea coastal strip of Yemen.

In 1938, Petroleum Concessions, Ltd., obtained a blanket exploration permit over the Aden Protectorate which was renewed periodically until 1960, when Petroleum Concessions relinquished its license and withdrew from the whole of the Aden Protectorate.

In 1961 Pan American International Corp. negotiated for and obtained a new 45,000-square-mile concession from the Sultans of the Qu'aiti and Kathiri states of the Hadhramant. These states form a part of the Eastern Aden Protectorate in the south of the Arabian Peninsula.

Pan American's concession area extends from the Gulf of Aden to the Rub al Khali or Empty Quarter of Saudi Arabia. The agreement is for a 10-year exploration period, with a possible 5-year extension, and a 30-year exploration period for each oil field discovered. The agreement further provides for the two states to receive 55 per cent of net profits or for the two states to take a participation of up to 20 per cent in the company's rights and obligations, in which event the division of profits will be on a 50-50 basis.

SYRIA

Syria Petroleum Co., affiliated with Iraq Petroleum, carried on geophysical work all over Syria from 1946 to 1952. Some ten exploratory wells were drilled, each on what appeared to be favorable structure. These wells were drilled to depths varying from 8,600 feet to 10,250 feet. Although sedimentary formations of all ages were penetrated, no oil in commercial quantities was encountered. The oil concession was abandoned in August, 1951.

In 1949, J. W. Menhall, a Syrian American drilling contractor was granted an oil concession in Eastern Syria on the Iraq frontier. Menhall in association with Atlantic Refining Co. drilled several wells in the concession area and discovered what is believed to be commercial production at Karatchouk. The UAR government expropriated the Karatchouk fields and all of the Mendall-Atlantic investments in Syria—for which compensation is still being sought.

The Syrian Region General Petroleum Authority has invited bids for drilling of 20 oil wells and three gas wells at Karatchouk (oil) and in the Jezirah area (gas). The Karatchouk structure is believed to be large but so far the oil recovered has been heavy (about 22° API gravity). In the fall of 1961 it was reported the Karatchouk oil field will be developed in the next three years by a new company, the Jezirah Oil Co., in which the State's Economic Development-Organization will have a 70 per cent interest.

Societe des Petroles Concordia S.A.R.L., apparently controlled by German interests holds a number of petroleum licenses in northeast Syria. Concordia completed three wells in 1960 including one dry hole. By mid-1961 Concordia had three productive wells at Souedie (extreme northeast corner of Syria, some 300 miles from the Mediterranean).

LEBANON

Iraq Petroleum's affiliate, the Lebanon Petroleum Co., drilled a well in Lebanon in 1947-48 to a depth of 10,060 feet, without encountering any trace of oil or gas—hence the concession was abandoned.

In 1952, the Lebanese Oil Co., in which Pacific Western had a one-half interest, obtained an oil concession in Lebanon over an area of 700,000 acres, but after drilling a dry hole, the American company abandoned its interest.

In 1955 a concession covering selected areas in Lebanon was granted to Compagnie Libanaise Des Petroles. This company is apparently owned 50 per cent by Lebanese and French nationals and 50 per cent by German interests. After two dry holes, it is expected this concession will be dropped.

The German interests (Gewerkschaft Elwerath and Deutsche Schactban) formerly associated with Libanaise Des Petroles will continue to carry on exploration work and drilling in Lebanon.

PALESTINE (ISRAEL)

In 1914, Standard Oil Company of New York (now Socony-Mobil) obtained 11 licenses to explore for oil in Palestine direct from the Ottoman government and had a trustee arrangement with three Turkish subjects for seven other licenses for mineral prospecting in Palestine. World War I suspended all operations on these licenses.

It may be recalled that British troops occupied Palestine during the hostilities. These authorities refused to allow the American company to do any work on their licenses. The Americans appealed to their government who in turn made representations to the British government. In due course, the Americans were advised all Palestine claims must await clarification after a mandate over Palestine was established and the war was over.

The United States government was not content with this reply, so the diplomatic argument continued for several years, in fact long after the war. Apparently, sometime in 1921, Standard gave up its claims to the Palestine licenses—perhaps, because by that time it appeared that the seven American oil companies, of which Standard of New York was one, would some day obtain an equitable share of Turkish Petroleum Co.

Several years after the members of Turkish Petroleum Co. had signed the Red Line Agreement (July 31, 1928), Iraq Petroleum Co., obtained permits to search for oil in Palestine and Transjordan but these permits were not exclusive. In 1938, a new mining law was enacted by the Palestine government and a year later 29 prospecting licenses were issued to Petroleum Development (Palestine) Ltd., an Iraq Petroleum affiliate. No drilling was undertaken during the war but in 1946, Petroleum Development began drilling a well but had only reached a depth of 3,464 feet by February, 1948, when operations were suspended because of the Arab-Israeli situation. When the new

Petroleum Law was passed by the Israeli government in August, 1952, all old concessions were cancelled.

Since passage of the 1952 Petroleum Law—which was framed on the basis of recommendations of Max and Douglas Ball, two well-known American oil consultants—a number of Swiss, Canadian, American[185] and other foreign interests as well as Israeli companies, individually or together applied for and obtained licenses to prospect for oil in various parts of Israel. Some of the exploratory wells drilled found encouraging signs of oil.

On September 22, 1955, oil was discovered at Heletz, (Huliquat) at a depth of 4,906 feet—this location is said to be the same as the one which Iraq Petroleum had drilled to a depth of 3,464 feet when internal trouble caused the cessation of drilling in 1948. The Heletz-Brur oil field had some 24 producing wells (all pumpers) at the end of 1961, in addition to one well shut in. This field was responsible for all of Israeli oil production through 1961—a total of more than 4 million barrels—and is currently producing something over 2,000 barrels daily.

In the spring of 1958, commercial gas was discovered west of the Dead Sea at Sohar-Kidad. At the end of 1960, eight completed gas wells were awaiting pipe line construction.

On September 1, 1960, oil was discovered at Negba some two and one-half miles north of the Heletz-Brur oil field, however subsequently Negba 4 and 5 (located within a half mile radius of Negba 3) were found to be dry.

In 1961 Naptha Petroleum discovered a new gas field at Caná im about 7.5 miles northeast of the Zohar gas field in the Negev area, but on a different structure.

At present oil licenses are held in Israel by six companies— Israel American Oil, Israel Continental Oil, Israel National Oil,

185. Among these American companies was Israel Oil Licenses and Pan-Israel Oil Co., controlled by William Buckley (recently deceased) well-known for his various Pantepec companies.

Israel Negev Petroleum, Lapidst Israel Oil Prospecting and Naptha Israel Petroleum.

TRANSJORDAN

In 1938, while Transjordan was still a part of the British Palestine Mandate, Iraq Petroleum Company organized Petroleum Development (Transjordan) Ltd., for work in that country. However, it was not until 1947 that the company was granted a 75-year exclusive oil grant over the entire country—some 37,000 square miles. This concession was terminated in 1954.

In 1957-58 Edwin W. Pauley, an independent operator, secured a concession in Jordan with the right of selecting 12,000 square miles. Considerable surface geology and seismic exploration was carried out. Subsequently, three deep wells were completed—all dry holes. More recently, Phillips Petroleum Co. acquired this concession from Pauley, and added more acreage to the concession by taking on area in the Dead Sea trough. For compensation, Pauley Petroleum, Inc. reserved a 9.6 per cent net profit royalty interest. Interest in Jordan's oil prospects waned in 1960 as Phillips released its 8,140,000 acre concession late in the year. The Pauley-Phillips venture drilled six deep wildcat wells in Jordan—all dry.

TURKEY

"Being on the fringe of the rich Middle East oil fields, and still nursing a grudge against Great Britain and Iraq for depriving her of the Mosul oil fields, Turkey, is preoccupied with the problem of oil, and oil has influenced her national thinking."[186]

When the new Turkey emerged in the early 1920's, many

186. Shwadran, Benjamin, *The Middle East, Oil and The Great Powers,* Frederick A. Praeger, New York, 1955, p. 431.

industries, services and natural resources were nationalized—
among them were petroleum and gas. Under the special law
covering exploration of petroleum, enacted in 1929, search for
oil began. Five years later a national agency, known as the
Mining Research Institute, began drilling for oil near Diyar-
bakir (Diarbekr) in southwestern Turkey, northwest of the oil
fields near Mosul in Iraq.

In 1948, six wells were completed as small producers—in aggregate less than 700 barrels per day. Nevertheless, a 200-barrel-
per-day refinery was built at the nearby railroad. Three years
later, another small oil field was discovered at Garzan in the
same region. This crude was heavy in gravity (average 20°
API) with a high percentage of sulphur. All the wells are pumpers—none flowed without agitation. By 1952 a dozen wells in the
Raman Dagh field, had been equipped for production out of some
20 wells drilled on that structure. Most of this crude was used
without being refined or topped, as fuel on the local railway.

Meanwhile, the staff of Mining Research Institute was
broadening its search for oil along the semiplains region south
of the main mountain range and more or less parallel to the
Iraq-Syria north frontiers. This search was not particularly re-
warding.

In 1952 a contract was awarded an American group to erect
a 6,250-barrel daily capacity refinery at Batman to serve both
the Raman Dagh and Garzan fields.

After 20 years of state monopoly of petroleum without the
finding or development of a major oil field, the politicians began
to think in terms of free enterprise and of inviting the cooperation of the international oil companies to establish an oil industry
of magnitude and substance in Turkey.

In furtherance of this awakening, in May, 1953, Max W.
Ball,[187] an oil consultant of Washington, D.C., was called to assist

187. Max W. Ball, in conjunction with Douglas Ball, had helped frame
the Israeli Petroleum Law in 1951-1952.

in drafting a new Petroleum Law. Nearly a year later, the new Petroleum Law was enacted. The terms of this Law were such that free enterprise and foreign oil companies could engage in the search for and development of petroleum resources in Turkey on a workable basis. Basically, this Law followed the 50-50 pattern of division of profits, as between country and producing company.

Within a very few months after the enactment of this new petroleum law, seven international oil companies had sought and were granted exploration licenses—among these were such American companies as Esso Standard of Turkey (an affiliate of Standard Oil of New Jersey), Turkish Socony Co., (Socony-Mobil affiliate), American Overseas Petroleum Co. (an affiliate of Caltex).

At the same time as the new Petroleum Law was promulgated, the national government of Turkey also established the Turkish National Petroleum Co., in which the state owned 51 per cent of the shares, to have exclusive rights over the existing oil wells and refineries and to control refining throughout the country.

Thus, in 1953, the Turkish government had effectively combined state ownership of existing oil wells and refineries with foreign free enterprise devoted principally to the finding and development of new petroleum reserves. In the last eight years this combination of state and free enterprise has intensified the search for oil by all scientific means.

Since 1953, other American oil companies have joined the search. As yet, no major oil yields have been discovered in spite of active competitive field activity. However, it is generally conceded that to date the possibilities of finding a sizable underground oil reservoir in Turkey have not been exhausted, though the chances of finding a field of the magnitude of Kirkuk, Burgan or Abqaiq appear quite slim.

Turkey has had some oil production since 1947, but the oil fields so far discovered have not been spectacular either in productive area or in volume of production. In 1954, the recorded average daily oil production in Turkey was only slightly more than 1,000 barrels—in the year 1961 the total oil production from all wells in Turkey is reported to have been 2,931,000 barrels, or say, 8,000 barrels daily. So far, Turkey's indigenous production of oil is not nearly enough to satisfy her internal consumption requirements.

At the end of 1960, 12 oil companies were actively operating in Asian Turkey—11 foreign and one national. By names these companies are: Mobil Exploration, N. V. Turkse Shell, Turkish Gulf Oil, Turkiye Petrolleri, (these first four were most active), American Overseas Petroleum, Bolsa Chica Oil, D. D. Feldman Oil and Gas, Deilmann Montan, Deutsche Erdol, Pan Oil, Pauley Petroleum and Tidewater Oil. During 1961, Tidewater, Bolsa Chica, Deilmann Montan and Deutsche Erdol are reported to have withdrawn.

All 1961 production came from the Raman, Kurtalan, Magrip, Garzan, Kayakoy and Kahta fields in southeastern Asian Turkey and the Bulgardag field near Mersin in south Asian Turkey. More than 95 per cent of Turkey's current production comes from fields owned or controlled by Turkiye Petrolleri A.O.

During 1960, light oil in commercial quantities was discovered by Mobil Exploration in the Bulgardag area of the Adana Basin in southern Asian Turkey inland from Mersin on the Mediterranean coast. By the end of 1960, Mobil Exploration had completed two wells in the Bulgardag field capable of flowing 1,200 barrels per day and 1,600 barrels per day respectively of 38.9° API gravity oil with very low sulphur. However, in 1961 Mobil abandoned the third and fourth wells drilled in the Bulgardag area and No. 5 yielded 640 barrels a day of 37° crude. Half a dozen wells drilled by Mobil at different locations within 25 miles of Bulgardag have all been unsuccessful. In 1962 the Adana Basin does not look as promising for large scale commercial production as it did during 1960.

At Mersin on the Mediterranean, a new refinery is under construction (1960) having an estimated capacity of 65,000 barrels per day. This refinery is being built by the Mobil-Shell-B.P. group and is expected to go on stream before mid-1962. Another refinery was completed in 1961 at Izmit near Istanbul. This refinery has a daily capacity of 17,800 barrels. It was financed by Caltex and Turkish Petroleum Corp.

9

Persian Gulf and Arabian Sea Continental Shelf Development

IN RECENT YEARS INCREASING ATTENTION has been given by oilmen to the prospects of finding sizeable oil fields offshore under the waters of the Persian Gulf and the Arabian Sea. Considerable exploration and drilling has been done seaward from Iran, Kuwait Neutral Zone, Saudi Arabia, Qatar and Abu Dhabi. By 1962, eight overwater oil offshore fields had been discovered in those areas; namely Bahregan Sar, Darius and Cyprus (Iran), Khafji (Kuwait Neutral Zone), Safaniya and Manifa (Saudi Arabia), Idd-el-Shargi (Qatar) and Umm Shaif (Abu Dhabi).

IRAN—OFFSHORE

In 1947, an all Persian company—the National Iranian Oil Co.—was organized as a government agency to hold the petroleum rights to all Iranian lands outside of the Anglo-Iranian leases. By the legislative acts of 1951, the Anglo-Iranian leases were also declared to be the property of the nation and since

259

then, no petroleum grants have recognized any exclusive private or foreign ownership to the underground.

SIRIP

National Iranian Oil Co.'s (NIOC) deal with Ente Nazionale Idrocarburi (ENI) was consummated July 31, 1957 without bonus payment. Under its terms ENI and NIOC each own 50 per cent of Societe Irano-Italienne des Petroles, (SIRIP). It is significant that both ENI and NIOC are state owned concerns. Three areas are involved, to wit, 5,600 square kilometers of the Continental Shelf (overwater concession) in the northeast segment of the Persian Gulf, 6,000 square kilometers along the Gulf of Oman covering both land area and overwater area and 11,300 square kilometers in the foothills of the Zagros mountains along the Eastern border of the consortium area. The combined area of the three parcels totals 22,900 square kilometers.

During 1960, SIRIP's first offshore test well, known as Bahregan Sar (sometimes spelled Barganshar), was bottomed at a depth of 11,012 feet. This hole encountered favorable oil horizons at 7,050 feet and 8,850 feet, and it is believed to be currently producing from those horizons. Early in 1961, Bahregan Sar No. 2 well was completed and preparations were being made to drill wells 3 and 4 from the same fixed platform.

During 1961 the Bahregan Sar field produced 1,098,000 barrels. It is reported SIRIP expects to increase production from Bahregan Sar to the order of 5 million barrels for the year 1962, and 14 million barrels for the year 1963.

The Bahregan Sar field is located approximately six miles offshore on the Continental Shelf zone of the Persian Gulf, southeast of Abadan.

IPAC

Iran Pan Am Co. (IPAC) is an Iranian Co., jointly owned by National Iranian Oil Co., and Pan American Petroleum

Corp., an affiliate of Standard Oil Co. (Indiana). In 1957, IPAC was granted two overwater (Continental Shelf) areas in the Persian Gulf—one for 1,000 square kilometers adjoining SIRIP's overwater concession on the north and the other for 15,000 square kilometers adjoining SIRIP's overwater concession on the south. These so-called continental shelf concessions have for their western boundary the median line of the Persian Gulf and for their eastern boundary the seaward limit of the territorial waters (3 miles offshore)—this later being the western boundary of the consortium concession.

IPAC's initial offshore test A-1 was spudded in 1959 and was bottomed in 1960 at 13,151 feet having encountered various oil shows. This well was located in 126 feet of water some 60 miles off the Iran mainland about half way between Kharg Island and the Shatt al-Arab.

Subsequently, the second exploratory test B-1 was drilled to a depth of 12,497 feet. B-1 is located in 152 feet of water about 22 miles south of Kharg Island some 20 miles from the mainland and about 60 miles southeast of A-1.

As of mid-1961 A-1 was still testing. However testing on B-1 was suspended early in 1961—it being considered a non producer.

During 1961, IPAC made two new offshore discoveries in overwater areas as Cyprus and Darius. These appear to be major discoveries.

In the Cyprus area, 45 miles west of Kharg Island, IPAC has drilled two exploratory wells. Cyprus No. 2 tested 6,000 barrels a day of 35.7° API oil from an open hole at 9,630 feet and has since blown out oil and gas below 10,700 feet at high pressures. Cyprus may well prove to be a commercial field.

The Darius area lies to the southwest of Kharg Island. About the end of 1961 Darius No. 1 well, located some 3 miles from

Kharg, tested at 35,000 barrels a day of 29° API crude from about 11,800 feet and produced some 163,000 barrels during the testing operation. Darius No. 2 is now drilling 2 miles southwest of the discovery well. The Darius area appears to be on a major structure, which extends to Kharg Island where the Consortium is now drilling.

It is reported that Pan American has expended about $40 million in IPAC's operation within the four years since the overwater concession was granted to IPAC—more than the $34 million it was committed to spend within that period—henceforth NIOC is due to foot half the bill for IPAC's development expense.

IRCAN

In 1958 Iran Canada Oil Company (Ircan) obtained an oil concession in Iran over approximately 386 square miles near the southern part of the consortium area and bordering on the Gulf of Oman including certain offshore area. Ircan is owned 50 per cent by Sapphire Petroleum, Ltd., (a Canada corporation) and 50 per cent by National Iranian Oil Co. (an Iranian company). No activity was reported for Ircan during 1960 or 1961.

KUWAIT—OFFSHORE

In January, 1961, Kuwait Shell Petroleum Development Co., Ltd., became concessionaire to one of the worlds most promising offshore areas. This so-called continental shelf of the Persian Gulf is adjacent to Kuwait state, lying more than six nautical miles from mean low tide. There is not immediately available any reliable estimates of the acreage involved in this overwater grant. However, it is assumed that the area may be as large or larger than the offshore concession pertaining to the Kuwait Neutral Zone.

Under the concession terms, Shell was obligated to commence exploration in nine months and to start drilling in 30 months. The agreement runs for 45 years. The agreement provides for sizeable cash payments as an initial bonus, annual rent before commercial production of 15,000 barrels per day is found and an increased annual rental thereafter until exports commence, as also a series of deferred bonuses until daily production attains 500,000 barrels a day. It is estimated that such bonuses and rentals could approximate more than $100 million by the time the 500,000 barrel-a-day target is attained.

The concession terms follow the same 50-50 pattern of the onshore Kuwait concession. However, this oil agreement contains some new ideas in company-country relationship in that it provides that the Kuwait government may purchase up to a 20 per cent interest in Kuwait Shell's operating company and may appoint two directors to Kuwait Shell's board.

A new drilling ship, the *Nola III,* built on the US Gulf Coast was scheduled to arrive in Kuwait during March 1962 and to commence drilling soon thereafter on Kuwait Shell's offshore concession.

The oil fraternity will follow Kuwait Shell's development of the Kuwait offshore area with keen interest. This concession is considered one of the choicest prospecting areas in the world today, lying as it does between Kuwait Oil Co.'s great proven fields on the mainland of Kuwait on the west and the (Japanese) Arabian Oil's proven Khafji field in the offshore of the Kuwait Neutral Zone on the south.

Kuwait Neutral Zone—Offshore

Arabian Oil Co., Ltd., a subsidiary of Japan Petroleum Trading Co., Ltd., acquired oil rights over the offshore area of the Kuwait Neutral Zone. This was in the form of two contracts executed in 1958 between the Japanese company and the Shaikh of Kuwait on the one hand, and the King of Saudi

Arabia on the other hand for their respective undivided one-half interest. Both of these agreements deviated from the 50-50 pattern.

The following reference to the Arabian Oil's 40-year concessions is quoted from the Petroleum Press Service, London, March, 1960, p. 103:

> Both agreements provide for annual rentals of $1.5 million a year, plus a rental of $1 million a year on discovery of oil to be backdated to the date of the agreement. They also both provide for a guaranteed annual minimum royalty of $2.5 million. In other respects they differ slightly, but have the common feature of affording the concessionary governments a share of the profits (more than 50 per cent) not only on crude oil production but on all other operations too. (See Petroleum Press Service, June 1958, page 207.) The Kuwait government will receive 57 per cent profits, which will be calculated separately for crude oil production based on posted prices, and for the other activities as a whole, whereas the Saudi government will receive 56 per cent of net income from operations inside and outside Saudi Arabia taken together. Both agreements require that the refineries must be built in Saudi Arabia and Kuwait (or the Neutral Zone) when total production averages 60,000 barrels per day for 90 days. The company is also obliged at a certain stage in its operations to engage in transportation and marketing. The two governments each have the option to buy 10 per cent of the company's shares and to purchase 10 per cent of production for local use at five per cent discount from posted prices. This will be the first modern instance of participation by the government of a producing country in profits from integrated operations, from the well to the user or retailer.

The Japanese company's first exploratory well, located in the Persian Gulf 28 miles offshore of the mainland in water 104 feet deep, unexpectedly struck gas at 1,507 feet on August 3, 1959, and burned wild for 11 days until extinguished by a group of expert Texas firefighters using explosives. Another overwater drilling rig was assembled in the United States and began drilling in November, 1959. On January 29, 1960 this second test came in flowing some 6,000 bpd of 26° API crude from a depth of about 4,900 feet subsea. This completion signaled the discovery of another major Middle East oil field. This offshore field is known as Khafji.

By May, 1961, Arabian Oil Co., Ltd. had completed 14 producing wells in the Khafji offshore field—all on the same structure. The current drilling schedule provides for a total of 26 completions by the end of 1961. It is estimated that each well will safely produce 6,000 barrels a day.

The first cargo of Khafji crude was shipped to Japan in April, 1961. During 1961 the Khafji offshore field produced some 13.1 million barrels.

At present temporary offshore facilities are being used to produce, store and load onto tankers the production from Khafji. Meanwhile, construction has begun on a $70 million permanent base onshore at Ras al Khafji near the southern end of the Neutral Zone. The new permanent facilities are designed to handle 200,000 barrels a day.

SAUDI ARABIA—OFFSHORE

Aramco's offshore concession in the Persian Gulf was acquired from the Saudi government in 1948, presumably in exchange for surrendering its grant to Saudi Arabia's undivided half interest in the Kuwait Neutral Zone. These overwater rights and obligations follow the same 50-50 pattern as Aramco's onshore concession.

Mention was made earlier to Aramco's offshore oil fields known as Safaniya (1951) and Manifa (1957).

Since discovery, Safaniya has been developed into a major oil field and has been producing for several years. By the end of 1960, 37 wells had been completed in Safaniya. Status: 20 wells producing, 15 wells shut in or standing and two observation wells. This field yielded 88,079,098 barrels of crude in 1961. Work is now under way to boost the crude output of Safaniya to 240,000 barrels daily. Safaniya may well be the largest off-shore oil field in the world.

Seven wells have been completed in the Manifa offshore area—six of which are rated as producers. This field has not yet been delineated and has not yet been put on stream. However, the producing structure is already known to be some 15 miles long by 10 miles wide and is said to contain six crude reservoirs.

QATAR—OFFSHORE

Shell Co. of Qatar has suffered misfortune along with good fortune in its initial offshore exploratory drilling operations some 50 miles east of the Qatar mainland.

Idd-el-Shargi No. 1 Shell's second exploration well, was abandoned dry at 11,883 feet in 1956. While the fixed marine drilling platform was being dismantled a very severe storm damaged the platform beyond repair. A new 6,000 ton mobile drilling platform was promptly ordered from the Netherlands but time of construction and towing to site did not permit resumption of offshore drilling until near the end of 1959. This new mobile marine platform, *Seashell,* is designed to withstand winds up to 100 miles an hour and waves 30 feet high while working in 90-foot water depths.

In mid-1960 Shell's Idd-el-Shargi No. 2 (total depth 8,320 feet) discovered oil in three horizons—4,725 feet, 7,110 feet and 7,900 feet respectively—as well as high pressure gas at about

6,800 feet. IS No. 2 is rated as a discovery. The mobile platform was then moved to a location about 30 miles northeast of Doha on the Qatar Peninsula where Hadet Shibeeb No. 1 was completed at 7,775 feet as a dry hole. From Hadet Shibeeb the mobile platform was moved back to the Idd-el-Shargi structure to drill IS No. 3. This wildcat was completed in January, 1961, at 8,325 feet having encountered the same favorable oil and gas conditions as in IS No. 2.

The Idd-el-Shargi structure gives promise of being an oil field of importance.

ABU DHABI—OFFSHORE

Abu Dhabi Marine Areas, Ltd., owned two-thirds by British Petroleum Co., Ltd., and one-third by Compagnie Francaise des Petroles, holds the oil rights over 12,000 square miles offshore of the area ascribed to the Shaikhdom of Abu Dhabi lying between the Trucial Coast and Qatar. The first exploratory well, known as Umm Shaif No. 1—20 miles east of the Island of Das and 80 miles north of the Trucial Coast mainland—discovered what may prove to be the first offshore oil field in the Persian Gulf, since Aramco's two offshore fields known as Safaniya (1951) and Manifa (1957) were found some 300 miles to the northwest.

Umm Shaif No. 1 tested 2,400 barrels of 40° gravity oil daily in 1958. However, Umm Shaif No. 2 was disappointing in that it only tested about 1,000 barrels a day. Wells Nos. 3, 4 and 5 had been bottomed by the spring of 1961, all on the same structure as the discovery well.

Production from the Umm Shaif offshore field will be delivered by submarine pipe line to Das Island—20 miles distant —where a sealoading tanker terminal is being built. Exports from Umm Shaif are expected to begin during the last half of 1962 at the rate of 10.5 million barrels a year.

Aden-Yemen—Offshore

BP Exploration Co., Ltd. holds an exploration permit over Kamaron and other British controlled islands off the coast of Yemen, including territorial waters. These islands are administered by the government of Aden. Work has been suspended by agreement with the Aden government.

10

American Oil Interests

As NOTED IN THE FOREGOING TEXT on Middle East oil, the American interests were excluded from participating in petroleum ventures in those parts until 1928. The break through occurred in Iraq, after which came the oil discoveries by Americans, either alone or with others, in Bahrain, Saudi Arabia, Kuwait, Qatar and in the Neutral Zone. In 1954, American interests were invited to join the consortium of international oil companies in Iran.

During 1961, American oil interests, directly or indirectly, were active in all the proven areas of the Middle East, except the Neutral Zone offshore, Abu Dhabi offshore and Qatar offshore. It is believed that discoveries have been or will be made in these Persian Gulf offshore concessions but as yet these areas have not been placed in production, hence, any estimate of reserves is premature.

Whereas before 1928 Americans had no share in the proven oil reserves of the Middle East countries, now the Americans' percentage share in the presently proven oil reserves is as follows:

269

Iran	40.	
Iraq	23.75	
Bahrain	100.	
Saudi Arabia	100.	(includes some offshore)
Kuwait	50.	
Qatar	23.75	
Neutral Zone	100.	(onshore and some islands)
Israel	—	
Turkey	—	

At the end of 1960, it is estimated that the proven reserves in the areas listed above approximated a total of more then 163 billion barrels of recoverable oil (see Appendix IV hereto) hence, the American share of such reserves can be said to be in the order of 96.6 billion barrels or nearly 60 per cent of all the presently known reserves of the Middle East.

Thus, in 30 odd years, by negotiation and by search and development, the American share of recoverable oil in the Middle East underground has risen from nothing to more than 1.7 times the estimated reserves of all the countries of the Western Hemisphere—which is no mean credit to American diplomacy and free industrial enterprise.

Appendix I

SUBSTANCE OF THE FAMOUS IRANIAN NINE POINT LAW

Reprinted with the permission of Lawrence and Wishart, Ltd. of London, publishers of, "Persian Oil," by L. P. Elwell Sutton, 1955.

1. With a view to arranging the implementation of the law of March 15 and 20, 1951, concerning the nationalisation of the oil industry throughout Persia, a joint committee composed of five Senators and five Deputies elected by each of the two Houses and of the Minister of Finance or his deputy shall be formed.

2. The government is required to dispossess at once the former Anglo-Iranian Oil Company under the supervision of the joint committee. If the company refuses to hand over at once on the grounds of existing claims on the government, the government may, by mutual agreement, deposit in the National Bank of Iran or in any other bank up to 25 per cent, of current revenue from the oil after deduction of exploitation expenses in order to meet the probable claims of the company.

3. The government is required to examine the rightful claims of the government as well as the rightful claims of the company under the supervision of the joint committee and to submit its proposals to the two Houses of Parliament in order that they may be implemented after approval by the two Houses.

4. Inasmuch as from March 20, 1951, when the Senate also approved the nationalisation of the oil industry, all revenues from oil and oil products are the unquestioned right of the Persian nation,

271

the government is required to audit the company's accounts under the supervision of the joint committee. The joint committee must also supervise closely matters relating to exploitation as from the date of the implementation of this law until the appointment of a board of management.

5. The joint committee must draw up as soon as possible and submit to the two Houses for their approval the statutes of the National Oil Company, in which provision is to be made for a board of management and a board of supervision composed of experts.

6. For the gradual replacement of foreign experts by Persian experts the joint committee is required to draw up regulations for the sending of a number of students to foreign countries annually on a competitive basis to engage in the various branches of study and practical experience connected with the oil industry, the said regulations to be implemented by the Ministry of Education after approval by the cabinet. The expenses connected with the studies of these students shall be met out of the oil revenues.

7. All purchasers of the products of the oil deposits recovered from the former Anglo-Iranian Oil Company may purchase hereafter annually at the current international price the same quantity of oil that they purchased annually from the beginning of 1948 up to March 20, 1951. For any surplus quantity they shall have priority in the event of equal terms of purchase being offered.

8. All proposals formulated by the joint oil committee and submitted to the Majles for its approval must be referred to the special oil committee.

9. The joint committee must complete its work within three months from the date of the ratification of this law, and must submit a report on its activities to the Majles in accordance with article 8. Should an extension of the period be required, it must submit an application for extension, giving valid reasons. Until the extension of time is for any reason disapproved by the two Houses, the joint committee may continue its activities.

Appendix II

THE IMPACT OF THE WEST, 1953

*Reprinted from pages 570-578 inclusive of,
"Kuwait and Her Neighbours," by Colonel H. R. P.
Dickson, London 1956, with the permission of
George Allen and Unwin, Ltd., publishers. See
page 171 of text.*

"My friend Dr. W. Harold Storm, a member of the American Mission of the Persian Gulf and now running a hospital in Hufuf, wrote a book entitled 'Whither Arabia?' In offering the following comments on the important subject of Western influence in Arabia, I have ventured to draw upon Dr. Storm's masterly summing-up of the situation, and where I make use of conceptions that are not my own, I do so with grateful acknowledgments to Dr. Storm and the publishers of his book, the World Dominion Press.

There are probably few parts of the world where the old and new exist side by side, as they do in Arabia. In the deep desert to-day, life as it was in Abraham's time can be seen in all its details. The Badawin nomad still relives the scenes of the Old Testament. His thoughts too are much the same as in the days of Job. His arrogance, independence, pride and self-sufficiency have only been intensified by Islam, while his religious life has been moulded into a rigid system of creed and formality.

Western influence, however, has changed the complexion of many of the sea-coast towns, into which centres the hungry Badawi comes in search of food and supplies. He looks at the changes about him with unmistakable scorn and returns to his desert home more contented than ever with it and the life there. Yet the wheels of progress grind on inexorably, and the sons of the desert cannot escape.

Probably no single factor has done so much to alter the thinking of the desert Arab as the motor-car. The Haj journey by camel across the Arabian desert from Kuwait to Mecca used to take at least forty days; now the trip is done by motor-car in six days. When the ruler of Sa'udi Arabia travels from his interior capital, Riyadh, to Mecca, he and his entourage are conveyed in ultramodern aircraft or anything from two hundred to five hundred cars, nearly every one of which is driven by a chauffeur from another country: Kuwait, Pakistan, Egypt, Somaliland, Syria and even Indonesia. It is not difficult to realize the tremendous effect of all this, for it is not only the motor-car that makes the change, but the driver, who brings with him new ideas, manners and customs. In Riyadh, for instance, one finds the drivers living in a small community outside the city wall. While this group elicits little thought or consideration from the members of the ruling class and the religious leaders, it has a constant stream of visitors from the town and desert. Ideas good and bad, with a background of Kuwait, Cairo, Damacus, Aden and Karachi, are being thereby disseminated among the Badu and are being steadily assimilated by these simple people.

The greater ease in transportation brings in its wake luxuries that tend to greater comfort. This very fact has a degenerating effect. No longer does the young Arab shaikh use his mare; he prefers to drive. Falconry, once the chief Arab sport, has developed into the systematic slaughter of thousands of hubara annually, for it is done by motor-car today. The gazelle too is hunted to such an extent in fast-moving automobiles that this beautiful animal is now nearly extinct. The old sense of sportmanship has been lost.

An even more noticable effect of the motor-car is on the psychology of the Arab. Competition for the best and most expensive car is aroused among the wealthy princes and town merchants; inability to own one brings discontent among the middle and lower classes. On the other hand, not all the results are bad. Distances are abolished, tribal independence lessened. Motor routes touch upon and penetrate the grazing lands of tribes once difficult of access; food supplies are more easily conveyed to distant camps. People and ruler are thus brought closer together.

More insidious is the effect of the motor-car on the ladies of the towns. Despite the fact that they must still ride in purdah, they are able to visit frequently places hitherto deemed inaccessible. More visiting is now done among the families of the same class, women hear more and see more, and it is likely that the motor-car will be an important factor in the eventual removal of the veil, though this is very, very far distant where tribal Arabia is concerned.

Although women in Arabia have not as yet been liberated in any real sense, certain amenities have been introduced into their rather drab lives. The radio brings them into a world of music, people, places and happenings of which their mothers did not even guess the existence. The Packard car and the Singer sewing-machine are found in the remotest Arabian villages and towns. Where formerly numbers of slave women spent hours and days laboriously preparing garments for members of the household on the occasion of feast days, now the work is accomplished in a few hours. These same women have a growing interest in cosmetics, perfumes, powders and soaps.

Modern medical science has also brought to Arab women relief from suffering and from anxiety over their own physical ills. Past generations were served by native women who carried on their ignorant practice of midwifery with no knowledge of cleanliness. Now the patient labour of British and American doctors, missionary nurses and others has created a desire for more scientific treatment and even a willingness, if need be, to enter a hospital. There is a growing interest in the proper feeding and care of babies and, as might be expected, this has brought about serious conflict in many Arab homes. The younger women, striving to follow new ideas of dieting, bathing and sleeping for their babies, meet with bitter opposition from the older women.

As the outcome of Ibn Sa'ud's inauguration of a wireless system throughout his kingdom, there are now a score or more stations in the larger centres, and a dozen or more mobile ones on wheels. These latter are used by the present ruler, the heir apparent, his brothers, the viceroy of Hijaz and others holding responsible positions, so that, no matter where they are in the desert, they remain in direct communication with the capital and other parts of the country. The slightest uprising can thus be quelled almost before it starts.

Other parts of Arabia are connected with various cable and

wireless stations. A change in price in the Bombay market is noted the same day in the bazaars of Bahrain, Muscat, Kuwait, Jiddah and Riyadh. Radios that tune in with Arab-speaking programmes from London, Beyrout, Jordan, Baghdad, Ankara and Moscow keep the people informed regarding world affairs. In the effort to unify Muslim thought, much Islamic propaganda is also broadcast. No sooner is some incident between Jew and Arab in Palestine announced than the Arabs hear of it and take sides and discuss it from their point of view. In Kuwait alone there are today some eight thousand receiving sets. Lebanese, Egyptian, Iraqi and Indian newspapers also interpret international affairs to every part of Arabia and the Arab world. Much anti-Christian literature is also spread abroad and the work of the missionary is often hampered by false reports of his activities. The recent deposing by the French of the Sultan of Morocco and his incarceration in Corsica caused heated controversy in the Kuwait bazaar and coffee shops two days later.

The desert Arab today, clothed in his ancestral dress, living as his fathers did before him, thinking the thoughts of the past, finds himself forced to face the modern progress of the world and to accept the influence over his life of such things as the motor-car and the radio.

The discovery of oil in Bahrain some years ago, and the still more recent finds in Saudi Arabia, Kuwait and Qatar, have brought modern methods, customs and the influence of Western civilization to all parts of the Persian Gulf littoral. From a rather obscure and delightful small Arab state, Kuwait, through the remarkable growth of her oil industry, has suddenly blossomed forth into the metropolis of the Gulf, even though Great Britain has made Bahrain her naval base for the Gulf, and that island is now the headquarters of Her Majesty's Political Resident.

A new and deadly dangerous factor has, however, emerged. It can be called modern materialism, and its influence and outcome are hard to estimate. In past days Islam came to grips with many religions and was never defeated, but now it would seem about to dissolve and break up in the home of its birth. With every motor-car and printed newspaper there enters the scientific materialism and unbelief of the West and that modern paganism which is the enemy everywhere of religious faith. How far this new type of unbelief will extend no one can say, but without question it is now coming in like a flood. Its influence has hitherto been limited to a small number of persons in the commercial centres, but to-day it is being felt in the remotest part of the desert and its power increases steadily. God-fearing Arabs and men of repute all over Arabia are to-day anxious and afraid.

Materialism, popularized by modern science, has weakened Islam in much the same way as Gnosticism undermined Christianity in the early centuries. Materialists claim, as did the Gnostics of old, that they are not antagonists but allies of religion. Therein lies a dangerous truth. Material progress, to be sure, is an asset to any religion, but when the acquiring of worldly possessions becomes the object of one's devotion—the driving force in one's living, instead of devotion to truth and righteousness—then religion does become affected. Material prosperity, which of itself is neither good nor bad, but, like fire, depends on how it is used, has tended to weaken rather than strengthen Islam.

Along with the growing influence of materialism and Westernization there has crept into the life of the Arab something of that spirit of nationalism found elsewhere in the world. This has not been so widespread or extreme as in Turkey and Egypt, but finds expression in an intense though somewhat perverted loyalty of the Arab to his race. The problem of Palestine has served to strengthen this loyalty, as have all the more recent plans and extensive propaganda for Pan-Arab unity.

In 1934, as we have seen, King Ibn Sa'ud, following a brief but decisive conflict, annexed 'Asir and also concluded a treaty of Islamic friendship with 'Imam Yahya of Yemen. This treaty was the precursor of other treaties and understandings between Muslim nations. Soon after it was concluded, negotiations began for a four-power pact between Turkey, Iran, Iraq and Afghanistan. At the same time 'Imam Yahya decided to adhere to the treaty of amity and alliance signed on 2nd April 1936 by the Governments of Iraq and Saudi Arabia. Another treaty was concluded between Saudi Arabia and Yemen on 3rd November 1937. This brought the two largest independent Arab Kingdoms into line with Turkey, Iran, Iraq and Afghanistan, the treaty between which was also signed in 1937. To further better understanding with Egypt, King Ibn Sa'ud ended not long ago the ten-year quarrel with the Egyptian Government, which agreed to send again annually to Mecca the Kiswah, or holy covering.

No one can venture to foretell the far-reaching effects of these political treaties. To the friend of the Arab it is most significant that Muslim nations are coming into better and closer understanding, which may lead to an alliance of the chief Muslim powers, but whether this will give rise to a revival of Islamic culture and religious zeal, or to the dissociation of political power from religion, it is impossible to forecast.

Foreign interests are largely British. Other countries, however, are concerning themselves with Arabian affairs. This is notably true of the U.S.A., which, following on the heels of the great American oil company, Aramco, at Dhahran, has sought to obtain political influence in Arabia. In response to a general demand the British Broadcasting Corporation has for some years been sending out programmes in Arabic. American warships now regularly visit the Persian Gulf and vie with their British friends in good-natured rivalry.

The course of events in Europe is now being followed with increasing interest in Arabia, and this growing intelligence is leading people everywhere to form more accurate judgments regarding European affairs. It is not very likely that Arabia under Islamic rule will play any important part in international affairs all at once, though it will still remain the centre of Islamic politics and the religious world of Islam.

The social and political movements that have taken place in Egypt, Pakistan, North Africa, Lebanon and Iran have begun to have their effects on Arabia proper. These new movements cannot fail in the end to exercise an increasing influence in the trend of affairs. Already we see nationalism getting hold, which is nothing but a challenge to the West, especially to England. As recently as 28th October 1953 a leading Arab of Kuwait said to me:

"You cannot blame us Arabs for wanting to copy the West and introduce such things as Trade Unions and other Western methods for protecting the rights of oil company labourers, when daily we are taught all about such things by means of blaring broadcasts on such subjects from England and America. If London has a strike of petrol-lorry drivers because they feel they are underpaid, why should we not do the same?"

The immediate and grave danger in a place like Kuwait state is, without doubt, the influx of Palestinians, Iraqis, Lebanese, Iranians, Egyptians and other foreigners on a scale undreamed of in the past, which to-day, with the town-development scheme in full blast, is the order. Whether these visitors come as displaced Palestinians, skilled workmen from Lebanon, unskilled labourers from Iraq and Persia, Arab journalists or business men from Beyrout, they one and all preach to the Kuwaiti "Arabia for the Arabs and Kuwait for the Kuwaitis" in its worst form.

Their approach is supremely clever, taking the line that Kuwait is an independent princedom, so why is there such strong British political influence in the place, and what is the idea of a British Political Agent? This must be put right, they say, and the Political Agent's influence eradicated—and the only people to do this are the Kuwaitis themselves. They criticize the British Order in Council —the Capitulations by which Great Britain is granted special privileges and the rights of exterritoriality—and say it must be got rid of; that the Political Agent should be a consul pure and simple or a junior British minister accredited to the court of the ruler of Kuwait. They undoubtedly advise junior members of the Al Sabah to aim for a state of affairs as in Saudi Arabia, and say how good is the Aramco set-up at Dhahran, and how well and truly do the Americans know how to work with the Arabs there, as well as with the Saudi Government. Throughout all these dangers it behooves both British and Americans, wherever they may be, to remember that the Arab of the unfriendly type, and who often holds extremist views, is always interested in spoiling relations between them. He is an adept at the game too.

This sort of vicious propaganda worries the senior and old-fashioned Kuwaiti, who likes the British, but conversely it pleases the young Kuwaiti extremist, who would like nothing better than to see Kuwait come under the political control of Iraq, a Muslim state and therefore better than the Christian British. Iraq not unnaturally encourages these ideas in a dozen different ways, working through the thousands of her nationals who are engaged as labourers, skilled and unskilled, on Kuwait's development scheme.

The Iraqis' latest line of approach is to dangle before the Kuwaitis the advantages of bringing in water from the Shatt al-Arab river in Iraq by means of a 32-inch pipe, which would enable large tracts of good soil in the vicinity of Kuwait town and Jahra to be turned into fruit and vegetable gardens, and would provide in addition a quadrupled supply of drinking-water for the town. They know that under this scheme the cultivators of the newly irrigated areas must of necessity be 'fellahin' of the Iraqi riverain tribe, so, in one step, they would have their nationals in occupation of a large part of Kuwait and ready to appeal for protection in any dispute, fabricated or not, that might arise between them and the Kuwait Government. The young men of the extremist party in Kuwait—and there are not a few of them—who favour coming under the political control of Iraq, know all about this. They not only bless the scheme, but also, by day and night propaganda, push their ideas in Iraqi and Lebanese newspapers.

A sad fact is that while the Kuwaiti youthful extremist or nationalist is more and more becoming anti-foreign and anti-British, the genuine old-fashioned Arab of the desert and the elderly influential merchant of the town, both of whom still like and respect the Englishman, with whom they have had friendly and commercial contacts for centuries, is slowly turning against the Westerner generally, for quite another reason. Deeply religious at heart these men see in the impact of the West, with its terrifying materialism, a very real danger to their old manners and customs, and in particular to their religion. They see their children going bad, taking to alcohol, giving up their religion, no longer saying their prayers, becoming grossly immoral, and refusing to obey their parents. In consequence they are saying to themselves that such a state of affairs must be due to the impact of the West, its money, its irreligion and its drink.

In sheer self-defence those of this older conservative generation are slowly becoming hostile. More fanatical than before, they are adopting the new cry, "Our religion is in danger"; and because they think that the West is getting hold of their country, sons and daughters, their cry today is, "Let us have nothing to do with the Westerner, for he is not what we knew him once to be." So the delightful Arab of the older school is also becoming anti-foreign, anti-British and anti-American, though not from the same causes as have led the younger generation to become so.

What is the answer to this tragic state of affairs? I venture to give it thus:

Let the West give up trying to force its concepts of civilization, such as better living, Western ideas of education, uplift, modern food and clothing, etc., and let it instead preach evolution and building on rock rather than sand. Let it preach that progress, though it cannot be stopped, must come slowly and surely, not as a devouring fire.

Let the West preach the virtues of character-building, the principles of religion, and belief in one God and His ordinances; and above all let it preach the universal sanctity of the Ten Commandments.

Let the West—and indeed all men of goodwill—be tireless in denouncing the evils that come with so-called civilization, commending instead only the good things that the West has to offer, for the evils that come in the train of such products of modern progress as alcohol, cinemas, etc. far outnumber the good."

Appendix III

(See Page 275 of text)

Reprinted From "The Times," Tuesday, March 4, 1952

With the permission of The Times Publishing Co., Ltd., London

KUWAIT'S BURDEN OF WEALTH
A NEW OIL CENTRE IN ARABIA

From Our Special Correspondent lately in Kuwait

Kuwait, an independent shiekhdom under British protection at the head of the Persian Gulf, after some centuries of quiet existence as an Arab trading centre has suddenly emerged as the fifth oil-producing country of the world. By Arabian standards Kuwait, even before the flood of industrial wealth began to descend upon it, was not a poor community and the Kuwaiti citizen, who does not like the picture sometimes drawn of him as a penniless Beduin who has come upon a bag of gold in the desert, will watch for this misapprehension in a foreign visitor and gently correct it.

The town was a community of merchants, dhow-builders, pearlers, and seafarers, whose services earned enough to maintain a settled life in a totally desert land. It was, however, an antiquated Arab city, and no more; unlettered, materially and culturally static, a society circumscribed by the total lack of power and water as well as by habitual conservatism. This desert State of perhaps 150,000 people will receive this year a revenue of about £20m. If this year's production from the Kuwait oilfield reaches 40 million tons, as is expected, the royalty and tax payable in 1953 under the agreement concluded in December will be in the neighborhood of £50m. Subsequently Kuwait's annual revenue from its oil may well be greater still.

To describe its ruler, the formal possessor of this immense revenue, by such round phrases as "the richest man in the world" is entirely to miss the point of what is happening in Kuwait. The need of budgetary techniques or of a separate Civil List has hardly been felt in Kuwait's modest past, and it may reasonably take a little time for such techniques to be evolved. The existing system is frankly patriarchal. It has served well in the past. Kuwait has an unusually stable and pacific history, and the ruling dynasty has been unbroken since 1756. No doubt some more elaborate administrative system will be needed to handle a revenue which will equal that of many an important State. There is, however, no question of the present ruler treating his vast revenue as a personal income to be used for his own or his family's private purposes.

A BENEVOLENT RULER

Sheikh Abdulla Salim is a serious and thoughtful man in his middle fifties, simple in dress, religious, and conservative in habits. No doubt it is largely due to his temperate and reflective character that Kuwait has been so largely free from the wasteful conspicuous expenditure that has followed sudden accretions of wealth elsewhere. If good fortune attends him he will be able to steer his people through the present testing period of adjustment. His governing preoccupation is to dispose of the revenue from oil wisely for the good of his people. He and his advisers are aware that the oil deposits of Kuwait, fabulously rich as they are—and for their combination of great volume with easy production and ready access to the sea they are probably unequalled—are an irreplaceable capital resource which will one day be exhausted. His intention is that while the revenue continues no fruitful outlay shall be grudged, but all the money not so spent shall be invested for the future. How this policy will be carried out and what its impact will be on a small and hitherto static Muslim society are perplexing questions. It is, however, a simple and sensible policy; more remarkable, it is in fact being applied. Its beginnings are already to be seen in action.

Kuwait's first need is water. The territory, some 6,000 square miles, is a sandy desert in which even the artesian water is salt. The neighbouring deserts of southern Iraq, muddy rather than sandy and still showing many traces of vanished cultivation, have the great river system of the Tigris and Euphrates to hand, promising that one day, with flood control and irrigation, they may be cultivated once more. But the Kuwait desert has never been cultivated. No river touches the State and a political frontier separates it from the logical sources of water, the Euphrates or its confluence with the Tigris, the Shatt-el-Arab. The town's traditional supply is brought from the Shatt-el-Arab in dhows which discharge into tanks at the quayside, from which the water-sellers load their skins. With its new fortunes the State will be able to afford to pipe water from the Euphrates and to pay for the privilege, if Iraq agrees. First, however, political prudence dictates that Kuwait should make itself tolerably self-sufficient in water, and this is to be done by the largest system of distillation yet conceived.

The world's largest existing water distillation plant (which was described in detail in The Times Review of Industry in December) is the Kuwait Oil Company's plant at its loading port, Mena-el-Ahmadi. From this plant, which uses the spent steam from the power generators to distill 600,000 gallons of fresh water a day from the sea, 200,000 gallons are piped daily to the town. The remainder serves the oil company's establishments, which are in effect a self-contained town separated from Kuwait town by more than 20 miles of clean hard sand. Outside the old city a new and still larger plant, designed to give one million gallons of water a day, is being built at State expense, and the design provides for future expansion to five times this size. It will be fired by oilfield gas. In the past the average Kuwaiti has used one and a half gallons of water daily, a quantity far too small to make sewerage possible; this has already been doubled, and next year it may rise to eight or nine gallons a head a day.

TOWN PLANNING

The prospect of water makes it possible for the new town plan to include an unheard-of amenity, a public garden in the central square. Around the square, at present a somewhat indistinct sandy expanse crossed by donkeys, camels, and a multitude of new American cars, clearing is going on and the shape of new traffic lanes is emerging. In the neighbourhood, sections of the old bazaar have been pulled down and replaced by colonnaded shopping streets, other sections are coming down, and still others are to follow.

Roads of sandy dust are being asphalted. The town is in many ways pleasant, though its single-storeyed houses and buildings, enclosed in their rough-cast walls the colour of sand, facing inward to their courtyards, have no special pretensions to antiquity or grace. Most of it is bound to be rebuilt as commerce grows and the means and tastes of the citizens are enlarged; it is to the good that the reconstruction will be governed by a town plan.

Kuwait does not know the tropical diseases that breed in water. Other diseases, however, abound, and a heavy task falls on the State medical service that is now being built up by the Kuwaiti health committee around a nucleus of British and Arab doctors. The present hospital was opened in October, 1949, for 120 beds; it now houses 180 beds. In addition a tubercular ward of 60 beds, established in another building to free the main hospital for general work, had to be expanded to more than 100 beds in its first few weeks. A permanent new tuberculosis hospital is approaching completion. As these figures suggest, tuberculosis at present overshadows other diseases. It takes an acute form and, even more than the townspeople, the desert Beduin are terribly vulnerable. The demand for medical and dental treatment has more than kept pace with the efforts to supply them, and indeed it is easy to imagine that a good free health service in Kuwait may draw the sick from neighbouring regions. The present plans envisage a department of some 25 doctors and dentists, with a new general hospital of 750 beds—at a cost of well over £2m.—on a site, now being cleared, outside the present town.

CHANGES IN EDUCATION

Perhaps the most profound of the changes now transforming Kuwait is the change in education. Until 1910 the only schools known in Kuwait were the Koran schools in which a mullah would instruct a few children in the scriptures. Two or three general schools were founded in the next 25 years, and in 1935 the enlightened policy was begun of importing teachers from more advanced Arab countries—Palestine, Lebanon, and Egypt. Expansion began, therefore, before the oil royalties came to pay for it, but until five years ago it was on a modest scale. Since 1945 11 new boys' schools and seven new girls' schools have been founded. Older schools have been enlarged and greatly improved. There are now 399 teachers instead of 119 seven years ago; the number of pupils has risen from 3,000 to more than 8,000, and is rising constantly. Education is free, the children receive a free meal a day, free clothing, and medical treatment. The equipment and teaching materials are unstinted.

Kuwaiti women are strictly veiled, their place is in the home, and except for some 130 teachers virtually none is in employment. It is the more remarkable that as many as 2,500 girls are now at school. The education of women in large numbers may make even deeper marks on Kuwaiti society than the coming of water or the reduction of disease. It is not to be supposed that the men now disinterestedly planning these changes have imagined and desired all their consequences. Change is, however, being sought deliberately, if all its possible effects are not. A boarding school for 500 boys is nearing completion outside the town. Young Kuwaitis are being sent to study in Egypt, Lebanon and the western countries with funds provided by the State and the oil company, and 27 (among whom are two of the ruler's sons) are now studying in England.

Kuwait is profiting by its extraordinary material luck to embark on an adventure; the construction, in a decayed and neglected region of the world, of a modern and advanced community. The adventure will be exacting in its demands, and, with all possible foresight, unpredictable in its outcome. Most people would think it worth attempting; none, having seen its beginnings and the seriousness that inspired it, could fail to wish it well.

MIDDLE EAST OIL PRODUCTION
By Countries—By Years
(Expressed in Thousands of Barrels of 42 U.S. Gal.)
ALSO ESTIMATED PROVED CRUDE OIL RESERVES—END 1960

Year	Iran	Iraq	Bahrain	Saudi Arabia	Kuwait	Qatar	Neutral Zone	Turkey	Israel	Total
1913	1,857									1,857
1914	2,910									2,910
1915	3,616									3,616
1916	4,477									4,477
1917	7,147									7,147
1918	8,623									8,623
1919	10,139									10,139
1920	12,230									12,230
1921	16,673									16,673
1922	22,247									22,247
1923	25,230									25,230
1924	32,373									32,373
1925	35,038									35,038
1926	35,842									35,842
1927	39,688	338								40,026
1928	43,461	713								44,174
1929	42,145	798								42,943
1930	45,828	913								46,741

Year	Iran	Iraq	Bahrain	Saudi Arabia	Kuwait	Qatar	Neutral Zone	Turkey	Israel	Total
1931	44,376	830								45,206
1932	49,471	836								50,307
1933	54,392	917	31							55,340
1934	57,851	7,689	285							65,825
1935	57,273	27,408	1,265							85,946
1936	62,718	30,406	4,645	20						97,789
1937	77,804	31,836	7,762	65						117,467
1938	78,372	32,643	8,298	495						119,808
1939	78,151	30,791	7,589	3,934						120,465
1940	66,317	24,225	7,074	5,075						102,691
1941	50,777	12,650	6,794	4,310						74,531
1942	72,256	19,726	6,241	4,530						102,753
1943	74,612	24,848	6,572	4,868						110,900
1944	102,045	30,943	6,714	7,794						147,496
1945	130,526	35,112	7,309	21,311						194,258
1946	146,819	35,665	8,010	59,944	5,931					256,369
1947	154,998	35,834	9,411	89,852	16,225					306,320
1948	190,384	26,115	10,915	142,853	46,500			13		416,780
1949	204,712	30,957	10,985	174,008	90,000	750		95		511,507
1950	242,476	49,726	11,016	199,547	125,722	12,268		108		640,863
1951	123,512	65,122	10,994	277,963	204,910	18,009		133		700,643
1952	7,800	141,100	11,004	301,861	273,433	25,255		146		760,599
1953	9,400	210,268	10,978	308,294	314,592	31,025		179		884,736
1954	21,500	228,432	10,992	347,845	347,319	36,450	5,995	399		998,932
1955	120,035	251,206	10,982	352,240	398,493	41,983	8,848	1,210		1,184,997
1956	198,289	233,421	11,014	360,923	399,874	45,345	11,725	2,200	152	1,262,943
1957	263,193	163,498	11,691	362,121	416,000	51,356	23,200	2,051	400	1,293,510

	Iran	Iraq	Bahrain	Saudi Arabia	Kuwait	Qatar	Neutral Zone	Turkey	Israel	Total
1958	301,526	266,102	14,873	370,486	509,383	63,910	29,310	2,268	650	1,558,508
1959	338,810	311,311	16,473	399,821	504,855	62,197	42,438	2,655	913	1,679,473
1960	390,755	354,592	16,500	456,453	594,278	63,908	49,830	2,573	1,025	1,929,914
1961	430,000	367,830	16,444	508,269	600,226	65,318	70,520	2,931	978	2,062,516
Total	4,590,674	3,084,801	262,861	4,764,882	4,847,741	517,774	241,866	15,961	4,118	18,331,678

	Iran	Iraq	Bahrain	Saudi Arabia	Kuwait	Qatar	Neutral Zone	Turkey	Israel	Total
Estimated Reserves (End 1960)	32,000	21,800	170	45,500	60,000	1,650	2,500	60	16	163,796

(Expressed in Millions of Barrels)

NOTE: The above production and reserve data-compiled by **World Oil** with the aid of oil companies and other sources-is reprinted in Appendix IV with the permission of Gulf Publishing Company, Houston, Texas.

The annual and cumulative production figures appearing in Appendix IV are not always the same as the author has stated in the text.

289

Bibliography

Anglo Iranian Oil Company, Ltd., *In Iran,* London, March 1947.
   A Short History of the Anglo-Iranian Oil Company, London
   1948.
   Our Industry, London 1949.
   Persia—Past and Present, London, 1950.
Arabian American Oil Company, 1960 Report of Operations to
   Saudi Arab Government.
Banker, The, "Middle East Oil—A Special Study," article in *The
   Banker,* Vol. CVI. No. 370, November 1956, London.
Barney, Rev. Frederick J., see under Mason.
Belgrade, K. B. E., James, H. D., *Welcome to Bahrain—A Guide
   for Tourists and Travelers,* Mark & Moody Ltd., Stourbridge,
   England, 1953.
Braidwood, Linda, *Digging Beyond the Tigris,* Henry Shuman,
   New York, 1953.
British Information Services (An Agency of the British Govern-
   ment)—"Anglo-Iranian Oil Company—Some Background
   Notes," ID 1059, New York, May 1951.
Brock, Roy, *Blood, Oil and Sand,* The World Publishing Company,
   New York 1952.
Bullard, Sir Reader, *Britain and The Middle East,* Hutchinson's
   University Library, London 1951.
Bustani, Emile, "Memorandum to the Arab Economic Council,"
   submitted by the Government of the Lebanese Republic, and
   based upon a project originated by Emile Bustani, American
   Press, Beirut, 1959.
   "The Arab World and Britain," reprinted from *International
   Affairs,* Vol. 35, No. 4, October 1959 by Royal Institute of
   International Affairs, London, April 9, 1959.
   "The Middle East Today," text of address before Devonshire
   Club Historical and Literary Circles, London, October 10,
   1959.

March Arabesque, Robert Hall Ltd., London, 1961.

Butler, Grant C., *Kings and Camels,* The Devin-Adair Co., New York, 1960.

Calverley, Rev. Edwin E., "The Harrison Story," Hartford Seminary Foundation, Bulletin #11, June 1951.

Calverley, M.D., Eleanor T., *My Arabian Days and Nights,* Thomas Y. Crowell Company, New York 1958.

Campbell, C. G., *Tales From The Arab Tribes,* Lindslay Drummond, London, 1949.

From Town and Tribe, Ernest Benn Ltd., London, 1952.

Told in the Market Place, Ernest Benn Ltd., London, 1954.

Cantine, James, see under Zwemer.

Case, Paul Edward, "Boom Time in Kuwait," *National Geographic,* Vol. CII, No. 6, Washington, D. C., December 1952.

Cheney, Hollis B., see under Mikesell.

Clare, I. S., *Library of Universal History,* 8 Vols., R. S. Peale—J. A. Hill, New York, 1897.

DeGolyer, E. L., "The Old Fields of the Middle East," in "Problems of the Middle East—Proceedings of a Conference," School of Education, New York University 1947.

Dickson, Col. H. R. P., *The Arab of the Desert,* George Allen and Unwin, London, 1949.

Kuwait and Her Neighbors, George Allen and Unwin, London, 1956.

Dickson, Violet, *The Wild Flowers of Kuwait and Bahrain,* George Allen and Unwin, London, 1955.

Dodge, Bayard, *The American University of Beirut,* Khayat's, Beirut, 1958.

Doughty, Charles M., *Travels in Arabia Deserts,* Jonathan Cape, London, 1936.

Douglas, William O., *Strange Lands and Friendly People,* Harper & Brothers, New York, 1951.

Duce, James Terry, "History of Oil Concessions in the Middle East," Article in *Bulletin of The Near East Society,* (Vol. 6, No. 7) New York, September 1953.

Duncan, David Douglas, Photographic Essay "Aramco," *Life,* Vol. 26, No. 13, Time Inc., Chicago, 1949.

Elwell-Sutton, L. P., *Persian Oil,* Lawrence & Wishart, Ltd., London, 1955.

Faroughty, PhD., Abbas, *The Bahrein Islands* (750-1951), Verry,

Fisher and Company, Inc., New York, 1951.

Fanning, Leonard, *Foreign Oil and The Free World*, McGraw-Hill Book Company, New York, 1954.

Feis, Herbert, *Seen From E. A.*, Alfred A. Knope, New York, 1947.

Fernald, Dorothy Hughes, "Seventy-Five Years of Union Congregational Church," Upper Montclair, N. J., 1958.

Foreign Relations, "Papers Relating to the Foreign Relations of the United States," 1927, II, Washington, D. C., 1942.

Feeth, Zahra, *Kuwait Was My Home*, George Allen & Unwin, London, 1956.

Ghirshman, R., *Iran*, English Version, Penguin Books Ltd., Harmondsworth, Middlesex, England, 1954.

Gibson, Ray, see under Oil and Gas Journal.

Hall, William H., *The Near East—Crossroads of the World*, Interchurch Press, New York, 1920.

Hamilton, C. W., "American Petroleum Interests in Foreign Countries—The Story of Foreign Oil Exploration, Production and Pipelines," statement made before The Special Committee Investigating Petroleum Resources, United States Senate, 79th Congress, First Session, June 27-28, 1945, United States Printing Office, Washington, D. C., 1946.

"American Corporations Engaged in Operations Abroad—A Private Point 4 Program in Action," address before The Foreign Policy Association of Pittsburgh, January 30, 1953.

"Can Private Enterprise Do The Job of Economic Development," *Bulletin of Foreign Policy Association, Inc.*, Vol. XXXII, No. 19, June 15, 1953.

"Human Relations—International," address before Fourth National Conference of the United States National Commission for UNESCO, Minneapolis, September 16, 1953.

The Middle East and Oil, pamphlet for Cyrus J. Lawrence & Sons, New York, September 1957.

Hamlin, Rev. Cyrus, *My Life and Times*, The Pilgrim Press, Boston, 1893.

Hart, Liddell, *Colonel Lawrence—The Man Behind the Legend*, Dodd, Mead & Company, New York, 1934.

Harvey, Reginald Charles, see under McGowan.

Hewins, Ralph, *Mr. Five Per Cent*, Rinehart & Company, Inc., New York, 1958.

Hitti, Philip K., *The Arabs,* Princeton University Press, Princeton, 1943.

History of the Arabs, MacMillan & Company, Ltd., London, 1949.

Lebanon in History, MacMillan & Company, Ltd., London, 1957.

Hope, Stanton, *Arabian Adventure,* Robert Hale, Ltd., London, 1951.

Hoskins, Halford L., *The Middle East,* MacMillan Company, New York, 1954.

Hotchkiss, Henry, "1960 Petroleum Developments in the Middle East," *Bulletin of the American Association of Petroleum Geologists,* Vol. 45, No. 7, July 1961.

India, Foreign Department, "Collection of Treaties, London, 1933.

Iranian Oil Operating Companies, 1958 Annual Report.

Iranian Oil Participants Limited, *Iran,* London, 1956.

Jarvis, C. S., *The Back Garden of Allah,* John Murray, London 1939.

Kamil, Hussein, Translation of Arabic pamphlet on "Kuwait—Its History and Progress and Growth of Its Civilization," by The Kuwait Mission in Cairo, Cairo 1947, Edited by Nils E. Lind.

Kinross, Lord, "The Richest State in the World," *The Listener,* London, September 11, 1952.

"The Story of the World's Richest Man," *United Nations World,* Vol. 7, No. 8, United Nations, August 1953.

Kirk, George, *The Middle East in the War,* issued under the auspices of the Royal Institute of International Affairs, Oxford University Press, London, 1952.

Kuwait Oil Company, Ltd., *The Story of Kuwait,* published by Kuwait Oil Co., Ltd., London 1957, Revised Edition 1959.

Laquer, Walter Z., *Communism and Nationalism in the Middle East,* Rontledge and Kegan Paul, London 1956.

Lawrence, T. E., *Seven Pillars of Wisdom,* Doubleday Doran, New York 1935.

Revolt in the Desert, George H. Doran, New York 1927.

Lebkicher, Roy, *Aramco and World Oil,* Russell F. Moore Company, Inc., New York 1952.

Lebkicher, Roy, George Rentz and Max Steineke, *The Arabia of Ibn Saud,* Russell F. Moore Company, Inc., New York 1952.

Aramco Handbook, Revised Edition, Arabian American Oil Company 1960.

Lewis, Bernard, *The Arabs in History,* Hutchinson's University Library, London 1950.

Lloyd, Seton, *Foundations in the Dust,* Oxford University Press, London, 1947.

Lockhart, Lawrence, "Outline of the History of Kuwait," *The Royal Central Asian Journal,* Vol. XXXIV, Parts III-IV, July-October 1947, London.

Loeb, Carl M., "Middle East Aspects of American Oil Companies" (Confidential Memorandum), Rhoades & Company, New York, January, 1949.

Longhurst, Henry, *Adventures in Oil—The Story of British Petroleum,* Sidgwick and Jackson, London, 1959.

Longrigg, Stephen Hemsley, *Handbook,* for Iraq Petroleum Company, Ltd., London, 1948.
    Oil in the Middle East—Its Discovery and Development, Oxford University Press, London, 1954.
    "The Liquid Gold of Arabia," a lecture, London.

Lowdon, James William, see under McGowan.

Mason, Rev. Alfred and Rev. Frederick J. Barney, *History of the Arabian Mission,* (1889-1925), The Abbot Press, New York, 1926.

Mikesell, Raymond F. and Hollis B. Chenery, *Arabian Oil,* The University of North Carolina Press, Chapel Hill, 1949.

McGowan, Charles William Neil, also Reginald Charles Harvey and James William Lowdon, "Oil Loading and Cargo Handling Facilities at Mina al-Ahmadi, Persian Gulf," Excerpt Part III, Proceedings of the Institute of Civil Engineers, London, June 1952.

Monroe, Elizabeth, "British Interests in The Middle East," *The Middle East Journal,* Vol. 2, No. 2, April 1948, London.

Moore, Jr., Frederick Lee, "Origin of American Oil Concessions in Bahrain, Kuwait and Saudi Arabia," Thesis presented to The School of Politics and International Affairs, Princeton University, 1948.

Morrison, S. A., "Arab Nationalism and Islam," *The Middle East Journal,* Vol. 2, No. 2, April 1948, London.

Murphy, Charles J. V., "Oil East of Suez," *Fortune,* Vol. LIV, No. 4, Time, Inc., Chicago, 1956.

Mylrea, Dr. C. S. G., "Old Times Evening in Kuwait," *Arabia Calling* (Arabian Mission) Summer 1950, #220.

Near East College Association, "A Century of Service and Friendship With Peoples of Many Lands," Summary Report, New York, 1959.

Near East Foundation, *A Brief Description of Its Policies and Programs,* Near East Foundation, New York, 1959.

Observer, The, "A Plan For The Middle East," Reprinted from *The Observer,* December 16, 1956, London.

Oil and Gas Journal, "World Wide Oil" (by Paul Swain and Ray Gibson) country by country report, Vol. 59, No. 52, December 25, 1961.

Pennings, Rev. Gerrit T., "Seeing Kuwait," Board of Foreign Missions of the Reformed Church in America, About 1910.

Penrose, Stephen B. L., "That They May Have Life," The Trustees of the American University of Beirut, New York, 1941.

Petroleum Press Service, *Coveted Kuwait* and *Shaikhdoms of the Persian Gulf,* Vol. XXVIII, No. 8, London, 1961.

Petroleum Times, The, *Review of Middle East Oil,* Export Number, London, June 1948.

Philby, H. St. J. B., *The Heart of Arabia,* 2 Vols., G. P. Putnam's Sons, New York, 1923.

"Two Notes From Central Asia—The Qariya Ruin Fields," *Geographical Journal,* London, June, 1949.

Arabian Days, Robert Hale, Ltd., London, 1948.

Arabian Jubilee, Robert Hale, Ltd., London, 1952.

Arabian Highlands, Cornell University Press, Ithaca, N. Y., 1952.

Phillips, Wendell, *Qataban and Sheba,* Victor Gollancz, Ltd., London, 1955.

Platt, Warren C. (Editor) "Peoples of Many Countries Will Benefit From Oil's Vast Middle East Development," *National Petroleum News,* Vol. 40, No. 47, November 24, 1948.

Potter, F. M., "A Tribute to the Late Ruler of Kuwait," Arabian Mission, New York, 1950.

Pratt, Wallace E., "The United States and Foreign Oil," *The Yale Review,* Vol. XLI, No. 1, Yale University Press, September 1951.

Redwood, Sir Boverton, *A Treatise on Petroleum,* 3 Vols., Charles Griffin and Company, Ltd., London, 1913.

Rentz, George, see under Lebkicher.

Rhoades & Company, see under Loeb (Carl M.) Rhoades & Company.

Rihani, Ameen, *Maker of Modern Arabia,* Houghton Mifflin, Boston, 1928.

Roberts, Glyn, *The Most Powerful Man in the World—The Life of Sir Henri Deterding,* Covici-Friede, New York, 1938.

Roosevelt, Kermit, *Arabs, Oil and History,* Harper & Brothers, New York, 1947.

Shaffer, Robert, *Tents and Towers of Arabia,* Dodd, Mead & Company, New York, 1952.

Shamma, Samir, *The Oil of Kuwait,* The Middle East Research & Publishing Center, Beirut, Lebanon, 1959.

Sanger, Richard H., *The Arabian Peninsula,* Cornell University Press, 1954.

Shwadran, Benjamin, *The Middle East Oil and The Great Powers,* Frederick A. Praeger, New York, 1955.

Standard Oil Company (New Jersey), "Joint Oil Producing Ventures in the Middle East," submitted to the Attorney General's National Committee to study the Anti-trust Laws, December 31, 1953.

Steineke, Max, see under Lebkicher.

Swain, Paul, see under Oil and Gas Journal.

Theisiger, Wilfred, *Arabian Sands,* E. P. Dutton & Company, Inc., New York, 1959.

Thomas, Bertram, *Arabia Felix,* Charles Scribner's Sons, New York, 1932.

Thomas, Lowell, *With Lawrence in Arabia,* The Century Company, New York, 1924.

Tweedy, Maureen, *Bahrain and the Persian Gulf,* East Anglian Magazine, Ltd., Ipswich, England about 1952.

Twitchell, K. S., *Saudi Arabia,* Princeton University Press, 1947.

United Nations, "Economic Survey Mission for the Middle East," Final Report, 2 Parts, United Nations, December 1949.

"Review of Economic Conditions in the Middle East," Preliminary version of the "World Economic Report," 1949-50, United Nations, January 1951.

United States Department of Commerce, Bureau of Foreign Commerce, "Economic Development in Kuwait," 1954-1955.

United States Senate, Special Committee Investigating Petroleum Resources, "American Petroleum Interests in Foreign Countries," Hearings 79th Congress, Washington, D.C., June 1945.

Van Ess, John, *Meet The Arab*, Museum Press, London, 1947.

Van Ess, Dorothy, "History of the Arabian Mission" (1926-57) manuscript "The Story of the Year," *Arabia Calling*, Spring 1952, # 227.

Villiers, Alan, *Sons of Sinbad*, Charles Scribner's Sons, New York, 1940.

"Some Aspects of The Arab Dhow Trade," *The Middle East Journal*, Vol. 2, No. 4, London, October 1948.

Ward, Thomas E., Private Memorandum 1948.

Watson, Charles R., *What Is This Moslem World*, Friendship Press, New York, 1937.

White, George E., *Adventuring With Anatolia College*, Herald-Register Publishing Company, Grinnell, Iowa, 1940.

Williams, Kenneth, "Oil and The Persian Gulf," *The Fortnightly*, London, May 1950.

Wilson, Sir Arnold T., *The Persian Gulf*, Oxford University Press, London, 1928.

Loyalties Mesopotamia, 2 Vols., Oxford University Press, London, 1930.

Wilson, Jr., Christy, *Apostle to Islam*, (A biography of Samuel M. Zwemer) Baker Book House, Grand Rapids, Michigan, 1952.

Woodhouse, Henry, "American Oil Claims in Turkey," *Current History* XV, March 1922.

World Oil, "16th International Outlook Issue," Vol. 153, No. 3, Houston, Texas, August 15, 1961.

World Petroleum, *Iraq Oil—An Expression of International Cooperation*, Vol. III, No. 9, Russel Palmer, New York, 1932.

Yale, William, *The Near East*, The University of Michigan Press, Ann Arbor, 1958.

Zwemer, Samuel M., *The Cross and The Crescent*, Zondervan Publishing House, Grand Rapids, Michigan, 1941.

Zwemer, Samuel, M. and James Cantine, *The Golden Milestone*, Fleming H. Revell Company, New York, 1938.

Index

298